HOW *to* RAISE *the* PERFECT DOG

CESAR MILLAN

with *Melissa Jo Peltier*

HOW *to* RAISE *the* PERFECT DOG

Through Puppyhood and Beyond

HARMONY

BOOKS · NEW YORK

Published in the United States by Harmony Books, an imprint of the Crown Publishing Group, a division of Random House LLC, a Penguin Random House Company, New York.
www.crownpublishing.com

HARMONY BOOKS is a registered trademark, and the Circle colophon is a trademark of Random House LLC.

Originally published in hardcover in the United States by Harmony Books, an imprint of the Crown Publishing Group, a division of Random House LLC, New York, in 2009, and subsequently published in paperback by Three Rivers Press, an imprint of the Crown Publishing Group, a division of Random House LLC, New York, in 2010.

Library of Congress Cataloging-in-Publication Data
Millan, Cesar.
How to raise the perfect dog/Cesar Millan; Melissa Jo Peltier.
p.   cm.
Includes bibliographical references and index.
1. Dogs—Behavior.   2. Dogs—Training.   3. Human-animal communication.   I. Peltier, Melissa Jo.   II. Title.
SF433.M556   2009
636.7'0887—dc22   2009027195

ISBN 978-0-307-46130-8

Printed in the United States of America

Design by Lauren Dong

20 19 18 17 16

First Paperback Edition

Since this book is about puppies, I'm dedicating it to my incredible sons, Andre and Calvin. Nurturing my own "pups" as they've grown; watching them begin to express their unique, inner essences and attempt to achieve their individual goals—these have been the greatest experiences of my life and have made me a much better, wiser person. I'm grateful I've been able to pass on my love of Mother Nature to them—a gift given to me by my grandfather—and I hope they will continue to convey this legacy to the rest of the world and, someday, to their own children.

CONTENTS

ACKNOWLEDGMENTS

A collection of dedicated canine professionals made invaluable contributions to the writing of this book. Both my coauthor and myself wish to extend our boundless thanks to my friend Martin Deeley, Director of the International Association for Canine Professionals and an internationally renowned trainer, specializing in retrievers and gun dogs. Martin selflessly made his wide range of knowledge—as well as his trademark dry wit—available to us 24/7. Hollywood animal trainer Clint Rowe also graciously shared wisdom from his more than three decades of working with dogs of all breeds and ages. We're proud to continue our professional and personal affiliation with him.

We are also in debt to the many fine veterinarians who remain stalwart supporters of our efforts, especially Charles Rinehimer, VMD, professor of veterinary technology at Northampton Community College (who has worked with us on three books now), and Paula Terifaj, DVM, of the Founders Veterinary Clinic in Brea, California, who also contributed greatly to *A Member of the Family*. Dr. Rick Garcia and his mobile veterinary hospital, Paws 'n Claws, were always available to answer questions and to provide thorough health care to all the puppies and dogs in my pack.

A top-notch breeder is hard to find, but in the writing of this book, we met and worked with several of them, particularly Brooke Walker of Covina, California, who provided us with our wonderful miniature schnauzer, Angel; and Diana and Doug Foster of Thinschmidt German Shepherds and Assertive K-9 Training in Corona, California. My old friend Jose Navarro came through with flying colors in producing our fine English bulldog, Mr. President, and of course I will always be grateful to Azael Espino, who gave me my perfect pit bull, Junior. Thanks also to Southern California Labrador Rescue, for bringing us Blizzard and for all the selfless work they do.

I'm proud to have begun a close association with Chris De Rose, Kim Sill, and the rest of the dedicated team at Last Chance for Animals. Their courageous work is already improving the way people treat the other creatures with which we share our planet. Thanks also to Stephanie Shain and the Humane Society of the United States for their campaign to end the cruelty of puppy mills.

As always, we thank our literary agent, Scott Miller of Trident Media Group; Julia Pastore, Shaye Areheart, Kira Walton, and Tara Gilbride at Random House; Steve Schiffman, Steve Burns, Michael Cascio, Char Serwa, Mike Beller, Chris Albert, and Russell Howard at the National Geographic Channel; and Fred Fierst, Esq. Cesar and Ilusion are incredibly grateful to John Steele, Michael Gottsagen, and the entire team at IMG—especially IMG's remarkable "Mr. Big"—for your continued encouragement and support.

For my pack, "Team Millan," I am especially grateful: Kathleen Daniels, Jennifer Dominguez, Carol Hickson-Altalef, Erick Millan, Rosalva Penuelas, Allegra Pickett, Delmi Salinas, and Susan Whalen. Nobody beats our "Super TV Crew": Nicholas Bunker, Brian Duggan, SueAnn Finke, Miles Ghormley, Todd Henderson, Chris Komives, Christina Lublin, Rich Mercer, Rita Montanez, and Neal Tyler. Also at MPH and CMI, thanks to Bonnie Peterson, George Gomez, Juliana Weiss-Roessler, Nicholas Ellingsworth, Todd Carney, Christine Lochman, Kay Bachner Sumner, and Sheila Possner Emery . . . and especially Crystal Reel, for her outstanding research, fact-checking, and unfailing can-do attitude. My wife and I are grateful to Stacey

Candella, for her dedication to our Cesar and Ilusion Millan Foundation and its mission, and to Adriana Barnes and family for their hard work on the new Dog Psychology Center. I want to acknowledge my neighbors Tim and Diane Archer for being patient and supportive with all our *Dog Whisperer* endeavors. And a special thank you to Frank and Juanita Trejo for all your love and encouragement.

Thank you to my wife, Ilusion, for her endless patience with me, especially with all the challenges that came with raising our puppy pack. And, of course, thanks to the one who keeps the puppies balanced, Mr. Daddy—the greatest nanny in the world!

MELISSA JO PELTIER wishes to thank: my MPH partners, Jim Milio and Mark Hufnail, for their unwavering support—"Three out, three back." Thank you, Cornelia Dillon, for helping me through one of the toughest times of my life. As always, props to my dear friend and cheerleader, Victoria Adams; my lovely stepdaughter, Caitlin Gray; and my husband, John Gray, who is the best life partner any girl could hope for.

Cesar and Ilusion, I'm so grateful you allowed me the honor of participating in your dream once again.

Finally, thanks to my one-of-a-kind dad, Euclid J. Peltier, for passing on your boundless energy, tireless work ethic, childlike sense of wonder, passion for learning, and indomitable life force. I love you very much.

INTRODUCTION

Several months ago, I walked into our Cesar Millan, Inc., offices and noticed our staff crowded around one computer screen, making "ooh" and "aah" noises. I nudged my way in to see what all the fuss was about. There in front of me, in a slightly blurry video, was a litter of six adorable Shiba Inu puppies—three male and three female—in a padded dog bed, playfully crawling over one another. When I learned that this was actually a live video feed in real time, I was fascinated—and impressed. Apparently the breeders—a San Francisco couple—had set up a video camera to serve as a kind of "baby monitor" so they could keep an eye on their charges at all times. The employees at the Internet company that set up the live feed fell in love with the puppies and began sending links to other friends. The link went "viral," and suddenly millions of people in more than forty countries were glued to their computer screens, watching the homegrown phenomenon that became known as the puppycam. During a time of national economic stress, viewers claimed that watching the Shiba Inu puppies calmed them down, distracted them from their worries, and had an overall positive effect on their mental health.

The puppycam experience inspired several of our *Dog Whisperer* staff members to set up their own webcams to start monitoring their dogs and puppies at home. Once the Shiba Inu puppies had grown up and moved on, there was always some new puppy adventure unfolding on one of our office computers.

Whatever your cultural background, the language you speak, your race, creed, or religion, you'd have to be made of stone not to be moved by the antics of puppies. Their apparent helplessness and adorable, clumsy attempts to explore a world that is new to them automatically awakens the nurturing instincts that nature has implanted deep in the genes of every male and female, child and grandparent. And as the testimonials from puppycam fans prove, loving puppies is good for us! Puppies bring us closer to our innocent, natural animal selves. They relieve our stress, improve our health, and remind us that true happiness exists only in the moment. Loving and raising a puppy can be one of the richest, most rewarding experiences of a person's entire life. And once that puppy becomes a full-grown dog, the bond created during those first eight months—the stage that I call puppyhood—can solidify into the kind of relationship that will sustain you throughout your dog's lifetime and beyond.

However, the fact that our human hearts routinely melt into butter whenever we see a pup doesn't automatically make us qualified to raise one. That's why I'm writing this book.

What is it about dogs that makes us believe the skills for raising them will come as effortlessly to us as raising our own human offspring? I don't know many humans who believe they would automatically know how to raise a baby elephant, leopard, or dolphin, should one happen to fall into their laps! I'm sure most people instinctively know that you don't raise a seal cub, a parrot chick, or a foal the same way you would a human child. Human beings have even learned hard lessons about trying to raise our closest cousins, the higher primates, as if they were hairier versions of ourselves. I recently read a heartbreaking book, *Nim Chimpsky: The Chimp Who Would Be Human,* by Elizabeth Hess, about a 1970s-era experiment designed to teach a chimpanzee language in a social context, by taking him from his mother in infancy and rearing him as if he were a human boy, in the midst of an upscale Manhattan family. Though Nim did manage to learn excellent skills in American Sign Language and could communicate with it for the rest of his life, his animal nature soon overwhelmed the human members of his naive adoptive family, who were forced to abandon him. He lived out the rest of his sad life in a kind of no-man's-land of foster homes and primate research facilities, never knowing if he was chimp, human, or something in between.

One of my cardinal rules in life is that we must respect animals as the beings they are, rather than as the near-human companions we might wish them to be. To me, having a true bond with an animal means celebrating and honoring its animal nature first, before we start to co-opt it into being our friend, soul mate, or child.

Although puppies may seem like wordless human babies to us, the truth is, puppies are dogs first. Raising a puppy to be a healthy, balanced dog is a very different process from successfully nurturing a baby to be a happy, confident young adult. As much as we may want them to be, puppies are not the dog equivalent of babies, especially by the time we usually take over as their caregivers. Whereas babies are essentially helpless creatures for many months, puppies come into this world as little survival machines, revealing their true animal natures almost immediately after they are born. A three-day-old puppy will already be striving to assert its dominance over its siblings by pushing them away from the mother's nipple. By two to three weeks, that same puppy will be able to walk on its own and will work further to establish its place in the pack. By the time a reputable breeder feels the pup is ready to separate from its mother and littermates—at approximately two months of age—that puppy is already developmentally years ahead of a human baby at the same age. When we adopt a

two-month-old puppy, it is far from helpless, although we often continue to view it that way, and treat it accordingly. In doing so, many
dog owners unknowingly disregard or disrespect a puppy's true nature: its "dogness."

By pampering our growing dogs as if they were helpless babies—
carrying them like purses, indulging their every whim, allowing them
the kinds of liberties we would never allow a growing child—we
thwart their progress from the very start. We can unwittingly nurture
fear, anxiety, aggression, or dominance. We can condemn our dogs to
lives of instability and stress. By putting our own psychological fulfillment before the very real developmental needs of a growing dog, we
may inadvertently create more behavioral issues.

In my experience, it's usually just lack of knowledge that drives
well-meaning dog lovers to make these crucial mistakes. Every dog
owner I've ever met has genuinely wanted only the best for his or her
pet. In this book, I hope to offer some strategies to help owners learn
to maintain the true canine identity of a dog before they make it into
their "baby."

One of the most important things to remember about puppyhood is that it is the shortest stage of a healthy dog's life. A dog is a
puppy from birth to eight months, then an adolescent from eight
months to three years. With good nutrition and veterinary care, a
modern dog's life span can last from ten to twelve to sixteen years or
more.[1] I see far too many humans falling in love with a tiny puppy's
cuteness but eventually losing interest in—or, worse, coming to
resent—the full-grown dog it is destined to become. This truly
breaks my heart. I believe that when we bring a dog into our lives at
any age, we take on a very important responsibility for that dog's
lifelong well-being. Owning a dog should be a joyful experience, not
a stressful one. Sure, it takes focus and commitment in the early
stages, but putting in that hard work up front will pay off in count-
less ways for years and years to come. The dogs in our lives teach us

how to revel in the moment, not obsess over our pasts or our futures. Dogs show us that simple joys—rolling around on the floor, running through the park, splashing in the pool, stretching out on the grass under a warming sun—are still the very best life has to offer. And dogs help us experience a deeper kind of connection—not just with animals but with the other humans in our lives and with ourselves.

If you are certain you want to commit to a dog for life, you truly have an incredible opportunity in front of you. This is truly your chance to create and mold the dog of your family's dreams, as well as nurture another living being into fulfilling all that nature destined it to become. Pups are programmed by their DNA to absorb the rules, boundaries, and limitations of the societies they live in. If you clearly communicate your family's rules to the puppy from day one, you can mold a companion that will respect, trust, and bond with you on a level that you never imagined possible. But, like children, dogs are constantly observing, exploring, and working to figure out how they fit into the world around them. If you consistently send them the wrong signals in the early days of your relationship, it will be a lot more difficult to rehabilitate them once those bad habits are ingrained.

I've raised hundreds of dogs in my life, through many different developmental stages, but when I decided to write this book, I wanted to make sure I was actually going through the process of following several puppies from birth into young adulthood. Every dog I rehabilitate or adopt, every puppy I raise, helps me better understand the nature of dogs and how we humans can give them the best, most balanced life possible. I hope the individual journeys of the dogs that appear in this book will help bring down to earth some of the concepts we'll be discussing.

Can you really raise "the perfect dog"? I absolutely believe you can. That's because I believe nature places the formula for perfection deep within every organism it creates. As human beings, we like to think we can improve upon nature, and perhaps in some areas we can. But when it comes to raising dogs, nature had it right the first time. Let's stop reinventing the wheel and start learning from life's best teachers, the dogs themselves.

1
MEET THE PUPPIES

Junior, Blizzard, Angel, and Mr. President

Junior

When I first imagined writing a book about raising the perfect dog, I wanted it to have a personal touch and a hands-on feeling. In my experience, it's easier to teach using real-life examples. I have raised many dogs in my life, but I wanted to reacquaint myself with all the different stages of puppyhood while I was writing about them so that I would be totally in tune with the behaviors I was describing. To do this, I decided to raise four puppies of different breeds—a pit bull, a Labrador retriever, an English bulldog, and a miniature schnauzer—bringing them up in my home and with my pack using the principles of dog psychology. I want to illustrate to you, my readers, how raising puppies as naturally as possible will prevent problems and issues and will avoid the need for intervention in the future. My goal was not to rehabilitate dogs but to raise balanced dogs and show owners how to maintain the natural balance that Mother Nature has already given them. Therefore, I wanted to select dogs with a certain inborn energy level—what I call "medium-level energy," which is the perfect energy level for even an inexperienced dog owner to deal with. We'll talk more about selecting for energy in the next chapter, but keep this concept in the back of your mind as you join me in the adventure of meeting the puppies.

JUNIOR, THE PIT BULL

Daddy and his protégé, Junior

Although my pit bull, Junior, made his first print appearance in my last book, *A Member of the Family*, I still consider him to be the most significant of the four dogs whose puppyhoods I've chronicled here.

When I began writing this book, Junior was a little over a year and a half old, smack in the heart of his canine adolescence, which lasts from about eight months to three years of age. Since the day I brought him home, *Dog Whisperer* cameras and my own records have recorded nearly every day of his progress, from clumsy toddler to the energetic, confident, yet serene teenager he is today. There are many wonderful lessons from Junior's upbringing that I am thrilled to share with you here.

It was of great personal significance for me to adopt a pit bull puppy as a role model, to be right by my side as I work to rehabilitate unstable dogs. The bad rap that pit bulls get here in the United States is, to my thinking, a crime. First of all, pit bulls are dogs first. They're not wild animals; they're domestic dogs like any other domestic dog. Of course, pit bulls are not always the right dogs for every family— but in blaming pit bulls as a breed for all those horrendous incidents we read about in the news, we're forgetting the basic fact that we humans have created the very characteristics we vilify in pit bulls, simply to fill our own needs. We are responsible for them. Over the centuries, we have genetically engineered these dogs to have strong jaws, relentless staying power, and a high tolerance for discomfort or pain. Those are the plain, unvarnished facts of their DNA. But even in the dog world, DNA isn't destiny. Pit bulls are not born aggressive to dogs or to people—we make them that way. Hundreds of thousands of pit bulls languish in kennels and shelters across the United States because they were originally conditioned by their owners to be "tough," but then they became too much for their owners to handle. Many of those dogs, destined for euthanasia, were bred to fight in the illegal dog-fighting culture, then abandoned on the streets when they didn't prove profitable for their hard-hearted owners. Properly socialized and raised with the same consistent rules, boundaries, and limitations that their natural pack would instill in them, it's been my experience that pit bulls make the most amazing pets.

The very pit bull attributes so often maligned by society can actually be rechanneled into the most positive outlets. For instance, the inborn characteristics of determination and staying power can be transformed into unwavering loyalty and patience. A balanced pit bull has the ability to wait calmly and respectfully for long periods of time, until its owner gives it a new command or direction to follow. With children or smaller puppies, pit bulls can be the epitome of the indulgent babysitter, because their bodies are built to easily withstand the climbing, pushing, and pulling that playful juveniles of both species can inflict. A well-socialized, balanced pit bull will put up with all sorts of childish antics and show stoicism and good humor. I am raising Junior to be much more "dog" than "pit bull," and between him and my senior pit bull, Daddy, I believe I can change the mind of anybody who harbors blind prejudice against the breed.

Any reader who has watched my television program is probably familiar with the soulful green eyes and stocky, golden body of my faithful companion, Daddy. At nearly sixteen years of age, Daddy has experienced everything a modern dog could possibly dream of—traveling all over the United States with me and even walking the red carpet at the Emmys. Daddy's original owner, the rapper Redman, sought out my help in raising Daddy when he was still a playful puppy just four months of age. It was absolutely the most perfect time to start shaping his young mind. Daddy was an eager and receptive pupil to both dogs and humans, and he has grown up to be the best, most positive role model imaginable for his much-maligned breed. He now has his own legion of fans and even has his own Facebook page! He definitely deserves his brilliant reputation. Today Daddy officially belongs to me. He and I share a bond that goes beyond anything nature or science can explain. I believe we have achieved a kind of ideal communion between human and dog, one that I like to use as an example to my clients to prove to them that this kind of healthy closeness with their pet is something very real and within their reach as well.

On dozens of *Dog Whisperer* episodes, when I'm called in to help unstable dogs, Daddy has unquestionably earned his props as my right-hand canine. More often than not, however, he's also my teacher, and I end up following *his* lead on how to proceed, not the other way around. Daddy possesses that rare quality that you can't get without a lot of experience and a lot of years on this planet—genuine wisdom. Because his energy is so completely balanced, sometimes just being in the presence of Daddy will turn a troubled dog around. On other occasions, if I'm not sure of how to proceed on a case, I'll bring Daddy in and closely observe his behavior. One of the most important points I've made in all my teachings—and that I particularly want to stress when it comes to raising puppies—is that a balanced adult dog can teach you more about "dog training" than any book, manual, or video. Daddy doesn't have any diplomas or certificates on the wall of his kennel, but he is the absolute master of dog rehabilitation, as far as I'm concerned.

As a senior dog, Daddy still takes the same delight in the small moments of life that he took as a puppy, but his advancing years are clearly catching up with him physically. I have recently begun to grapple with the reality that he won't be able to play the role of my best pal, sidekick, and co–Dog Whisperer forever. I've heard some dog lovers who, when considering the demise of a lifelong companion, make statements like "There will never be another one like him" or "I could never love another dog, because no other dog could be as wonderful." Of course it's true that there will never be another dog exactly like Daddy, but when I called this book *How to Raise the Perfect Dog*, I wasn't being glib. I really do believe it's possible to raise another dog to be as balanced, stable, well behaved, and as perfectly in sync with me as Daddy has been. I had a plan—Daddy himself was going to pass the baton of his greatness to the next generation—by helping me raise his ideal successor!

PASSING THE BATON

A longtime friend of mine, a vet tech who also happens to be from my home state of Sinaloa, Mexico, understands and agrees with my philosophies about raising dogs and also owns a female pit bull that I know to be calm and balanced—an easygoing family dog that had always been a dream "nanny" to his own small children. My friend informed me that he had selectively bred this dog and that she had a new litter of puppies. Knowing of Daddy's impending retirement and my growing concerns about it, he invited me to come take a look at them, saying, "Who knows, you might find the next Daddy."

When Daddy and I arrived at my friend's house to see the litter, I was relieved to find the bitch just as affectionate, gentle, and submissive with human kids as I had remembered. She had the ideal temperament for a family dog and was also an active, alert, and attentive mother to her pups. The temperament of a pup's parents is vital, because temperament is a characteristic often passed down from generation to generation. My friend showed me a photo of the puppies' father—also a well-bred, healthy pit bull, as well as a prize show dog. Though I couldn't meet the sire in person because he was already back in his home state, I know that show dogs by definition need to have a degree of self-control, patience, and stability above and beyond that of the average household pet. As I looked over the litter of cuddly, clumsy eight-week-old puppies, one dog immediately caught my eye. He was all gray with a little white on his chest, and he had the most gentle powder blue eyes. He was what is known as a blue pit. But what attracted me most to him was his energy. Though he didn't resemble Daddy at all physically, his serene demeanor reminded me of him instantly.

I was immediately drawn to this particular pup, but in this case I wasn't the most experienced dog whisperer in the room. This was a job for Daddy. Any dog can tell you much more about another animal—dog, cat, or human!—than a human can, which is why I always take my dogs' instincts very seriously. In fact, I frequently bring Daddy or another of my most balanced dogs with me to business meetings, to see how the dogs respond to any people I am meeting for the first time. If one of my easygoing, calm-submissive dogs inexplicably shrinks away from, ignores, or otherwise avoids a certain person, I always pay close attention. My dog may be trying to tell me something I need to know.

I escorted Daddy into the room full of playful pit bull puppies—a dignified elder statesman making an appearance in a boisterous kindergarten class. I had noticed one of the puppies acting a little dominant around the children in the family—climbing on them and mouthing them—so I tried introducing him to Daddy. Daddy immediately growled at him and turned away. At Daddy's age, he hasn't got the energy or patience for ill-mannered, pushy youngsters. Another pup I picked out—a lower-energy fellow—didn't interest Daddy at all; he totally ignored him. Older dogs don't waste their precious energy on puppies that annoy them. But how would Daddy react to the gray pup that had so attracted me? I was praying that our energies and instincts would be on the same wavelength for this very important decision.

I gently lifted the little gray guy up by his scruff and presented his rear to Daddy, who showed immediate interest. He checked the puppy out by sniffing, then signaled with his head for me to put him down on the ground. When I lowered the puppy, the little guy automatically bowed his head in a very polite, submissive way to Daddy. It was clear that at only eight weeks of age, his mother had already taught him the basics of canine etiquette—respect for your elders. Daddy continued to smell him, and it was obvious there was an attraction there. But the most wonderful thing happened next! When Daddy finished checking the puppy out and began to walk away, the puppy immediately started to follow him. From that very first moment, I was certain that this little gray bundle of fur was going to be Daddy's spiritual "son." And America would soon have a new, calm, well-behaved pit bull role model to look up to.

HOW *NOT* TO RAISE MARLEY

Blizzard, the Labrador Retriever

John Grogan's *Marley and Me* was on the *New York Times* bestseller list for fifty-four weeks, then was adapted into a feature film that grossed more than $215 million worldwide. It even spawned a sequel named (much to my chagrin as Dog Whisperer!) *Bad Dogs Have More Fun.* Through Grogan's heartfelt, evocative writing, Marley has become the symbol of one of the most popular family pet breeds in America, the Labrador retriever. Labradors are the number one pet dog in America because of their friendliness, energy, and happy-go-lucky demeanor, and Marley epitomized that same goofy, exuberant, bouncy behavior. But Marley took that behavior too far, to the point of being out of control. "Marley," writes John Grogan, "was a challenging student, dense, wild, constantly distracted, a victim of his boundless nervous energy. . . . As my father put it shortly after Marley attempted marital relations with his knee, 'That dog's got a screw loose.' "

Marley became the inspiration for me to adopt a yellow Lab as the second dog whose puppyhood I would chronicle for this book. As much as I laughed and cried reading John Grogan's memoir of Marley, and as much as I appreciated having the chance to work with the Grogan family and their current Lab, Gracie, I wanted to offer a different perspective on the life of a Labrador retriever. In other words, I wanted to write the chapter on how *not* to raise the next Marley.

I turned to Crystal Reel, the intrepid researcher at our *Dog Whisperer* production company, MPH Entertainment, to help me find the perfect

Labrador puppy. Though there are plenty of Labrador breeders in Southern California, we decided to show our support for one of our area's excellent rescue groups that save the lives of lost, abandoned, and rejected dogs every day. Crystal contacted Southern California Labrador Retriever Rescue, an eleven-year-old nonprofit organization dedicated to the mission of rehabilitating and rehoming Labrador retrievers and educating the public about these wonderful dogs. Over several weeks, Crystal coordinated with SCLRR volunteer Geneva Ledesma, screening several potential puppies available for adoption. We finally narrowed the search down to two dogs, and Geneva and her fellow volunteer, Valerie Dorsch, agreed to bring both dogs to meet me at the original Dog Psychology Center in downtown Los Angeles.

The month of October can still feel like summertime in Southern California, but there was a morning breeze easing away the heat as I slid open the gates to my downtown Dog Psychology Center, revealing the two Labrador puppy candidates from which I would choose my Marley. Geneva and Valerie each held the leash of one of the rescues. The first, a sleek and solid black Labrador pup, had been picked up as a stray running loose in a field. The other, yellow like the Marley of literary fame, had been dropped off at a shelter with a couple of his littermates. Both were male, around two months old, and both were incredibly cute. Both had also just finished with their second set of shots, so their medical histories were in order, despite the fact that they were rescued off the street.

Since my goal for this project was prevention, not intervention, I wanted to choose a puppy with a naturally calm-submissive demeanor and raise him to remain that way, so he could become the perfect family dog. It took only seconds for me to determine that the yellow Lab was the right guy. He sniffed around a little, slightly curious, then sat back on his haunches and relaxed. Within a few minutes, he was stretching his body out on the sun-warmed pavement. The black Lab, on the other hand, was already acting a little skittish, nervous, and overexcited. His body was turned away from us and he was pulling back on the leash, holding himself slightly back. Now, I could easily work with him and rehabilitate that state. But I wanted to do something different for this book—I wanted to use the natural balance Mother Nature has already programmed into dogs and show you, my readers, how to nurture and maintain that state.

Both Valerie and Geneva were shocked that I chose the yellow Lab, because they thought I'd be attracted to the more "active" puppy. "I thought the yellow puppy was lazy," Valerie commented. Despite being experienced "dog people," they were not able to discern nervous energy from playful energy. Once I pointed out the indications of the black Lab's anxious energy, Geneva began to see what I was talking about. "Can I ask you, how do they become like this?" she queried tentatively. "Are they born this way?" I told her that sometimes scary early puppyhood experiences can make a dog unsure, especially if he doesn't have an attentive mother or a pack leader to guide him through the experience the right way. A normal dog is a curious dog, even if he is a little tentative at first. When you see extremely fearful, shrinking behavior from the beginning, that's a potential red flag.

Some puppies are born weak or scared, the proverbial "runts of the litter," and the brutal truth is, in a natural habitat, those puppies probably wouldn't make it. As humans, we tend to feel bad about them. But we have to learn to help them overcome that state of mind. Otherwise, we will keep them that way, by feeling bad about them. It's a wonderful thing to rescue dogs that have become lost in the physical world, but we also need to learn how to rescue them from their fearful psychological worlds. No dog should have to live his whole life in fear. And that kind of rehabilitation starts with our own calm-assertive energy. It's easy to go running up to a nervous puppy and, in a high voice, cry out, "Oh, it's okay, sweetie, it's all right!" We think by showering them with what *we* define as love, affection, and comfort, we can help them. But for a nervous puppy, an approach like that will only intensify his anxiety or excitement. I showed the ladies how to use scent to distract the black pup's nose, to help release his brain from being "locked" into that negative, nervous state. I passed a can of organic dog food just in front of him, without invading his space. Just a whiff of the food and the little guy perked up, then sat back on his haunches. His ears relaxed. I didn't use words. I didn't use petting. By remaining calm, strong, and silent but engaging his strongest sense—smell—I was able to snap him out of his anxious state of mind.

"The truth is," I continued, "this yellow guy, in the hands of an owner who doesn't give rules or gives only affection, affection, affection, could easily become overexcited or anxious or nervous, too. My goal is to nurture his beautiful, natural state for the first eight months of his life. Because by eight months, that's it. Puppyhood is done. At eight months, they hit adolescence, so they begin to challenge, but if they are raised with rules, boundaries, and limitations, they will always know how to go back to balance."

While I had been chatting with the ladies from Southern California Labrador Retreiver Rescue, my little Marley had become so relaxed, the sun had lulled him into a deep, peaceful sleep. I reached for my can of dog food again. "With puppies, sometimes we can create a nervous or spooked reaction from them if we startle them while they are sleeping," I explained. I waved the can of dog food under his nose, but he didn't wake up until he sensed the black Lab nudging his way over to get a sniff at the food as well. "See how he was not shocked or surprised when he awoke?" I pointed out. "It's a normal behavior among puppies, with their littermates, to nudge one another, step on one another, wake one another up. So I'm triggering the brain to wake up in a familiar way, not a startling way, since my hand is not familiar to him yet."

Having made my choice, I was ready to introduce the new puppy into the pack. But with puppies, every first impression is important, so I had to do it right the first time. Attracted by the food, the mini

Marley happily followed me toward the inner area of the Dog Psychology Center, to the fence behind which the pack eagerly awaited their newest and youngest member. He sniffed the fence cautiously, then his tail started to wag. If he had been too excited or too bold, the pack would have perceived it as a negative, but the little guy kept his head held low, in a respectful manner. He was ready.

A quick note here about puppy health and safety (which we'll consider in more depth in future chapters). Before introducing the new Labrador puppy to my pack, the ladies from SCLRR and I had to be sure that the health of the puppy and the health of my other dogs were being protected. The SCLRR volunteers first made sure that both puppies had clean bills of health and had their first two rounds of shots. Even with shots, however, a pup's immune system is still developing until four months of age, and it is during these crucial months that he is still susceptible to diseases, particularly the parvovirus. Parvo is passed through the feces of infected dogs. Therefore, before SCLRR would sign off on allowing whichever puppy I chose to interact with my dogs, SCLRR wanted me to verify that all the dogs at the Dog Psychology Center were also up-to-date on their immunizations, that our facility was sanitary, and that we had not had any recent outbreaks of parvo or other contagious diseases. Once the SCLRR volunteers were sure of this, they okayed the Labrador to be with my dogs. In this case, there were two parties—the rescuers and the new adoptive owner—looking out for the puppy's health and welfare. We must be responsibly cautious during this window of a puppy's life, while his immune system is still developing, but at the same time, we can't deprive him of normal socialization experiences, which are equally as important to his overall well-being.

I put one hand on the scruff of his neck and lifted him off the ground. That gesture immediately sent him into a relaxed state, although I was supporting his full weight with my other hand on his lower body. Bringing him low to the ground, I presented him to the

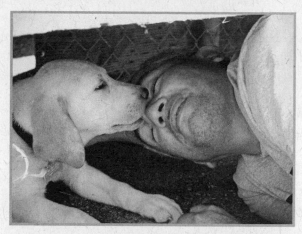

Blizzard shows Cesar some affection.

pack. His tail was partially between his legs, signaling a little anxiety, so I waited until it relaxed before placing him on the ground. The other dogs sniffed him gently, accepting him immediately. Within ten minutes, he was happily and confidently exploring his new environment. This little guy may have looked exactly like the Marley of literary and cinematic fame, but he was going to have an entirely different experience of life.

FOLLOW YOUR NOSE

Angel, the Miniature Schnauzer

Having selected my Labrador puppy from a rescue group, I wanted to go to a top-notch breeder to find a dog in the terrier category that would become the next puppy for this project. A characteristic of the terrier breeds is that they are exceedingly scent-driven dogs. Since "nose-eyes-ears" is the formula I always teach my clients to employ when communicating with all dogs, I wanted to have a nose-dominant breed among the puppies I raised for the book. A dog's nose can get him into trouble if he's bored, but if that scent-driven energy is properly channeled at an early age, your dog's nose can become your key to his heart—and his mind.

Brooke Walker is a statuesque redhead who oozes positive energy, and if given the opportunity, she can talk all day about her life's passion: breeding show-quality miniature schnauzers. From the first moment I met her, I could tell that Brooke really knows her stuff. I asked her how she came to be interested in this particular breed.

"After I retired from thirty-eight years as a flight attendant, I knew I wanted a dog and I hadn't had a dog in a number of years. So I went to a dog show and visited with the breeders, asked a lot of questions. That's a great place to go to learn about dogs, because every breeder imaginable is there and breeders like to talk. The miniature schnauzers caught my eye because they have an elegance about them; they're just an elegant, handsome breed."

Of course, like most breeders, Brooke has become even more an aficionado of her chosen dog over the five years she has been raising them. "Miniature schnauzers don't shed; they don't have dander. They are the perfect size—you can take them on an airplane in a carry-on and they fit right under the seat so you don't have to put them in the plane belly. I travel with my dogs all the time."

It had rained the day before I drove down to Costa Mesa, California, to pick out my schnauzer from Brooke's latest litter. The home environment was serene and peaceful, neat and tidy, despite the fact that there were three two-month-old puppies, a breeding pair, and a senior male dog running around on the property. That's an excellent sign right there. If you go to check out a breeder and walk into chaos, with jumping, yelping, or nipping dogs all over the place, it's important to remember that this is the environment in which your puppy had its first formative experiences. A dog raised in a chaotic environment will naturally absorb that unstable energy from the moment it is born. I've worked with several clients with miniature schnauzers who've told me they just assumed that hyperactive energy and incessant barking were part of the "package" of the breed. Brooke's pack quickly disproved that myth. The atmosphere was quiet and calm, although her pups were still curious or playful.

We sat on Brooke's well-tended flagstone patio and observed the pups as they wrestled and explored, delighting in every new sight and sound they encountered. Watching along with us was their vigilant mother, a schnauzer named Binky who was nearly two years old. While she seemed relaxed and interested in our human activities most of the time, every now and then one of her pups' antics would catch her attention. I noticed that when the female pup harassed one of her brothers a little too long, Binky jumped down from her perch on the stone firepit and, in a split second, gently mouthed the offender and put her on her side. A mother dog allows her pups to play dominance games with each other, but when they get too intense, she will step in and manage the situation. As soon as the female pup relaxed, as if to say, "Okay, Mom, I got the message," the mother went right back to nosing around Brooke and me. Such is the speed, precision, and matter-of-fact nature of a mother dog's corrections, and it is this calm-assertive, gentle but firm, natural discipline that I advocate owners emulate with their own dogs. Observing and imitating good canine mothers such as Binky is exactly how I learned my own techniques.

Brooke had three schnauzer pups to show me—two males, one with a blue paper collar and one with a green, and a female with a pink collar. The female was the smallest of the three. Upon observing her pouncing on her green-collared brother, however, I could tell that her energy level was still quite high. Brooke's clear favorite, and the dog she assumed I'd choose, was Mr. Blue Collar, a coal black schnauzer with glistening silver eyebrows, chest, feet, and tail. She introduced him as "the pick of the litter." "He was the first to do everything. He was the first to climb out of his whelping pen. He was the first to bark. He was the first to go over to the other puppies when he was just in 'swimming' mode, and he was even the first one to get on all fours. He has a lot of natural intelligence, a lot of leadership qualities."

Her description of the first two dogs' energies placed the green-collared male at the bottom of the family hierarchy. But it was clear to me that he was not a fearful or anxious dog, and his energy was medium level, not low. To test their different temperaments, I put each of the three pups up on three different garden chairs. Mr. Blue immediately jumped right off the chair and came running back to me; he wanted to be in the middle of things. When Brooke put him back on the chair, he jumped right off again. It took a little longer for the female, Ms. Pink, to jump off, but eventually she couldn't take the waiting anymore and followed her dominant brother's example. Of all the dogs, only Mr. Green was able to sit on the chair and just observe. He didn't whine, he didn't squirm, he simply waited, alert, to take his next cue from me. I asked Brooke about her experience with him. "I think he is going to make a fabulous pet because he is so, so loving. He's more mild-mannered than his brother, less independent. But personally, I like the more independent dogs because I find they're very easy to train."

Like the ladies from Southern California Labrador Retriever Rescue, Brooke also seemed genuinely surprised when I chose Mr. Green Collar—the medium-energy dog—as the dog I wanted to raise for this book. I reminded her that, although as Dog Whisperer I enjoy higher-energy dogs, most potential owners are not as experienced as she and I, and can easily let an independent, dominant pup overwhelm them once they bring him home. My goal for this book was to find pups that would start out life with the perfect, inborn "medium" energy level—suitable for any average or even inexperienced dog owner or family—and to share with my readers exactly how to main-

Angel and his littermates

tain that state of mind during the crucial months of puppyhood and beyond.

After choosing Mr. Green, I asked Brooke if she could find me a towel or cloth that carried the scent of his canine family of origin, to help ease his transition from his first pack into my pack. Brooke did much more than that. She presented me with his "papers"—including his passport certifying that he is a miniature schnauzer male, his AKC certification, documents showing the date, place, and type of inoculations that he had already received, and the recommended dates for his next round of shots. She also gave me a brochure with rich information about the miniature schnauzer breed, a trimming chart, and a little "going-away" gift basket containing treats, a teddy bear dog toy, and a grooming brush. That's the "personal touch" that you're going to get when you adopt a dog from a top-notch breeder. For breeders like Brooke, every dog is not just a dog. It's absolutely a family member, and while her life's mission is to find these dogs great homes, every pup that she sells will take a little bit of her heart with it when it goes out the door.

I'm a major supporter of shelter or rescue organization adoption, and I always encourage people who want to go this route for finding the right dog. The problem of canine overpopulation in America is staggering, and two to three million dogs are put to death each year simply because there are no homes for them. Every dog that finds its way into a family from a shelter or rescue group is one less dog that will lose its precious life simply because it was unwanted by a human. And there's a special satisfaction that comes from giving a rescue dog a great life. But for those of you who do decide to go the breeder route, finding someone like Brooke is like striking gold. When you bring home a puppy from a breeder with Brooke's level of high ethics and years of experience, you are not just bringing home that one dog, you are bringing home the rarefied bloodlines of many generations of dogs—in essence, you are owning a little bit of canine history. Brooke says the three most important qualities she breeds for are health, temperament, and conformation—that is, maintaining the integrity of the breed. In the next chapter we'll talk more about how to find breeders like Brooke.

One of the ways such breeders preserve their chosen breed's lineage is to make sure their puppies do not fall into the wrong hands. A huge red flag indicating a less-than-reputable breeder is someone who will sell you a puppy sight unseen, without asking you any questions about your experience with dogs, your home environment, and your intentions for caring for the dog. An important item for most breeders is the adoption contract. Brooke had me sign a contract that stipulated that I would not neuter Mr. Green until the eight-month puppyhood period was up. Personally, I prefer to neuter male dogs at six months, to prevent them from ever experiencing the overwhelming, uncomfortable urge to mate. But I understand Brooke's criterion—as a breeder, she wants the pup to grow to full adolescence before she decides whether or not to mate the dog, to continue its valuable bloodline. I also agreed that, at the end of the puppyhood period, I would return the dog to her if I decided not to keep him or didn't find a place-ment both she and I agreed was suitable. I greatly admire Brooke's de-votion to her litters.

During the half hour or so we spent going over the puppy's paper-work, Mr. Green sat next to me, quietly chilling out. That's pretty amazing for any puppy. Then and there, Mr. Green confirmed for me that I had chosen the right miniature schnauzer puppy to raise for this book.

After signing the papers and saying good-bye to Brooke, I brought Mr. Green to my car, first putting the blanket from his mother's bed on the seat to attract him. Of course, I had to lift him from the ground onto the car's running board, but I wanted to let him go onto the seat by himself as much as possible. With a puppy, patience is key, and the first time you separate a puppy from his first pack is one of those occa-sions when you need to call up all the patience you can muster. I held a bully stick—which is like a rawhide bone but is actually a dried bull penis—in front of his nose, and let him follow the scent as I gently pushed his rear up into the car. From there, I was able to easily guide him into the crate in which he would ride to his new home and family in Santa Clarita. Once I got him home, my boys were so impressed by his sweet temperament, they promptly gave Mr. Green the new name Angel.

HAIL TO THE CHIEF

Mr. President, the English Bulldog

Now that I had in place America's next favorite pit bull, my happy-go-lucky Labrador, and my nose-driven terrier breed, I wanted to choose a breed with completely different inborn characteristics for the final puppy in the project. I've always had a special affinity for bulldogs—

and in America, I'm not alone. According to *USA Today*, bulldogs have made their way onto the AKC's "top ten most popular dogs in America" list for the past two years.[1] I imagine many of you reading this are considering a bulldog-type dog as a possible breed for you. There are lots of stereotypes about bulldogs—that they are all lazy couch potatoes, that they don't need much energy or stimulation, or that they are consistently laid-back, mellow, and gentle in temperament. In many cases, these stereotypes can prove true, but there is another side of the coin.

The truth is, the bulldog originated in the British Isles, its name a reference to the purpose it was originally genetically engineered to fill—as a star player in the brutal but unfortunately popular sport of bullbaiting, in which a bull was placed in a pen or a hole, and one or more dogs were set upon him, to clamp down on his neck with their jaws. The first bulldogs—descendants of ancient Asian mastiffs mixed with pugs—were specifically bred for ferocity, staying power, and an astonishing resistance to pain. When bullbaiting was made illegal in England in 1835, a kinder, gentler generation of bulldog lovers took over the line, eventually breeding out most of the fierceness of the original Olde English bulldog. But those characteristics of pugnacity, persistence, and what many call "stubbornness" remain deeply lodged in every bulldog's DNA. With some individual dogs, it can be quite a challenge to properly channel those breed-related tendencies.

One thing that is little known about bulldogs of all varieties is that they are in a sense handicapped from birth by the fact that they have been designed by humans to have pushed-in, flat noses and small windpipes. Mother Nature didn't plan this kind of nose in her blueprint for canines, but back in the bulldog's history, humans theorized that a flatter snout allowed for a stronger jaw to clamp onto the bull. The fact that bulldogs wheeze and snore is often a subject of good-humored sympathy among bulldog owners, and this is one of the side effects of their unnatural physical design as dogs.

Another result of their unique physical design means that bulldogs' sense of smell is generally not going to be as powerful as that of other breeds, which puts them at a disadvantage when it comes to tracking and makes it harder for them to find their way back if they get lost or separated from their pack. They can also fall into a pattern of using their eyes more than their noses in responding to the world around them, which is not natural for a dog and can cause them to get into more conflicts with other dogs right off the bat, if they engage in eye contact with a stranger too soon or at the wrong time. Since I believe that a dog's nose is the key to his behavior, I wanted to raise an English bulldog the right way, by going the extra mile to give him the kind of scent-driven upbringing that the rest of my dogs get to experience. I wanted to bring out the best of his species-related qualities—patience, loyalty, and affection—in order for him to grow up more dog than bulldog.

My dream English bulldog would come to me the same month I got Angel, from a longtime acquaintance of mine who specializes in breeding English bulldogs with mild, reliable temperaments. My friend knew I wanted a medium-energy-level dog and one of his bitches had just given birth to one. This chunky, white-and-brown guy who looked like he was wearing baggy pajamas was the only dog of his mother's litter; in fact, he was delivered by C-section, the way most bulldogs must be—another side effect of human genetic engineering that's made bulldog pups' heads and barrel chests so much bigger than their mothers' narrow hips and birth canals can bear. Our researcher, Crystal Reel, came with me to pick up the new bulldog puppy. She was ecstatic because English bulldogs are her favorite breed. I let her name the little guy, who is now known as General George Washington, or Mr. President for short.

If you've watched episodes of *Dog Whisperer,* you may have seen two of the many bulldogs I have been called in to rehabilitate—Jordan, from season one, and Matilda, from season three—both obsessed with skateboards. They would attack them, grab them in their jaws, clamp down, and hold on for dear life. Obsessive mouthing behavior—chewing, pouncing, and never letting go—is one of those ancient bulldog traits I described and one that you as an owner need to manage or discourage early on. Puppyhood is the time when you have the best chance of dialing down the volume on this breed-related behavior that resulted in the old cliché "stubborn as a bulldog."

Mr. President started showing his bulldog nature as soon as I brought him home. He was the only one of the four puppies raised during the writing of this book that ever had a chewing issue. When the puppy reaches two months of age, however, owners have the perfect opportunity to stop or redirect that behavior before it escalates into a problem. With Mr. President, I began by distracting him with various pleasing scents, not only to redirect his naturally obsessive energy but also to encourage him to use his nose more. If his intensity level is too high, a very light touch to his neck or haunches snaps him out of obsessive behavior immediately. I'll discuss redirecting and correcting unwanted behavior more in Chapter 4.

Hand correction to Mr. President's neck

THE PUPPIES COME HOME

By the time I began writing this book, I had my four puppies in place. Junior was a full-blown adolescent, a year and a half in age. Blizzard, the yellow Lab, had just turned four months old, and both the little miniature schnauzer, Angel, and the English bulldog, Mr. President, were just over two months old. Since I was in the process of moving my original Dog Psychology Center in downtown Los Angeles to a new 43-acre plot of land in the wild, hilly terrain of Santa Clarita Valley, I had already dispersed many of the dogs in my pack to permanent homes, to temporary foster homes, or to the facility in Templeton, California, of my friend and protégée, Cheri Lucas, where she keeps her own pack of fifty dogs for rescue and rehabilitation. This meant that the new puppies would be raised at Casa Millan—our midsize, suburban ranch-style home in Santa Clarita Valley—with daily excursions to the outdoor oasis of my new Dog Psychology Center property just a short drive away, as I worked to prepare it for its opening in the fall of 2009. All told, our core family pack (including my wife, Ilusion, and sons, Calvin and Andre) now comprised the four puppies, Junior, Blizzard, Angel, and Mr. President; my grandfatherly pit bull, Daddy (fifteen); our Chihuahuas, Coco (five) and Minnie (two); our Jack Russell terrier, Jack (four); Apollo, a Rottweiler (approximately two and a half); and a two-year-old Yorkie, Georgia Peaches, a puppy-mill survivor that I had recently rescued while in Atlanta for a speaking engagement. Because the Dog Psychology Center was in flux, I also regularly brought home dogs from the *Dog Whisperer* show that needed more intensive rehab, so the pups would be exposed to a revolving cast of different breeds, ages, and levels of stability.

My puppy experiment was ready to begin. The goal was to raise four balanced dogs of different breeds, to maintain the stability they were already born with, and to prevent any future issues from forming. Throughout the rest of this book, these puppies will appear in costarring roles with me as they go through their different developmental stages, so you can see exactly how I applied the concepts of dog psychology to their rearing.

I felt inspired and invigorated as I set up a line of baby gates and rearranged the row of comfortable kennels where our dogs sleep in my large garage, which has an open door that leads to the side yard. Eager to help, Calvin and Andre pitched in to prepare our home for this exciting new experience. For the next seven months, my whole family and I would be immersed in the pure delight of watching these dogs as they lived through the magical season of life that is puppyhood, and on into their adolescence.

2
PERFECT MATCH
Choosing the Perfect Puppy

Georgia Peaches

Growing up on my grandfather's farm in rural Sinaloa, Mexico, I lived among scruffy farm dogs, our loyal friends and coworkers in the fields and around the house. You wouldn't call these dogs "pets" by American standards, in that their lives were spent near us but not as a part of us. They were our dogs, yet they lived in a world separate from our human lives, content and balanced in their own dog culture. I watched a lot of litters born among these dogs, and though the puppies were sweet and appealing, I never really experienced the extraordinary "cuteness" of puppies until I came to America and was exposed to the hundreds of breeds in this country: French bulldog puppies, with their flattened snouts and oversized brown eyes, or Lhasa apso or Westie or poodle puppies, all heartbreakingly adorable balls of fluff. When I saw some of these more attractive breeds as pups, I began to better understand why Americans tended to "baby" their dogs—something that is not a part of the culture in Mexico.

All baby animals are appealing, but in my personal opinion, puppies simply corner the market in cuteness. Even the most hard-hearted human can't help but stop and sigh when passing a puppy on the street. I have many clients who are ruthless businesspeople in their professional lives but who absolutely melt into butter at the sight of a juvenile dog. According to Canadian psychologist and animal behavior expert Dr. Stanley Coren, "Very young mammals have pheromones that give them a characteristic 'baby smell.' One of the purposes of these pheromones is to excite protective instincts, or at least non-hostile instincts, in its own species. However, because of the similarity amongst all the mammals, we tend to find that other animals will respond to it."[1] Coren's words offer a partial explanation for the deep "friendships" we have seen develop between an older, more protective animal and another of a different species. Whether it be Koko the gorilla and her pet kitten, or a lioness and a wolf cub, the innate drive to care for an infant runs deep within all mammals.

But a puppy's cuteness can be its—and our—downfall. The "cute response" we feel when we get the irresistible impulse to bring home a puppy is an emotional response, not a rational one. John Grogan perfectly captures the universal experience of "puppy love" in his wonderful memoir of a lovable but unpredictable Labrador, *Marley and Me.* "The deal I had struck with Jenny when we agreed to come here was that we would check the pups out, ask some questions, and keep an open mind as to whether or not we were ready to bring home a dog. . . . I said, 'Let's not make any snap judgments.' But thirty seconds into it, I could see I had already lost the battle. There was no question that before the night was out, one of these puppies would be ours."[2]

I can't tell you how many times I have heard variations on that same theme when I'm called in to help rehabilitate a dog with issues. Unfortunately, those stories don't always end with a best-selling book and hit movie. Sometimes they end with the disillusioned, frustrated owners tearing their hair out, and eventually dropping off their puppy or dog at a rescue or shelter. Sometimes those abandonments result in an innocent dog losing its life.

When you bring home a puppy, you are actually bringing home what in a few short months will be a full-grown dog—not a stuffed animal that will stay small and cuddly forever. Animal lovers, especially those of us who work with dogs day in and day out, take very seriously the staggering number of dogs languishing in kennels and pounds. In recent years, responsible breeders, rescue organizations, and even shelters have become much more aware of the consequences of homing one of their puppies with an owner who isn't realistic about his or her ability to care for a puppy. Often they will require the potential owner to fill out a contract and will even perform a "home visit" to make sure the owner's environment is appropriate for raising a dog. Angel's breeder, Brooke Walker, makes all new owners of her pedigree miniature schnauzers sign a contract stating that if the circumstances change and they're no longer able to have a dog, they will return the dog to her for rehoming. She also microchips her dogs so that if they are ever lost, they can be traced back to her.

Two certified trainers and award-winning breeders I have worked with, Diana Foster and her husband, Doug, have been running their business, Thinschmidt German Shepherds in Corona, California, for thirty-four years now. They not only breed pedigree German shepherd puppies with excellent temperaments for pets, they also train them. Diana describes the detailed grilling she gives potential owners before agreeing to adopt out one of her purebred shepherd pups: "We have a lengthy discussion with them. The first thing I ask is if they ever had a shepherd before. Some people don't understand how much of a dog it is, 'cause they're so cute when they're little. But they have to understand what these dogs are bred for and the size and the strength and how important the early training is. I ask them why they want a shepherd. What's the reason? Is it going to be a guard dog that stays outside all the time? If so, we won't sell them one of our dogs—that's not what we breed them for. Our dogs are family. Right away I ask them if there are children in the family. Do you have any dogs? Are they males or females? Are you active? Is the dog going to be with the family? Where is he going to sleep? We provide a diagram with our suggestions of how to set up your home to get it ready for the dog. We don't want to send one of our dogs off until we have a very good idea of what its life is going to be like."

Like the Fosters, Brooke Walker carefully considers whom she allows to take home one of her prize miniature schnauzer puppies.

If it's a two-career couple with toddlers, they're not going to have the kind of time it takes to raise one of these puppies right. My dogs are great with kids—that's not the problem—and the dog is going to survive as long as it's cared for, of course, but if the dog is not getting enough individual attention, that's not the kind of life I want for one of *my* puppies. I ask, where will the dog fit in, in the dynamic of the family? If they have a yard, it has to be fenced, that's absolutely imperative. For people who live in a small place, they have to give me the commitment that they're going to walk their dog—and I'm not talking around the block. Psychologically they have to have that long walk. Miniature schnauzers' noses are always going; they need the stimulation of changing sights and sounds and places.

Brooke also has a checklist in place that prospective adoptive owners have to complete before she'll allow them to take possession of the dog.

First of all, I ask that anybody who takes a puppy has a reputable veterinarian already in place. I ask them to show me at least a business card, proving that they've spoken to a vet and have him or her on board. People who've had dogs before usually have their vet already, but new dog owners have to find one they trust before I'll let them take the puppy home. I want them to come to visit the puppies at two weeks of age, but if this is their first schnauzer, I also insist that they go to a dog show and spend some time around the grown dogs. They have to be as much in love with the adult dog as they are with the puppy, because I want my dogs to have a home for life.

If you are unsure about your ability to care for a puppy, ask yourself if *you* could pass Brooke's stringent requirements for ownership of one of her prize puppies:

• Do you have a vet? Is he or she a specialist or at least very experienced in treating small-breed dogs or terriers?
• Is your vet aware of the fact that you are getting a new puppy?
• Have you set an appointment for a health evaluation of that puppy within three days of bringing your puppy home?
• Have you had a puppy before? What breed? Where did you purchase it? How long did it live? What can you tell me about your experience with your previous dogs?
• Do you kennel/crate-train your dogs?
• Do you have children? What ages? What responsibilities will they have regarding the puppy? Do your children act appropriately with dogs now?

• Do you have a fenced-in yard? How large and how secure is it? Do you have a pool? Is it completely secure so that there are no ways of getting into it accidentally without a parent present?

• Do you work? How many hours would be the longest that the dog would be alone? (Brooke says she favors retired folks—their dogs are always with them. She's an advocate for dogs being taken everywhere with their humans . . . except to the movies.)

• Are you able to afford to care for a dog? Will you take the dog for regular vet checks? Will you feed high-quality food and avoid overfeeding? (No table scraps and no begging!)

Brooke insists on the following steps:

• Prospective buyers must come to her home at least once and visit a dog show to see the adult schnauzers before they get on her list of potential parents.

• When they come for puppy pickup day, they need to spend at least one hour for a brief socialization with their new puppy. At that time they are required to bring a crate, a water dish and bottled water, a leash, and a harness that will fit the puppy.

• Brooke requests periodic progress reports. She thinks of her buyers as family, and they are always invited for play days that she holds once a month for siblings and other schnauzers. Socialization is important to a dog's mental health.

• Buyers must sign a sales contract prior to getting the puppy.

• Brooke's contract stipulates that if owners have a change in life circumstances that requires that they give up the dog, the dog must be returned to her. If they have a family member willing to take over the dog, Brooke wants to meet them and have them answer some basic questions.

• Brooke would like to be informed of any illnesses, regardless of how seemingly insignificant. If the dog should die, she wants to be informed and will pay for a necropsy so that she can record any information that will be helpful for the future of her breeding program.

Diana Foster and her husband are just as serious as Brooke when it comes to selecting the right owners for their prize German shepherd pups. "The hardest part of being a breeder is trying to overcome ignorance," says Diana. "A German shepherd is a lot of dog, but people only see how cute the puppies are and assume it's going to be easy. We breed dogs with wonderful temperaments, but they don't raise themselves. When people obviously aren't getting the picture, they can't believe it when I turn them away."

The Monks of New Skete, also renowned German shepherd breeders, describe another example of this phenomenon in their excellent book, *The Art of Raising a Puppy*. When they showed one prospective owner the application form she would have to fill out before being able to purchase a puppy, she exclaimed, "My heavens, you'd think I was adopting a child!"[3] To be honest, this woman wasn't too far off in her assessment. As a father, I can attest to the fact that while raising a healthy, balanced dog is nowhere near as *complicated* a task as raising a healthy, balanced human, it is absolutely no less of a *commitment*.

WILL YOU MAKE THE TIME?

Unlike adult dogs, puppies in their first six to eight months of life require consistent supervision, and they'll continue to need a significant time commitment from you well into their adolescence. In a natural pack, puppies are constantly being watched and corrected by the adults in their lives and are never alone for long periods of time. This doesn't mean you have to be with your puppy 24/7 for eight months—the reality of our human lives means we have to teach a puppy to master something that is completely unnatural for him, and that is to be left alone. Proper crate training at an early age can successfully accomplish this and prevent the separation anxiety issues that I see in my work almost every day. I'll address both crate training and separation anxiety in Chapter 4. But bringing home a puppy does mean that you should be open to rearranging your family's schedule for a while. Puppies also need regular stimulation through play, and if you don't have another dog to undertake that task for you, you run the risk of an idle mind getting into trouble when you're not paying attention.

FIRST-TIME OWNERS: LIFESTYLE CHANGES

Chris Komives filming a dog up close

Sometimes when we're joking around on *Dog Whisperer* locations, I like to lighten the mood by pondering what breed my human pack members might've been if they'd been born dogs. Curly-haired cameraman Chris Komives is *definitely* a terrier, in both looks and behavior. Chris is the guy who goes in before I arrive and gets all the close-up "bad behavior" footage, and he is relentless about getting exactly the right shot, no matter the difficulty, discomfort, or even danger. He himself admits he's a bit of an obsessive personality. It took a lot of work for me to teach him how to approach unstable dogs, patiently ignore them, use "no touch, no talk, no eye contact," and wait beside them in a quiet, calm-assertive state for as long as it takes until they relax, get used to him, and get used to the bulky high-definition video camera he carries. Chris has taken all my lessons seriously and has become an excellent amateur assessor of dog behavior. Sometimes he will arrive at a house and the owner will say, "Don't get near her, my dog is dangerous!" Chris is usually able to tell if that's really the case or if it's the owner that's causing the situation. Usually once Chris gets to be alone with the dog and follows all my protocols, everything is fine.

After shooting five seasons of *Dog Whisperer* with me, Chris and his wife, Johanna, a senior policy analyst at the Government Accountability Office, were eager to get some hands-on practice with a dog of their own. They decided they wanted the fulfilling and challenging experience of raising a puppy together.

"Never having had our own dog before, we wanted to experience one from start to finish," Chris told me. "We also wanted to maximize the amount of time we'd have the dog in our lives, so that meant a puppy. When it came time to choose a breed, having seen so many types of dogs on the show gave me a lot of direction into the type of dog for us. Since Cesar had told me if I were a dog, I'd be a terrier, that's the group we looked into."

Chris and Johanna researched terrier breeds and decided they wanted a soft coated wheaten terrier.[4] They chose to go the breeder route, rather than seek a rescue or a shelter dog. "By choosing a purebred with known lineage, we were confident in avoiding expensive vet bills for the life of the dog. Working with Cesar also gave us credibility with some of the breeders with whom we were applying. Some breeders are reluctant to give a purebred like a soft coated wheaten terrier to a first-time dog owner because of their concern for the quality of life of the puppy. When I answered the application questions so specifically, the breeder wanted to know how I had such extensive dog knowledge. When I told her I was a cameraman on *Dog Whisperer*, the deal was done!"

But Chris and Johanna are a busy, two-career couple. In planning for the arrival of their new puppy, Eliza, they soon realized their entire lifestyle was going to have to change. "I knew from Cesar what we were in for, and that we'd be making a lot of changes and a few sacrifices, too. I actually took two full weeks off work to be home with Eliza while she adjusted to our house. I knew from Cesar that the puppy needed at least two long walks a day, and we never varied from that. I got up an hour earlier than usual every day in order to walk her, and in the evening, I walked her again before feeding. That routine has continued to this day. When I had to go back to work, we hired a dog walker twice a week to take her out in the afternoons. Though it

Chris Komives with Eliza

wasn't always possible with my shooting schedule, I tried to get home at lunchtime whenever I could to let her out of her crate on days when the dog walker wasn't booked." To make sure that Eliza was never crated more than four hours at a time, Johanna arranged to work from home on the days the dog walker wasn't available or when Chris was shooting too far away to make it home in the afternoons.

KOMIVES FAMILY SCHEDULE FOR ELIZA'S FIRST MONTHS

5:30 a.m.: Wake up, walk Eliza, obedience/agility/other challenges in short intervals.

6:15 a.m.: Return, feed Eliza, shower, and get ready for work.

7:00 a.m.: Put Eliza in back hallway, go to work.

7:30 a.m.–4:30 p.m.: At work—check on Eliza's webcam. Twice a week, dog walker takes Eliza with pack around 12 noon for one hour.

5:00 p.m.: Return home, walk Eliza, obedience/agility/other challenges in short intervals.

6:00 p.m.: Feed Eliza.

7:00 p.m.–9:00 p.m.: Eat dinner, keep Eliza on her "place," groom Eliza (brushing, trim nails, clean ears, etc.).

10:00 p.m.: Put Eliza in back hallway, go to bed.

"I knew from my on-the-job training, so to speak, that the first six months are vital for establishing the routine with the puppy as well as the rules," Chris recalls, "so I became very focused on raising and caring for her—unfortunately, to the detriment of my other relationships. I tend to have a somewhat obsessive personality anyway, and I channeled this into Eliza. After a month or so, Johanna requested we find something else to talk about besides the dog."

As the Komiveses learned, puppies require commitment, focus, and energy. If you are not prepared to care for a dog for the rest of its life, then please don't fall for an adorable face and bring a puppy home on a whim. But the good news is, raising your dog from puppyhood is your best chance at creating the kind of intimate human-dog bond that we all dream about. Puppies are born without issues, and if they are raised by a good canine mother for the first eight weeks of their lives, they usually come to you unscathed by the quirks and neuroses that bother many an adult dog. Puppies come with a built-in leash attached, because they are programmed to *follow*. They also naturally seek stability and balance, and they are hungry to learn and absorb the rules, boundaries, and limitations of your family pack. Putting the right time and dedication into the first eight months of your puppy's life offers you an incredible opportunity to nurture and influence the dog of your dreams—your faithful companion for a lifetime.

WHERE TO FIND A PUPPY

"How much is that doggie in the window?"

Actually, the cost of that puppy—to animal welfare and to society—is far higher than simply the dollar amount on the price tag.

There are three legitimate ways to go about adopting a puppy— from a shelter, from a breeder, or from a rescue organization. But many a softhearted dog lover has been lured by the winsome puppies in the windows and cages of the chain and independent pet stores that dot the streets of American cities and the aisles of our sprawling shopping malls. Most well-meaning animal lovers who purchase a dog from a pet shop or over the Internet or from a classified ad are unaware that those same puppies may be among the hundreds of thousands in America having been raised in horrendous, unsanitary, inhumane conditions in factory-like atmospheres known as puppy mills.

"I've been inside a lot of puppy mills, from one end of the country to the other," says my friend Chris DeRose, founder of Last Chance for Animals, a nonprofit activist group that works as a kind of "animal FBI," gathering prosecutable evidence of systemic animal cruelty through detective work, whistle-blower information, and undercover operations. "And the one thing I can tell you is, puppy mills are ugly." In most puppy mills, dogs live and die in their own excrement. Because they spend their early lives trapped inside wire cages, sometimes their feet get caught, and they lose paws and limbs to injuries and infections that are never treated. There is no regular veterinary care, and the dogs aren't tested for genetic health problems, so chronic eye, ear, and digestive tract infections are common. Many puppy mills that exist in areas with extreme temperatures have no heating or air-conditioning, so the dogs routinely die from overexposure to heat or cold. The worst sufferers in puppy mills are the breeding pairs, the mothers in particular. They are forced to produce litter after litter, until they are physically used up. Then they are disposed of—often with unimaginable violence and cruelty.

What's often ignored in the puppy mill discussion is the significant role that a puppy mill background plays in the growing epidemic of serious behavior problems we see in America's dogs. I've been called in to help dozens of dogs whose troubling behaviors I can pretty accurately trace back to their having been born under these oppressive conditions. That's because dogs raised in puppy mills don't have a natural style of life during the first weeks and months that are most crucial to their normal physical and mental development. They can't learn how to be dogs, because their mothers don't know how to be dogs. Recently, Chris DeRose took me inside my first puppy mill to help rescue and rehabilitate some of its saddest victims, the ones these so-called breeders were willing to relinquish to us (after all, these dogs

*Cesar with the Last Chance for Animals team and
some rescued puppy-mill dogs.*

were already so damaged, they would never make them any money). I saw dogs that were at such a high level of stress and anxiety, they didn't know how to calm down—ever. I saw dogs trembling with shock, depressed dogs, sick dogs—even hopeless dogs. Anyone who has ever owned a normal, upbeat, joyful dog knows that hopelessness is a very aberrant quality for a dog—especially a puppy—to exhibit. It was a truly sobering and life-changing experience for me.

I am a big believer in the theory that the mental health and environmental stresses placed on a mother (of any species) play a role in the issues her offspring inherit. Imagine a female dog, like her mother and grandmother before her, raising litter after litter of puppies, never leaving the confines of a 4-foot-by-4-foot wire cage. Her puppies are going to come into the world stressed, and they're going to get more and more anxious as the weeks go by and they absorb their mother's unstable, depressed, or jittery energy. Once that puppy gets to the pet shop window, she may look adorable, but the deck is already stacked against her. Because of the inborn behavioral (not to mention physical) problems that will show up more as the puppy grows out of her cute stage, this dog is more than likely to end up abandoned at a shelter and possibly put to death. Why should the puppy mill owners (and pet shop owners) care? They've already pocketed their money.

I was doing a seminar in Atlanta, Georgia, last year when a rescue group there presented me with a little female Yorkie with extreme anxiety, fear aggression, and a host of other behavioral problems. She was a puppy mill dog. This little girl was going to be put down unless someone stepped in. I ended up bringing her back to Los Angeles with me, and now she's a member of my home-based family pack. In the beginning, even my normally very patient wife threw up her hands in frustration at her behavior. "Georgia Peaches," as we named her, spent all her time hiding in corners and under and behind furniture, aggressively attacking anyone who got near her. She peed and pooped wherever she stood—even in her kennel. Puppy mill dogs have only one option—to pee where they sleep—something healthy dogs never do in nature. Eventually I was able to rehabilitate her so that she is no longer a behavior problem. She is still somewhat tentative, but she lives and plays happily with our other dogs and doesn't show any of the signs of stress or aggression she did when she first arrived. She's not human-aggressive anymore. But as far as housebreaking goes, she is still a work in progress. Growing up in a puppy mill kills off even the deepest instincts of many dogs.

Many well-meaning people suspect that a pet store puppy may have been raised in a puppy mill but buy it anyway, honestly believing they are doing a good thing by "rescuing" an individual puppy. I can understand that line of thinking—most of us who love dogs cannot stand to see *any* dog, especially a puppy, go without a loving home. But according to Stephanie Shain of the Humane Association of the United States, "All these well-meaning people are doing is opening up another cage for yet another puppy mill dog to fill. It's all about economics; it's all about money. If people stop buying puppy mill puppies, the puppy mills stop making money."

The Humane Society is determined to put an end to the horror of puppy mills in our lifetime, but since puppy mills are still legal in most states, the only way to do that is to make this trade in canine flesh no longer profitable for its investors. If unpurchased, the puppy in the window of an unethical pet store will eventually end up at a shelter or rescue organization once she is past her "cute" expiration date. That's the time to adopt, if you sincerely want to help and believe you are patient and *experienced* enough to handle the many behavioral and health problems that might come along with that dog. The puppy mill "breeders" don't profit, the pet stores don't profit, and you will be helping go one step further toward solving the problem of puppy mills and putting them out of business forever.

HOW TO FIND THE RIGHT BREEDER

It's easy to avoid pet shop puppies or puppies being hocked on the Internet, but how do you tell a responsible breeder from a "backyard breeder" or a home-grown amateur? First of all, I want to say that there is nothing inherently unethical about bringing home a puppy from your neighbor's backyard. Just know that you will probably have no guarantee at all that the puppy isn't predisposed to chronic genetic health conditions or behavior problems. This is why, if you are an inexperienced dog owner or fear you can't afford the possibility of long-term, expensive vet bills, I urge you not to go this route. Some backyard breeders may truly have the best intentions, but most will have little or no experience selecting for health and temperament, and they may not know anything at all about the lineage (including genetic health or behavior histories) of the puppies' parents. Unfortunately, there are many other backyard breeders who don't think about the dog's welfare at all. They have little concern for the puppies they bring into the world, except to use them to make a little extra money.

If you have decided you want to go the breeder route to purchase your new puppy, it's in your best interest to find people like Brooke or the Fosters, with high standards and excellent reputations. As their examples have shown you, a great breeder will ask you a *lot* of questions. Some of them may even seem quite personal. Don't be shocked if the breeder asks to come to visit your home to see firsthand where the dog would live and to make sure your yard is secure. This is how seriously responsible breeders take the placement of their dogs— they do not want to contribute in any way to the growing population of abandoned and unwanted dogs in the United States! A trustworthy breeder will also be only too happy to answer any and all questions *you* may have, about the breeder, his or her practices, the dog you are thinking of buying, and the complete histories of all litters, older dogs, and their bloodlines. *Think twice about any breeder who does not freely share this kind of information with you, or acts as if you are taking up too much of his or her time.*

Purchasing a puppy from a responsible breeder will probably cost you a premium—from the high hundreds to thousands of dollars— but remember, you are not only paying for the puppy, you are paying for a buffer against costly veterinarian bills during your dog's life, as well as a lifetime *relationship* with the person responsible for bringing the puppy into this world.

So where do you find these dream breeders? Call the Humane Society of the United States or visit their website, www.HSUS.org. They provide their own thorough checklist of criteria for selecting a good breeder. The American Kennel Club's website is also an excellent resource, www.akc.org. Remember, many breeders specialize in raising a certain *kind* of dog, even within their specific breed expertise. In searching for Eliza, Chris and Johanna Komives made sure they had the right category of breeder for the puppy they wanted. "We did choose our breeders based on their statement that they breed for temperament," Chris told me. "The breed standard is for a happy self-confident temperament with less aggression than other terriers. Other breeders we inquired with were more concerned with the soft coat and its color than the demeanor of the dogs."

QUESTIONS ALL REPUTABLE BREEDERS SHOULD BE ABLE TO ANSWER

- How long have you been breeding dogs?
- How many litters do you have every year?
- Why did you select these particular parents and why did you plan this litter?
- What are the potential health problems of this breed and what have you done to prevent such problems in your line?
- Do you have proof of health tests for the parents?
- Are the parents on the premises? If not, why not? If yes, can I meet them?
- Were the parents in any kind of conformation or performance events (dog shows)?
- What steps have you taken to properly socialize the puppies?
- What are you feeding the puppies and why?
- Do the puppies have all of their shots?
- Have the puppies been dewormed?
- Do you require a signed contract of sale?
- Do you offer a health guarantee?

ANY REPUTABLE BREEDER WILL . . .

- Never sell you a puppy that is less than eight weeks of age! Puppies absolutely need at least eight weeks of rearing by their canine mother before they are ready to be placed with human owners.
- Require you to sign a contract of sale. This contract will explain in detail the terms of the sale and what is expected of you as the new owner.
- Require you to have the puppy spayed or neutered before you can receive the registration papers and/or you will only be given a limited registration, which prohibits subsequent puppies from being registered with the AKC . . . unless you plan to breed the dog, or if specific arrangements are made otherwise.
- Offer a health guarantee of some kind. Some breeders will guarantee the health of the dog for life; others may guarantee the dog for a certain number of years. These health guarantees normally cover any *genetic* problem that prevents the dog from living a normal, healthy life.
- Offer to be available through the life of your dog to answer any questions you may have.
- Offer to help you find a new home for your dog should you ever find yourself in a situation where you can no longer keep it.[5]

Another great option is for you to visit an official dog show. There you can meet a variety of breeders, get to know them, and see firsthand the dogs they have raised. Dog show aficionados tend to know one another, and breeders know other good breeders (they have to, in order to keep their bloodlines diverse), so even if you don't find what you are looking for right there, you are sure to get a lot of good references. At a dog show or conformation event, you can also get a close-up experience of the adult dogs of the breed you are considering, and a better idea of whether or not it is the right breed for you.

FINDING A RESCUE ORGANIZATION

If you think you know the breed of puppy you are seeking but really want to give an abandoned dog a home, and if you don't think you can swing the premium prices charged by a top-notch breeder, you have the option of contacting a breed-specific rescue organization, like the Southern California Labrador Retriever Rescue, our friends who brought us Blizzard, or like Daphneyland, a rescue organization for basset hounds that helped us out for the production of my video *Your New Dog: The First Day and Beyond.*

Dogs arrive at rescue groups for a variety of reasons: sometimes they are dogs that were lost or abandoned; sometimes they are dogs that were returned to a shelter or kennel because of behavioral or health problems; and sometimes they are dogs whose owners had legitimate reasons for relinquishing them, such as a change in life circumstance or a death in the family. Reputable rescue groups are diligent about obtaining any needed veterinary care for their animals. They spay and neuter the dogs that arrive there, and often even go the extra mile by working to rehabilitate dogs with behavioral issues. A number of the cases I have handled have come to me from rescue establishments that were having trouble rehoming a dog with problems. My wife and I started the nonprofit Cesar and Ilusion Millan Foundation in part to give financial aid, training, education, and other support to these essential groups. Great rescue organizations are not in it for the money; they are nonprofit groups. Like great breeders, the people who run them genuinely care about dogs and are actively doing something to help solve the problem of dog overpopulation. They are often staffed primarily by volunteers, and any fees they charge are usually marked as donations that go right back into the many costs involved in rescuing and caring for their animals.

A reality check: puppies that come into rescue groups are usually snapped up as soon as they come in, but you can always get your name on a waiting list, so you can be contacted immediately when any new puppies arrive.

Just as with finding the right breeder, you should be diligent in your choice of rescue organizations. The first thing you should do is check business records to confirm a rescue group's nonprofit status and to make sure the group is not a front for a puppy mill, a backyard breeder, or simply people trying to make a little extra money from "animal hoarding," a pathological behavior that can often be a danger to the public health. The Humane Society of the United States is the best clearinghouse for finding a reputable group in your area. Petfinder and Pets911 are also excellent resources.

A REPUTABLE RESCUE ORGANIZATION WILL . . .

- Have 501c3 (nonprofit) status, or be in the process of applying for it.
- Provide preadoption veterinary care for and spay and neuter all dogs older than six months.
- Present a clean, sanitary facility and healthy, well-fed animals.
- Be knowledgeable about all the dogs in its rescue and have completed some form of temperament testing to ensure it will be matching its dogs with compatible owners.

- Ask you detailed questions (though probably not quite as many as a breeder) about your lifestyle, environment, experience with dogs, and ability to provide for the dog. Some organizations, like some breeders, may insist on a home visit.
- Offer to take back or help rehome its animals if an adopter can no longer care for them. This is usually a stipulation in the adoption contract.
- Provide you with any available health records and other pertinent history of the animal you are adopting.

FINDING YOUR PUPPY AT A SHELTER

Rescuing a dog from a shelter is an admirable endeavor, one that I always support and encourage. If you are confident enough in your ability to accept all the "unknowns" in a dog's background, there is no reason in the world why you should not do so. Most of the dogs at a shelter or pound are adult or adolescent dogs, usually of mixed-breed origins. Some of the dogs at a shelter that appear to be "purebred" may well have puppy mill origins; pet stores have no use for puppy mill puppies when they outgrow their "cuteness" phase, so they often end up in shelters. On occasion a pregnant or nursing bitch is brought into a shelter. At other times animal control will clear out the puppies produced in a hoarding situation, or have to take in puppies due to their abandonment in a death, a move, an eviction, or a foreclosure. To find a puppy at a shelter in your area, go early and get your name on a waiting list.

The Humane Society of the United States provides us with guidelines for discerning whether your local shelter meets the minimum acceptable standards:

ANY RESPONSIBLE ANIMAL
SHELTER SHOULD . . .

- Accept every animal, or partner with another local shelter or facility that does.
- Accept surrendered animals without charging a mandatory fee.
- Maintain a clean, comfortable, safe, and healthy environment for each animal.
- If applicable, hold stray animals for a minimum of five operating days, including Saturdays.
- Screen prospective adopters using established adoption standards.
- Use sodium pentobarbital administered by well-trained, compassionate individuals when euthanasia is necessary.
- Spay or neuter all animals at the time of adoption, or require adopters to get their animals sterilized soon after placement and follow up to ensure compliance.[6]

Penny Dunn, director of the Washburn County Area Humane Society in Spooner, Wisconsin, spoke to us about her criterion for accepting puppies at her shelter. "We'll gladly take in any and all breeds. But the number one thing we do is ask the person who wants to bring in the puppies to have the momma dog spayed first. Every now and then someone will find one or two individual puppies and bring them in, but the reality of the situation is that most of the time people know exactly where the puppies came from and we all have to work together to prevent any future unwanted animals."

We'll talk more about spaying and neutering in Chapter 9.

SETTLING ON A BREED

When President Barack Obama was elected to our country's highest office, he was faced with a dilemma. He was going to have to make good on a campaign promise—made not to the American people but to his two daughters, Malia and Sasha—to adopt a puppy after the election chaos was over. For weeks on end, the news media was obsessed with the still-hypothetical Obama puppy. On Sunday-morning talk shows, pundits from both political parties debated the merits of one breed over another. What is the ideal presidential dog? Which breed would be most compatible with Malia's allergies? Breeders and dog lovers all across the United States sent the White House thousands of missives, filled with photos of potential puppies, and reams and reams of unsolicited advice.

It's easy to see why the Obamas, who had never owned a dog, might have experienced some confusion over this particular executive decision. There are more than 150 separate dog breeds recognized by the American Kennel Club, and hundreds more breeds and variations of breeds in addition to those. Selecting the appropriate breed of dog is an important factor to consider when choosing a puppy for your family, especially when considering size and special needs, lifestyle choices, environmental compatibility, and factors such as food and exercise requirements. But in my opinion, the energy level of the puppy is a much more accurate gauge of whether you and your dog will be compatible mates for life. That's because all breeds of dogs are *dogs* first. I think of any dog first as animal, then as dog, then as breed, and last, the dog's name, or what most people term her "personality." When humans took on the task of custom-designing dogs for our own needs and desires, we didn't create the characteristics we selected from scratch, we merely adapted and refined basic dog traits that were already there. In other words, we took what Mother Nature had already given the canid species and reshaped it to our liking. I think of breed in a dog as that extra "boost" that kicks the dog's natural instincts into hyperdrive.

All dogs are predators, but over thousands of generations, we've created sporting breeds to be exceptionally focused predators. All dogs like to dig and chase small prey, but terriers are superdriven to dig and find rodents. All dogs love to run, but greyhounds can run up to forty miles an hour, and huskies can run for hours and hours on end. All dogs have the natural ability to fight or wrestle with one another, but the bully breeds have been genetically engineered to fight to the death. The more pure the bloodline, the more that genetic "boost" will probably play a part in your dog's behavior. That's why some owners claim that their "mutts" make mellower pets, because, they theorize, their DNA has been somewhat diluted, and their breed-related drives diffused as a result.

As a general rule, the more purebred the dog, the more intense the desire it will have to fulfill its genetic purpose. Therefore, it will require more focus and attention from you in making sure that those breed-related needs are constantly challenged and fulfilled.

When thinking about what might be the right breed for you, you must do your homework ahead of time. Read up on every breed you are interested in, paying special attention to the original job it was bred to do. Then ask yourself, Can I provide the right environment, the proper amount of time, and the appropriate stimulation to fulfill those inborn breed-related needs? For instance, if you are in love with the scruffy face and petite size of terriers, are you prepared to designate a part of your prized garden so it can fulfill its biological need to dig? Or are you so in love with your lawn that any damage to it causes you to fly off the handle? If you admire the sleek physique and elegance of a pointer or Weimaraner, do you have the time and energy to play hide-and-seek or hunting games with it in the park several days a week? Or will you keep it cooped up in your apartment and only walk it to the corner? If you desperately want a high-energy Australian shepherd, will you be willing to take it to sheep-herding class or play agility games with it, on a regular basis? When we fulfill *all* the needs of our dogs—with consideration to them as animals, dogs, and breeds—they will reciprocate by being the most loyal, loving friends we could ever imagine. When we leave them unfulfilled, on the other hand, we create issues that can make their lives and ours absolutely miserable.

WELCOMING THE FIRST PUPPY

The Obamas did their breed research and settled on a Portuguese water dog, an ancient breed from the AKC's working group known as a friendly, playful, very active family pet. Portuguese water dogs are also nonshedders, animals better tolerated by people with allergies like Malia's. To set a good example for the country, the Obamas had originally intended to rescue a shelter dog, but they soon found that locating a young puppy of the correct breed from a shelter would be a daunting mission, even for the president of the United States. "It's harder than finding a commerce secretary," the president complained. The Obamas learned that the Kennedy family were also fans of Portuguese water dogs, having raised a number of these fine animals in their large extended family throughout the years. Senator Ted Kennedy contacted the breeder for his own dogs, and learned that a six-month-old puppy was being returned to the breeders for rehoming. By taking a rehomed puppy, the Obamas were able to give a nod to the rescue community, avoid the issue of illegal presidential "gifts," and still give the girls the experience of having a young dog from their chosen breed.

The media was in full circus mode when the Obamas finally took possession of their new puppy, Bo, in April 2009. An excited environment is not the ideal energy to project when a new puppy is introduced to his new home, but unfortunately, such is the nature of life in the presidential fishbowl. As White House staffers held back the dozens of press corps photographers wildly snapping away, the curly-haired, midnight black Bo—already a large dog at six months of age—proceeded to lope about the South Lawn on his white, bootlike paws, pulling Malia behind him. I was watching the live feed of Bo's first official appearance from my Burbank offices, talking via satellite to Wolf Blitzer in CNN's Situation Room. "Uh-oh," I blurted out, forgetting I was on mic. "They're gonna need a lot of help." I'm not sure Wolf understood what I was trying to express. While much of America was seeing simply a happy, playful, picture-perfect puppy, by virtue of what I do for a living I was seeing something else. Bo's first impression of the Obama family was as an overexcited pack of somewhat disorganized followers.

What the First Family needs to remember is that Bo does not see them as the president's family. He simply sees them as the energy they project toward him. President Obama has been naturally blessed with a strong calm-assertive energy—that's why he seems nearly unflappable in so many tense situations. But I have plenty of clients who are leaders among humans in the entertainment and business worlds whose dogs think they are pushovers. Sometimes leadership abilities don't translate well between human and dog worlds.

Did the Obamas choose the right breed and energy-level dog for their family? They are all athletic, high-energy people, which is a good thing, because Portuguese water dogs, by virtue of their working nature, are not couch potatoes. "I wouldn't say he's excessively high in energy," claims Bo's breeder, Martha Stern of Boyd, Texas. "But he's still a little bit more than middle-of-the-road. On a scale of five, he's probably a three." If the Obamas can find time in their busy schedules to walk Bo a lot every day (that's a proper walk, with Bo *next* to them—not pulling them along on the leash!), they'll start to drain his overabundant energy and to create the kind of bond between human and dog that can cut through even a high-energy dog's excitement. They also need to make sure he's tuckered out and hungry at meal-times—that will give the dog a routine and help him see that the family is the source of his food. Of course, being the First Family, they have plenty of household help and support, not to mention access to the best dog trainers in America, to fill in the gaps. But I'd like to see a First Dog who honors and respects his president and family as his indisputable pack leaders. Nearly every resident of the recent White House, to my mind, has failed my "pack leader" test when it comes to having a well-behaved, calm-submissive dog. I have my fingers crossed that the Obamas may prove to be the exceptions.

SELECTING FOR ENERGY

Above and beyond breed, finding an individual dog with the right energy level for you is the most important first step you can take in creating a fulfilling lifetime with your pet. Yes, many dog breeds "come with" a certain activity level attached, but each individual dog's personal energy level will vary. An older German shepherd with low energy may make a better pet for a laid-back family with children than a boisterous golden retriever puppy. For an inexperienced dog owner who wants a small dog, a medium-energy terrier may well make a better choice than a nervous, high-energy Chihuahua. When it comes to choosing a puppy, understanding how to read a dog's energy level is as vital a skill to hone as an encyclopedic knowledge of dog breeds.

Dog Energy Levels

Every dog is born with a certain energy level. Those levels are:

1. *Very high:* Constantly on the move, from dawn to dusk. Can walk or run for hours on end and still have energy to spare.
2. *High:* Very athletic, prefers very vigorous activities, but tires normally and is ready for sleep at the end of the day.
3. *Medium:* Seeks out normal physical activities, sometimes vigorous ones, but balances them with equal periods of rest.
4. *Low:* Your basic couch potato dog. Prefers rest to activity. A couple of regular walks a day will be plenty of exercise for him.

As a good rule of thumb, I recommend that people choose a dog with the same energy level or a lower energy level than their own. If they have other dogs at home, it's even more important not to choose a dog with an energy level higher than that of the dogs or humans already in the family pack.

Some breeders employ a method called puppy temperament testing,[7] an exam administered by a professional at around seven weeks of age that attempts to predict what kind of "personality" the grown-up dog will probably have. Based on the puppy's responses to several basic challenges, the test attempts to quantify responses in such areas as social attraction; following; restraint; forgiveness; acceptance of human dominance; willingness to please; touch, sound, and sight sensitivity; and energy levels. Breeders use the results of these tests to help categorize their dogs from cautious to aggressive and to assess how likely they are to be suited to certain specific jobs, such as therapy dog, search and rescue dog, police dog, and so on. If you are getting a puppy from a breeder, you might want to ask her if she has the results of these tests for the dog that you are interested in. They may aid you in assessing whether the puppy's personality is right for your lifestyle.

However, even those breeders who use these tests religiously will tell you that their results don't always tell the whole story. When evaluating energy, other factors can make a big difference, such as the dog's direct bloodline, its birth order, or, more important, its day-to-day interactions with other dogs. When you are evaluating an adult dog at a shelter, you may find it hard to separate a dog's true energy from the issues it carries with it from previous life experiences or placements. Happily, with puppies, there are no issues to get in the way of your selection. Puppies are clean slates, born with a certain energy level, and in most cases, that same energy will be with them for the rest of their lives.

MEET THE PARENTS

As you've already learned, breeders will carefully choose their breeding pairs—both females (dams) and males (sires)—seeking to control and shape the temperament of the offspring. In other words, breeders who want calm, sweet-tempered puppies that will make good pets, therapy dogs, or show dogs will choose sweet, calm-tempered mothers and fathers. Breeders who raise search and rescue dogs or agility dogs may be looking for more active energy in their dam and sire. Those breeding for guard or police dogs may be looking for some territorial traits in their mating pairs, and those who illegally breed pit bulls for fighting unfortunately select the most aggressive, ferocious dogs to mate for the next generation. That's why it's important that a breeder be willing to let you meet the parents of your new puppy whenever possible.

Brooke Walker let me spend a lot of time around Angel's mom and dad, and they were playful and active yet calm and stable dogs. Mr.

President's parents were both the kind of laid-back, mellow English bulldogs everyone desires as pets. With puppy mill puppies you purchase at a pet shop, you will never be allowed to meet the parents. That's because they may be in a warehouse hundreds of miles away, crammed among dozens of other dogs in tiny cages. The bitch will probably already have another litter gestating by the time that puppy hits the pet shop. Imagine the effect on the temperament of a dog living in those inhumane conditions. Imagine the stress placed on the mother as she is forced to give birth in a cramped enclosure again and again and again, until her body gives out from the strain. There's no way that a mother's experiences don't have an enormous impact, both on her own temperament and energy and on the lifelong psyches of the puppies she brings into the world.

LOVE AT FIRST SIGHT

In *Marley and Me,* there's a funny scene where, after having selected Marley from a backyard breeder's litter but before the dog is ready to come home, John Grogan picks up a book about Labrador retrievers and gasps when he learns that a dog's temperament can often be traced back to its parents. Marley's breeders had hesitated to let them meet the sire, a dog that turned out to be "a manic dervish tearing blindly through the night as if demons were close on his tail." Marley's hyperactive father aside, the Grogans had been exposed to plenty of warning signs that highlighted Marley's very high energy level. In the book, John humorously recounts what is an all-too-common puppy selection experience.

> One of the males seemed particularly smitten with us. He was the goofiest of the group and charged into us, somersaulting into our laps and clawing his way up to lick our faces. He gnawed on

our fingers with surprisingly sharp baby teeth and stomped clumsy circles around us on giant tawny paws that were way out of proportion to the rest of his body. . . .

"I think it's fate," Jenny said.

"He certainly seems to like us," I said.

Like the Grogans, most people selecting a puppy will instantly fall in love with the first dog that climbs all over them or begins licking them. They say to themselves, "He loves me. He chose me. He wants to come home with me." Of course, feeling that we are "chosen" by a dog makes us feel good about ourselves and good about the dog we are going to bring home—both important factors in a human-dog relationship. But we have to keep in mind that in many ways, this attraction that we perceive is just a beautiful story. Any healthy, curious puppy will be attracted to most new things and people that enter its environment. The truth is, the puppy who, like Marley, leaps out of his box to be with you may already be displaying dominant tendencies.

Now, a dominant, active puppy with a high or very high energy level may be exactly the energy that you are looking for. You may be looking for a future champion agility dog to run obstacle courses with you. You may be a daily long-distance runner, like my colleague, *Dog Whisperer* field producer Todd Henderson, who needs a very active dog to keep up with him. Todd adopted Curly, a very-high-energy Lab-greyhound mix from the show—a wonderful dog that was far too boisterous for his previous owner, Pete, a laid-back New York City dweller. Remember how Angel's breeder, Brooke Walker, wanted to give me Angel's more dominant brother, Mr. Blue Collar, whom she called "the pick of the litter"? Brooke says she prefers more assertive puppies, because in her experience, they have been easier to train as show dogs. But remember, both Todd Henderson and Brooke Walker are also highly experienced dog owners, with naturally confident, calm-assertive energies. If you are inexperienced with dogs, or if you know yourself to be a softer, more submissive, more laid-back sort of person in general, the little Marley that jumps out of the box and charges you is probably not a good energy match if you want a compatible pet for life.

Interpreting a high-energy puppy's natural curiosity as "love at first sight" isn't the only way we can misread a dog's communication through the hazy filter of our own emotional needs. Some people are looking for a spiritual connection with a dog, so they'll select a puppy based on his "soulful eyes." Other people want a puppy because they want to feel needed. They will see a puppy that seems nervous, timid, or withdrawn and choose it because they feel sorry for it. Then there are the people who choose based entirely on looks. In the first season of *Dog Whisperer,* we met an owner who selected Emily because the puppy had a heart-shaped pattern on her flank. Emily was a very active pit bull, and the owners ended up keeping her cooped up in a fenced backyard, unintentionally creating a red-zone dog-aggressive pet that needed serious rehab later. I've met people who brought home a puppy simply because it looked like Spuds MacKenzie, Petey from *The Little Rascals,* Lassie, one of the 101 Dalmations, or the Beverly Hills Chihuahua. I believe it is very important that people be attracted to the way their dog looks, but choosing a dog on looks alone makes even less sense than choosing your human mate solely for that reason.

Choosing a puppy based on energy level is a skill anyone can learn. At one month of age, all puppies are adorably clumsy in the way they move, but food is always a motivator, and the mother is pretty much the number one focus of their lives. So I will call the breeder in advance and find out what time the mother usually feeds her puppies, which happens on a certain schedule, the same time every day, about five times a day. That's when I'll schedule my visit. By one month of age, the puppies are already walking. I'll ask that the puppies be kept in a separate area, then bring in the mother for feeding, and observe in what order the puppies waddle to the mother. By doing this I can read the energy of each puppy right away. I'll see which is the pushiest, which is the most anxious, which has the most submissive energy, and which has the most medium or laid-back energy. Right there, I will be able to classify the puppies as low, medium, high, or very high energy.

You can also use the method I employed when choosing Angel from his siblings, by sitting all the puppies on chairs or a bench and observing how long they are willing to wait before getting distracted or jumping off. Low- and medium-energy puppies are perfect for inexperienced dog owners, families with kids, or owners who already have a higher-energy dog at home. In fact, the great majority of the problems I'm called in to correct are the result of an owner who is living with a dog with a higher energy level than the human. Higher-energy puppies are for the Todd Hendersons, Brooke Walkers, and Diana Fosters among us—very active people or very experienced dog owners.

Although Chris Komives is a very active, high-energy person, his wife, Johanna, is quieter and definitely medium-level energy, and it's always best to seek a dog that matches the lowest-energy family member, so everyone in the household will find it easier to be the dog's pack leader. "Because we were looking for a terrier, we knew we'd be getting a medium- or high-energy dog," Chris said. Being novice dog owners, the Komiveses planned on taking my advice and wanted a medium-energy dog for their very first puppy. However, their breeder had other ideas. "In working with breeders, they have a lot of say about which puppy from the litter you'll be getting. Unfortunately, because of the breeder's confidence in me as a *Dog Whisperer* cameraman, she gave us what she called the 'pick of the litter.' Now, I only recently learned from Cesar when he brought home Angel, that the 'pick of the litter' is the highest-energy, most dominant pup. So that didn't work out as planned. In the breeder's defense, I did talk about doing agility with Eliza, and a higher-energy dog is more appropriate for this activity." Eliza's higher energy level did present the Komiveses with a few unexpected challenges when she became a teenager, which we'll discuss in upcoming chapters.

When it comes down to choosing energy, however, experience trumps activity level, as far as I'm concerned, because even most long-distance runners have to go to work during the day. Lots of hands-on experience with dogs, on the other hand, gives you the kind of leverage that only instinctual knowledge can bring. A person with a physical disability may not be very active, but he may also be able to handle a high-level-energy service dog, because he understands leadership, patience, and knows how to channel that dog's energy into doing things like turning on lights, opening doors, and guiding the person to the bus stop. A person with instinctual calm-assertive energy and confidence, combined with experience, can manage even the highest-energy dog, even if that person has physical limitations.

Finally, since dogs speak in energy 24/7, a dog can tell you more about another dog's energy than any human system of measurement. When I first took Daddy to meet the pit bull puppy that would carry his legacy of calm-submissive energy to the next generation, I allowed him to show me the energy levels of the puppies I was considering. Remember how Daddy growled at the puppy I had noticed displaying dominance toward my friends' children? Daddy knew right away that the puppy's behavior was not his cute "friendliness" or "spirit" but the kind of dominant energy that can cause problems within a pack. Daddy ignored another puppy, one that was displaying a lower energy level but also some early symptoms of nervousness and anxiety. He instantly gravitated to the calmest, best-behaved puppy in the litter. Take your cues from Daddy and don't let your emotions get in the way of finding the perfect puppy for you.

3
MOTHER KNOWS BEST
Learning from the Pros

Binky and her pups

My first instructors in the different stages of puppyhood were all professionals—professional canine mothers, that is. I'm proud to say that I learned about raising puppies from the very best—the female working dogs on my grandfather's farm in Mexico. Mother Nature is all about balance, and it is always to nature that I turn whenever I want to explain about the correct way to bring up puppies. As human beings, we often look at the animal kingdom with a superior eye—after all, the Bible tells us we have dominion over the animals, right? Modern science is even more arrogant about our relationship to animals. The truth is, while human beings can create, design, and build all manner of clever systems, innovations, and shortcuts to try to improve on nature, there is one thing we can never better, and that is a natural animal mother raising her offspring in the wild. This is one case where the original blueprint is still—and always will be—the best. When my clients are having a hard time understanding what leadership truly means to a dog, I refer them back to the experts by asking them to observe the way a mother dog births, rears, and nurtures her young to be good, obedient followers and pack members. In many ways, everything we need to know about raising puppies is right there in front of us, in the miracle of a good mother dog and her offspring.

I can vividly recall my childhood wonder at the everyday phenomena of animal birth, life, and death constantly unfolding before my eyes when I lived on my grandfather's farm. I could not get enough of observing the intricate rituals by which the mothers raised the pups. The best mothers made it look so effortless. It was as if they were following a program. Imagine a computer program where you input an application, and then the computer shows you "Click to the left and you will find this. Click to the right and you will find that. Click underneath and you will find this . . ." over and over again, and it's perfect, every time. The dogs on the farm were running an amazing program; it had a natural flow, and it was very precise. It was gentle but had a feeling of surety and assertiveness behind it. These female dogs that I grew up with usually had their own mothers as role models, but even an inexperienced bitch can be an outstanding mother. That's because this flawless program for raising puppies lies deep within their DNA.

One such first-time mother who came through with flying colors was Angel's own mother, a miniature schnauzer named Binky who was just over a year and a half old when she was first bred. Angel's breeder, Brooke Walker, shared with me some details of Angel's birth, a tale that illustrates not only the meticulous procedures of a conscientious breeder but also the innate wisdom and calm-assertive energy of an exemplary canine mother.

BINKY'S FIRST LITTER

"The first thing I'll do when I want to breed a girl is I'll go to my vet to do a full cytology on her, to make sure there isn't any blockage to her being able to deliver on her own," Brooke recounts. "You have to think ahead. So then I have them draw a sample of her blood and test the progesterone levels, so that I know when she's ready to be bred." After performing this canine form of the "rhythm method," Brooke is able to predict accurately when the puppies will arrive. Binky was bred on August 22, 2008. That meant that fifty-eight or sixty-three days later, the puppies are mature enough to be born. Using this formula, Brooke knew that the first day Binky could whelp would be October 18 of that same year . . . the day that would become Angel's birthday!

"When a bitch has been pregnant for a month, I go down to my vet, and I have him do an ultrasound. So we see how many puppies there are. The uterus of a dog is very different from a woman's," Brooke explains. "It's like a horn. There are two areas where the whelps, or embryos, grow. And nature just takes care of that so well. There are usually two in one horn and two in the other horn, or three and three, or three and two. With Binky what we had was two in the left horn, two in the right horn, and right in the center was a twin."

Brooke was very excited by the idea of an identical twin puppy, which was something she as a breeder had not experienced before, but her vet seemed much more reserved about the situation. She would soon learn the very grave reason for his reticence.

As the weeks passed, Brooke prepared her bedroom to be the whelping area.

"I set up the whelping pen in my bedroom, because for the first forty-eight hours I don't leave the room." Of course, in nature, a wild canine doesn't want or need the assistance of a human, or even another pack member, when giving birth—in fact, a pregnant female will wander away from the pack to make a nest, and all the other dogs will respect her signals and give her a lot of space when she is going through the birthing process. A pregnant female in a pack of dogs commands tremendous respect and status. But as a cautious breeder, Brooke wants to be available at all times in case there is an emergency with the puppies or the mother—especially a first-timer such as Binky. "I put the expectant bitch into her whelping pen a couple of days before so that she can feel comfortable in it." Since bitches select their own nesting areas in the wild, it's not always a done deal when the human is the one to decide where the birth will take place. This was true of Binky. "She jumped right back out at first. I had to very kindly encourage her, putting her toys and blankets in there, a tempting treat, praising her for spending time in there." After the first day, Binky felt good enough to settle into her pen, which was a box 3½ by 3½ feet with raised walls, to keep out drafts; a raised area; newspapers, blankets, and a heating pad on the floor; and a railing around the side known as a "pig's rail," to prevent any situation where a puppy might get crushed if it happens to crawl behind the mother. Everything was in place for the big day.

Novice or not, Binky rose above and beyond her call of duty. "That's what is so beautiful about nature. She just instantly knew what to do. Sure, she did cry a little when her vulva was starting to enlarge, and when she was having her first contractions. The first time out, all of those areas are enlarging and the first delivery can be a little bit painful." But Binky soldiered on. Angel's sister, Ms. Pink, was the first of the puppies to make an appearance. "I recorded the time that she went into labor and I recorded the time that the puppies were born. I also had a scale waiting nearby. So Binky had her first puppy at noon, and it was a female. She was 5 and ⅜ ounces. I also try to find if there's a significant something or other about their markings so that you can tell them apart. So you can make sure when you're weighing every day that you're seeing a weight increase in the first three days."

The moment her first puppy was born, Binky proved she was going to be a canine supermom. She appeared both fascinated and thrilled by her new infant, immediately licking her clean and biting off the umbilical cord as if she had done it a thousand times before. Brooke always stands by to help make sure the puppy gets to the nipple and to make sure the placenta comes out. In nature, the mother will usually eat this nutrient-rich afterbirth, but Brooke has discovered that too much of a good thing can cause problems with her schnauzer moms. "I always allow my bitch to have one at least because they're really nutritional. But it gives them really bad diarrhea. The first litter I had, I didn't know left from right. I only knew what my books had taught me. I let her eat all five of her afterbirths and, oh my goodness . . . the mess . . ."

Once Binky's first daughter started nursing, the stimulation caused Binky's body to prepare again for the next birth. Binky's second puppy, another female, came next, at 12:30 p.m. Then there was a long, long wait. Brooke wasn't worried at first—unlike dogs that bear big litters, miniature schnauzers can take as much as four hours to deliver completely—but when 4:00 p.m. rolled around and there were no more puppies in sight, she knew something was wrong. "Someone who didn't take the time or didn't have the knowledge could have thought the whole thing was over, that she was just resting. But I knew that she was definitely straining. She was having contractions and nothing was coming. She was getting to the point where I felt like she was getting too tired to get the job done."

Brooke called in her reproductive vet, to give Binky a shot of Pitocin to induce contractions, and a very big puppy began to crown. Now Brooke understood why her vet had been concerned about the twin they had spotted in the ultrasound. "I've since done a lot of research on it, and it's very rare that a situation like that turns out happily. It's

BROOKE'S MINIATURE SCHNAUZERS
WHELPING CHART

DAME: Brookehaven's Binky

SIRE: Ch. Brookehaven's Turner

Oct.18

WHELP DATE: Oct/08/08 – Saturday

MARKINGS	SEX	PHYSICAL CONDITION	AFTERBIRTH	TIME CONTRACTIONS STARTED	TIME DELIVERED	BIRTH WEIGHT	20th Date wt.	21st Date wt.	22nd Date wt.	23rd Date wt.	24th Date wt.	25th Date wt.	Nov1 Date wt.	Nov8 3wks Date wt.	Nov15 4wks Date wt.	Nov22 5wks Date wt.	6 wks
1.Pink	F	dark	yes		Noon	6 3/8	6 5/8	7 7/8	8 5/8	9 1/4	11	13 1/4	1.3#	11b.9	2.0	2.3/4	2.14
2.Orange	F	bright	yes		12:50	7 1/4	7 5/8	8 1/4	9 1/4	10 1/8	13	15 2	1.3 3/8	11b1/4#	2.4	2.9	3.6
3.Blue	M	bright	yes	Alpha	4:30	6 3/8	7 1/8	8	9 1/8	10	12 1/8	11b	13 3/4	21b.	2.9	2.14 1/2	3.14
4.Green	M	dark	yes		5:00	6 1/8	7 1/8	9	9 3/8	10 3/8	13	14 3/4	1.2 3/4	1.9 3/4	2.0	2.5 4	3.4
5.													girls eyes open	girls eyes open			
6.																	

Bred 8/22

Binky ultrasound 9/19/08 – 4 win

57 days – puppies born – 5 pups – 1 twin   #3 edema puppy removed at WHELPE

3wks – walking & responding to my voice

Binky's first litter-whelping chart

almost always an abnormality." Binky's twin was hydrocephalic, which means it had an abnormally large head. "We needed to massage her and help her pull it down. And then, the minute it was out, she started pushing out number four, at 4:30, and number five at 5:00." That number five was my man, Angel, the last of the siblings to enter the world.

Binky's hydrocephalic puppy illustrates a fact that I believe humans very much need to understand—motherhood, for a dog, is not an emotional experience, it is an instinctual experience. Her hydrocephalic puppy was born dead, and Binky totally ignored it. She made no attempt to revive it or to clean it. Her only concern was delivering her living puppies and making sure they were safe and healthy. She just knew right away that it was imperative to move on to her viable pups. "It was like, phew, that's over, now let's get on with what we're getting on with," Brooke observed. "Of course, as a human watching, if she had grieved, I would've gone to pieces. Which wouldn't have helped anyone."

As humans we are very attached to the process of mourning, even if that means grieving a being we haven't met yet. I had such a misfortune in my own human family, a younger brother who was born dead, and the heartbreak of that experience still enshrouds my entire family like a thick fog. My mother still feels great sadness and guilt about this tragedy that occurred more than thirty years ago. For dogs it's all about the greater good, the survival of the whole litter, and, in the bigger picture, the survival of the pack. A mother with a dead or sick puppy may make an attempt to revive it, but she will never linger to mourn. Her immediate concern is for her puppies that are living. In this way, a bitch will never nurture weakness in her offspring. From the moment they are born, the canine mother gently but firmly lets her new offspring know that they must follow her rules if they want to survive. Mother dogs do not "coddle" their young. In fact, if one of the pups in her pack has trouble finding a place to feed, she will help him only up to a point. If he can't keep up with the rest of the litter, she may even let him die. When it comes to raising puppies, we humans have to remember that this calm-assertive pragmatism is the natural state of mind of their very first pack leader—their mother. We never want to lose the empathy and tenderness within our hearts that make us want to care for puppies in the first place, but we do need to acknowledge the example of the mother dog herself, and keep in mind that puppies naturally respond to this matter-of-fact way of being in their world. Their feelings will not be hurt when you set the kind of firm rules their mother will set. In fact, they are just waiting for those rules, so they can be assured of secure, balanced futures.

EXPERIENCING A DOG'S WORLD FROM DAY ONE

On October 18, 2008, Angel entered his new world with his eyes and ears closed but his nose wide open, already familiar with the first and most important scent, the scent of his mother. During the two-week neonatal period, Angel and his siblings were mostly reactive. Their whole purpose in life was to feed and to sleep. However, even at this phase, there was already a hierarchy forming among the littermates. Brooke describes how Angel's more dominant brother, Mr. Blue, was always the first to feed, the first to push the others out of the way. This is what I mean when I say that a dog's basic energy level is inborn. This doesn't mean that Angel's big brother will grow up to be a hard-to-control dog. Because of his excellent genes and the socialization exercises that Brooke puts all her puppies through before they are adopted, with the right calm-assertive owner, Mr. Blue will most assuredly mature to be a first-rate, obedient pet. But his inborn energy level does mean that Mr. Blue's natural tendency in new situations will be to take charge if there isn't another leader around to give direction.

Angel, on the other hand, has an inborn tendency to sit back and see what happens before he steps in to fill a leadership gap. That is the classic response of a medium-energy dog.

The First Two Weeks: The Neonatal Period

Puppies mature much faster than humans. The first two weeks of life for a puppy could be compared with an entire human infancy. But even at this helpless stage, the puppies are showing that they will fight to stay alive. Puppies may seem so tiny and helpless in this first phase of life, some uninformed humans will be reticent to handle them at all or to expose them to any undue stress during this time. The truth is, even in their newborn state, puppies' brains are developing quickly and beginning to lay out the blueprint of how they will respond to and experience the world around them. Informed breeders like Brooke know that a carefully controlled program of handling at this stage is vital. It prepares puppies to be better problem solvers and to more effectively handle stressors, challenges, and new experiences later in life:

> I want my puppies handled, so that having humans around them is a part of what they have always known. One of the first things I do is, I blow very gently on the puppies' faces. I want them to associate my scent with nurturing, just like they associate their mother's scent with nurturing. At one week of age, they get their toenails clipped, and again every week after that. I also let them experience the gentle blowing of a hair dryer from week one. Even though they can't see or hear it yet, I want them familiar with its scent and the feeling of the warm air on them. Many of my puppies become show dogs, and I want grooming to be a part of their life routine right from the beginning, so it is never a foreign or upsetting event for them.

Like most responsible breeders, during the first two weeks, Brooke has a routine in place for handling her puppies a few times a day, for three to five minutes at a time, in order to accelerate their physical and psychological development.[1]

When the puppies are three days old, Brooke brings in her vet to do a series of physical procedures. The first is tail docking, less common in other areas of the world but still standard procedure for show-quality miniature schnauzers in the United States. Brooke explains that this procedure—along with its frequent partner, ear cropping—didn't originate for aesthetic reasons. These practices actually began as necessary operations for the survival of these working terriers when they were first "designed" 110 years ago.[2] "Miniature schnauzers were bred to rid barns in Germany of hordes and hordes of rats—not just one or two rats like we see in houses today, huge armies of them. If rats are together, they will launch a mass attack on a dog. If a dog has a long ear or a long tail, those places are vulnerable to attack. So originally, the ears and tail were taken care of strictly for practical reasons."

During the same session, Brooke has the vet remove the puppies' dewclaws. A dewclaw is something like a human thumb in its placement, but it grows a bit higher up on the paw than the rest of the toenails on that paw and never comes in contact with the ground. It's a vestigial structure that is now nonfunctional or has some function only in some breeds—the sheep-herding Great Pyrenees, for instance, have double dewclaws on their back paws that were thought helpful for stability when herding sheep on rocky mountaintops. The majority of dogs have dewclaws only on their front paws. Dewclaws can hang loose, get caught, or cause minor or, rarely, serious irritations to the foot of a dog, particularly a terrier that is bred to dig. "Dewclaws on schnauzers are nothing but problems. It's always the nail that they catch. So taking them out right away is something that we just do as part of the course," says Brooke.

However, vets say that many dogs do just fine without having their dewclaws removed. When we think about removing something like a dewclaw on a puppy, we have to put it in the context of the fact that we have genetically engineered dogs away from their original design. Some features of the original design no longer function within the body of the new breed. Procedures like removing a dewclaw are the direct consequence of our having rearranged Mother Nature in the first place.

The most important thing to understand about your puppy's first two weeks on the planet is that he is experiencing the world completely differently from the way a human baby would experience it. He knows three things—scent, touch, and energy. His mother is a scent, a warm body that provides comfort and food, but she is also a source of calm-assertive energy. She is gentle but definitely firm and assertive when she pushes a puppy away if she doesn't want to nurse, or picks him up and moves him to where she wants him to be, or turns him over to clean him and stimulate his digestive system. She does not treat her litter as if they were breakable, and she does not "feel bad" if she needs to tell them in the language of touch and energy, "No, you are nursing a little too hard right now, back off." Your puppy's first experiences in life were filled with very clear rules, boundaries, and limitations.

Neonatal Period	
Birth to two weeks	• Sleeps 90 percent of the time • Only senses are touch and scent • Nurses, crawls, seeks warmth of littermates and mother • Needs stimulation to urinate and defecate • Can usually right herself if turned over • Nervous system is rapidly developing

The Transitional Period: Weeks Two to Three

Between twelve and fourteen days, the puppies enter what is known as the transitional period, which lasts another week or so. Compared to human babies, their transition from infant to toddler occurs at lightning speed. The puppies will start standing on their wobbly little legs, jostling for position, and even begin to play dominance games with their siblings. They are more deliberate in their activities. And the bitch becomes noticeably firmer in her discipline and corrections. There is absolutely no time in the puppy's early development that his mother is not modeling leadership and enforcing distinct rules, boundaries, and limitations.

This is also the phase that begins and ends with the puppy's acquiring his final two senses. According to Brooke's chart, Angel was born on October 18 and first opened his eyes on November 1. The landmark end of this stage in the puppy's life occurs when he opens his ears—for Angel, that day was November 8, twenty-one days after his birth. A conscientious breeder will continue handling the puppies the way she did during the neonatal phase, and will also begin exposing them to different sights and sounds. For Brooke, this is the time when she allows outsiders—including future or prospective owners—to come to see the dogs. "I have ironclad rules about when people come down to visit the puppies. No shoes, and they always have to sanitize their hands. But I want my puppies handled. I want them to hear other human voices. And I want them to hear different sounds, like squeaky toys and the hair dryer. The vacuum is one that I insist on, because the vacuum is so terrifying to most dogs." Having taken on many *Dog Whisperer* cases where dogs were terrified of vacuum cleaners and hair dryers, I can personally appreciate the hard work breeders like Brooke put into this early desensitization.

Like Brooke, Diana Foster can't emphasize enough the importance of exposing puppies at this early stage to some of the different environmental sights, sounds, and smells they will be encountering once they're out there in the "real world":

> Once the ears are open and they can hear a little bit, we do a lot of handling, picking them up, touching them, but we also start playing sound tapes. We do that at three weeks. We have realistic tapes of the sounds of firecrackers, vacuum cleaners, kids screaming, cars honking, doors slamming—everything you can think of from regular family life—because at that age, there's no fear in the puppies yet. They have the comfort of their mother. We have the nice heat lamp on. They're warm. They're fed. They don't shake. They don't jump, and so what happens is, all these sounds get into their subconscious. This prevents the worst things that could happen down the line, like a German shepherd that gets freaked out when a kid yells. When that happens, the dog snaps at somebody. He ends up at the pound or being put to sleep, and it's not even the dog's fault.

By the arrival of their three-week milestone, Angel and his siblings were all walking around clumsily and responding to the sound of Brooke's voice. They were about to enter what is probably the most significant time in a puppy's early development, the socialization period.

Transitional Period	
Two to three weeks	• Eyes open • First formation of teeth • Stands on all fours and takes first steps • Begins to lap with tongue • No longer needs stimulation to eliminate

Socialization: Weeks Three to Fourteen

These next six to nine weeks are among the most crucial in your puppy's life, a time during which he will learn the lessons of how to be a dog among dogs, from his mother, littermates, and any other adult dog with which he is living. From weeks three to six,[3] puppies still interact primarily with their siblings and their mother. They will venture a few feet away from the mother or their "den" but quickly come running back. This first phase of the socialization period is the time of "becoming aware"—of their own bodies, their surroundings, their littermates, and the comfort of their mother.

The second phase of the puppy's socialization, starting at about five weeks, is where the power of the pack comes in. His primary pack at this point consists of his mother and his littermates. Through trial, error, and an abundance of spirited playfulness, he learns from his littermates how to navigate through a social world. They teach him how hard he can bite or pounce, how to dominate, how to submit, and other basic skills of communicating with others of his kind. If your puppy were a canid being raised in the wild, the rest of the adult members of his pack would all jump in at this point and participate in making sure he grew up to be a good canine citizen. Canid societies—whether they be wolf, African hunting dog, or *Canis familiaris*—are incredibly orderly worlds in which the rules of the pack are established for every member, right from the beginning, with no exceptions. The whole pack adapts when puppies arrive, and they rearrange their lives to participate in the rearing. Even in the Dog Psychology Center, certain dogs in my ever-changing pack take it on themselves to become "nannies" or "schoolmasters" to any new pups or adolescents who happened to join our merry band.

When her pups are about six to seven weeks of age, a mother dog begins to be a little less possessive of them and lets other members of the pack help lessen her workload. Among packs of wild canines, the rearing of the young is truly a family affair. Sometimes adults other than the mother even share the job of feeding the maturing pups, returning from hunts and regurgitating food for them. More important, the whole pack always shares in the education of the pups, including disciplining them. The adult dogs work together to form what amounts to an amazing, comprehensive, and cooperative "public school system," to build a healthy, productive new generation. If another adult member of the pack feels the pups are getting a little too boisterous in their play, she may use physical touch—a nudge, or even a firm but nonaggressive bite—to communicate. If an adult or adolescent senses a pup doesn't understand the manners of the dinner table, she may emit a low growl to warn the pups away from her food. Every dog recognizes that having obedient, well-adjusted, socially literate puppies is necessary for the survival of the entire pack.

However, domestic dogs don't live only with dogs; they live with and must rely on us humans. In a way, your puppy needs to grow up "bilingual"—speaking the languages of both dog and human—before he can go out into the world. Tens, maybe hundreds of thousands, of years of evolving with us side by side have given our dogs an inborn proficiency in understanding our energy and body language, a proficiency that is just as impressive as that of our closest evolutionary cousins, the other primates. Nevertheless, being domesticated doesn't bring automatic understanding. "Human" is still very much a second language to puppies. To become good pets, puppies need positive interactions with humans on a daily basis during the period between five weeks and nine weeks. They also need to be exposed to the different kinds of stimuli that await them out in the modernized world. That's why a diligent breeder participates as actively as the canine mother during the socialization period of her puppies' lives, to expose each puppy to different aspects of human culture and to introduce him to the oddities of the half dog–half human society into which he's been born.

Socialization Period			
Stage 1: Becoming Aware	3–4 weeks		• Can hear and see • Sense of smell much more acute • Begins to eat food • Begins to bark, wag tail, and bite siblings
	4–5 weeks		• Walks and runs well but tires quickly • Chases and plays prey-killing games • Bares teeth and growls • Begins pawing
Stage 2: Curiosity Period	5–7 weeks		• Weaning begins • Very curious • Plays dominance games with littermates
Stage 3: Behavioral Refine-ment	7–9 weeks	7 weeks	• All senses function • Will investigate anything
		8 weeks	• Becomes fearful and startles easily • Is cautious about anything new in environment

Diana Foster describes the routine she and her husband, Doug, go through with every German shepherd litter that they raise.

At about five weeks of age, we start bringing the puppies indoors one at a time, so we can get them used to being in the company of humans without their littermates. They're so dependent on being with each other and being with the mother, when we first bring them in and put them down, they'll start whining. So we'll hold them for a little bit, then we put them back with the mother. It's good to give them a little bit of stress so they learn how to handle it, but a few minutes a day is plenty. We do it in short increments, so the dog gets used to being away from the whelping box, and around people.

The Fosters also make sure their shepherd puppies continue being exposed to a series of new, real-life stimuli and stressors during this time:

We try to have them situated on the property where there's the most commotion. We have five acres, but we never put them in the back pen or up on the hill where they can't see everything that's going on. Instead, we have a huge pen in the front, and that's where we have a lot of people who pull up to come look at our dogs. The kids get out of the car screaming. There are other dogs barking. There's music. There are my kennel workers. There's the trash truck. Since we can't take them out in public when they're that young, we bring the environment to them, so when they hear a loud sound, or something scares them, they may go screaming to the back of the pen. I tell my kennel workers, "Do nothing. Don't go over to them. Don't talk to them. Don't pick them up. Allow them to work it out for themselves." And little by little, they start coming toward whatever made the noise and getting a little braver, and then they realize the big bad thing's not going to hurt them, and then they're fine. The less you do, the better. If I were to write a book about raising puppies at this age, I might even call it something like *Do Nothing!*

Dogs also love routine, which is important for their development, both at this early stage and throughout their lives. Brooke Walker keeps a strict regime around her house when socializing her miniature schnauzer pups.

As soon as the grass dries if there's morning dew, I'll take them out in the yard. They all potty instantly. They get their breakfast. They stay out, they play. They go back for their nap. They come out. They get their lunch, they potty, they play. They go back in. It's such a routine. I feed three times a day once the mother has stopped feeding. Normally, mothers feed for four weeks. Binky was an exceptionally involved mother; she fed and cleaned those babies straight through five weeks.

Brooke told me that I was the only person she ever let adopt one of her puppies before ten weeks. Usually, she likes to have the housebreaking and crate-training process completed by the time her puppies leave her home.

Housebreaking is easy. They come outside in the mornings and I praise them when they pee and poo outside. They come out, I praise. They go potty, I praise. Lots and lots of praise. My owners are always calling me to say that they are amazed their puppy came to them already housebroken. I also always have older dogs around, and they are just wonderful teachers; my puppies are so much wiser about the world by eight to ten weeks old because of the older dogs' being such great examples for them to follow.

Diana Foster and Brooke Walker both crate-train during the socialization period, starting at about six weeks, after the puppies are weaned. That's a very smart thing to do because, as we'll see in the next chapter, the most difficult, most unnatural thing you'll ever need to teach your dog is the skill of being alone without you or without his pack. By training a puppy to be alone for short periods of time in his crate while he's still in the phase when the most basic blueprints of living are being etched into his brain, he learns that "alone time" is a part of his pack's behavior—even though it is absolutely, totally foreign to a dog's DNA.

"As they get a little older—more like seven or eight weeks—what I like to do is mix it up," Diana explains.

Sometimes I'll have them together as a litter. They'll run around and play and sleep together, and then I like to separate them all. I'll put each puppy in a little crate by himself, and I'll put each one in a pen by himself. I start to get them used to that because I know once they go to a home, they're not going to have each other to keep them company. We start with very short increments, like maybe half an hour. I'll put them in the crates, and they're all screaming. After ten or fifteen minutes, they all just go to sleep.

"There's not a dog that leaves my house that doesn't love a crate," Brooke boasts. "I throw a treat into the back of the crate and say, 'Do you want a cookie? Okay, it's in your crate.' So the crate becomes 'Oh wow, this is my favorite spot anyhow, 'cause I get a cookie when I go in there.' I let them take their naps in there, then I let them out. I start with short periods of time, gradually getting longer. And so crate training is the easiest thing in the world to do."

Exploring a Brave New World

During the "behavioral refinement" phase, the puppies become bolder and strike out on their own into new areas. They want to investigate and explore absolutely everything. This is the time when serious breeders start exposing the puppies to as many new stimuli as possible. Brooke takes behavioral-enrichment play seriously—she wants to raise curious, intelligent, adaptable schnauzers, so she provides them with a huge selection of interesting toys and games to choose from.

My backyard is like Disneyland. I just love introducing them to this yard. They play on the patio, they play in the dirt; when they get courageous enough, they'll explore the high grass I have growing in my garden, or they'll explore inside my hedges. I teach them a lot of skills in their exercise area. Since they are terriers, they love to go into holes, so I provide carpeted cat tunnels for them to climb inside and run through. They love that, and when they get big enough, they climb to the top of them. I provide lots of different toys: pull toys so that they can pull against one another, toys with sounds or bells in them, different types of balls for them to chase, different things to stimulate them. I cycle between different toy combinations every single day.

Says Diana Foster of her German shepherd pups,

At this point, they don't need the mother for survival anymore, but we like to keep them with her as long as possible, because of the natural way she disciplines them. For instance, she tells them not to touch her bone or stops them if they start getting too rough with her. Her correction is quick. The puppy may yelp and run away with his tail tucked. And what does the average person do? Pick them up. "Oh, you poor thing. Come here!" Everyone wants to rescue them and feel sorry for them when anything new happens. What they're doing is reinforcing the fact that something bad just happened. But in their world, what happened wasn't bad! It was just a learning experience. Their real mother couldn't care less. She allows the puppy to work out the situation on his own. That's how he grows, that's how he learns. He may run away whimpering, but after just a couple of seconds, he's back playing with his friends. It's not a big deal. It's only a big deal to the humans. I'm like Cesar. I sit for hours and I just watch the dogs. And you can learn so much just by observing what they do, especially a really good mother.

Angel's mom, Binky, was such a good mother that she remained involved with the disciplining of her pups right up until the day each one was adopted out. That's an important part of the reason Angel was so alert and open to accepting rules and structure once he came to live with my family.

Early Socialization: The Cautious Phase (Eight or Nine Weeks)

At around eight or nine weeks of age, a puppy usually hits a phase where he goes from being outgoing and recklessly curious to becoming extremely cautious again. This is to be expected, and in nature it's a stage that passes quickly. The best breeders take special care at this age not to overprotect their puppies but instead help them to develop real self-confidence on their own. "I make sure my puppies are safe and not being bullied or harmed in any way by the rest of the pack," says Brooke. "But to rescue a puppy every time will only lead to a very fearful dog. I want to prepare all my puppies for being gone from me, their siblings, and their mother. At eight weeks, I take my puppies to Fashion Island here in Newport, California. There are many colors, noises, and smells that they haven't experienced before. There is a special fountain that pops up water from the ground in irregular sequences. Although schnauzers are not supposed to be water dogs, I have yet to have a puppy that didn't get into that fountain and enjoy trying to catch the bubbles!"

This cautious period can sometimes coincide with the time a breeder releases a puppy to his new home. New owners often interpret a puppy's understandable reticence as something that must instantly be comforted. When they don't permit him the honor of overcoming his own insecurities in his own way, they can actually undo some of the meticulous hard work that his natural mother and his breeder have put into his education up to this point. "I am currently trying to teach a friend this lesson," Brooke confides. "Her dog falls apart the minute she is around and curls up and hides from other dogs. But when he is here on his own, he is playful, eats well, and walks properly on his leash. I use a firm voice for his commands and restrain myself from the high-pitched baby talk that I use when they are newborns. The long and short of it is, keep the puppy safe, but never rescue." To prevent a puppy from developing fear or anxiety issues, owners shouldn't interfere with the nature of the learning process, which includes feeling uncomfortable and also making mistakes. For puppies, this means we must let them investigate every new situation in the order of nose-eyes-ears, while allowing them to work through their own strategies for meeting new challenges ... even frightening ones. We'll discuss this more in the next chapter.

Follow Mom's Example

No reputable breeder will permit you to bring a puppy home with you before it is eight weeks of age, but I believe it's important for people to understand all the different influences that go into making your dog who he is *before* the day he finally becomes yours. That's because, if a puppy is raised by an instinctual, thorough mother like Angel's mom, Binky, you will already have a great head start on your job. Your dog will already have instilled in him the concept of rules, boundaries, and limitations and will come to you armed with a freshman-level understanding of the most important canine social dos and don'ts. There's no question that Binky gave her all in caring for Angel and his littermates, but she didn't let her emotions get in the way of imposing the natural laws and structure every dog needs if he is going to grow up to be a good canine citizen and a model member of another pack. If your puppy has had a top-notch breeder like Brooke or Diana, he'll have the added advantage of having passed a beginner course in the peculiarities of the human world, including the feeding ritual, the concept of indoor-outdoor borders, and even a little crate training or housebreaking thrown in for extra credit.

Your primary job as his new pack leader is to continue furthering his education, using the same natural common sense.

4

PUPPY COMES HOME

Easing the Transition from Litter to Family

Mr. President as a puppy

You've done your research, found the right breeder, rescue, or shelter, selected a puppy with the correct energy level, and are as certain as you can be that she will grow up to be your perfect canine companion for life. Now it's time to bring her home. I always say, when you're a pack leader, everything you do means something to your dog. Every action, every emotion, every signal you send—accidentally or intentionally—will be input into her computer and used to reevaluate who you are and what function you should play in her life. With puppies, all those tiny moments matter even more. Your puppy's brain is still developing, and she is looking to you to model the behavior patterns she will follow from now on. Junior, Blizzard, Angel, and Mr. President all started out as calm-submissive, medium-energy, issue-free puppies. But even I—yes, I, the Dog Whisperer—could mess up their already perfect programming if I didn't pay attention to every interaction I had with them from the first day forward, especially during those earliest weeks in which my puppies were making the transition from their first pack—their mom and littermates—to living with my pack—my human family and my other dogs.

THE TRIP HOME

When you pick up your dog from the breeder's, shelter, or rescue, the previous caretaker will talk you through adoption or sales contracts, as well as fill you in on the details of her health history, including documented records of any shots she has had up until now. When your puppy comes home with you, she should already have had at least her first round of immunizations, against distemper, hepatitis, para-influenza, and parvo, something we'll address in more detail in the next chapter. Ideally, you will have already been to visit your puppy at least once before the actual adoption. Many breeders like their new owners to handle the puppies after they are two or three weeks old, to begin to get them familiar with the scents of their new pack leaders—remember, dogs memorize and recognize an individual's scents in much the same way we humans remember faces, except dogs' noses are hundreds of times more accurate than human eyes! In other words, your new puppy would be able to pick you out of a police lineup with far more accuracy than you would be able to recognize her in a lineup of similar-breed dogs!

Your dog's powerful sense of scent works to your advantage in other ways. To help ease your puppy's transition away from her first family, make sure to bring with you some clothing or toys that bear the scent of her mother and littermates. They will provide needed comfort for her first few days apart from the support system she has come to depend upon. You will also have with you a kennel or carrying case to transport your puppy. If this is the carrying case that will become your puppy's permanent "crate" at your home, you can ask your breeder to start getting the puppy used to that particular crate a week or so in advance. You can even provide an item—a towel or undershirt—to put in the crate that has your scent on it, *as long as it is totally sanitary and has never come into contact with any nonimmunized dogs or other pets!* The more we can use our dogs' noses to help them prepare for new situations, the easier any change will be for them.

KENNEL/CRATE TIPS

Choosing a Crate Style

WIRE CRATES

- Stay cooler in hot environments
- Give more ventilation
- Give a 360-degree view to the puppy
- Can be covered with a towel to minimize distractions
- Often fold flat for storage

Note: Make sure to keep the floor lined with comfortable paper, cardboard, or bedding.

HARD PLASTIC CRATES

- Are easy to clean
- Have comfortable, smooth floors that can be easily arranged with bedding and a raised sleeping area
- Are lightweight and better for portability
- Provide a ready-made "den-like" environment—naturally calming for excited puppies and helpful in soothing separation anxiety issues

---

The choice is yours, but whichever style you choose, be sure the crate is big enough so that there is enough room for the dog to stand up and turn around, and in which she can lie down and sleep in a comfortable position. It's also best to allow some extra room for your puppy's rapid growth.

When it comes time to bring your puppy to the car, you may be carrying her from the breeder's in her crate, or you may choose the option that I prefer: walking her to the curb and allowing her to go into the car (and into her open crate inside the car) of her own volition. There's a reason that I suggest to owners that they allow their puppies to propel themselves into new situations as much as possible: puppies are not marsupials, and they are not primates. When their mother wants them to go somewhere, she lets them figure out a way to follow her there. If they are too slow, somehow stray off the path, or get blocked by an object that's in their way, she will go back, pick them up by the scruff, and move them back to where they need to be. Then she will continue on her journey, and they will once again have to figure out how to follow her. She doesn't spend her days carrying her litter from place to place. If she did, her pups would never learn to fend for themselves, and that would be disastrous for the pack as a whole.

We need to keep our puppies' mothers in mind at all times when helping them make the switch from their early lives to what will be their living situation for the majority of their puppyhood. Becoming a *partner* in your dog's life from day one means helping her through challenging new circumstances but never rescuing her from those situations or doing all the work for her. Nature, with the added help of the mother, has already created a time-tested, nearly foolproof strategy for a dog's education. We have to be aware that sometimes our best intentions drive us to actually block puppies from getting the benefits of Mother Nature's lesson plan. Those best intentions, for too many owners, usually involve carrying their puppies around everywhere like babies, so the puppies never get a sense of how they got to where they're going. This is very much against their nature and can seriously stunt their learning and development.

To use my method for introducing the puppy to the car and her kennel, park the car as close as possible to the pickup spot so you will be able to let the puppy follow you there. Many great breeders, like Brooke and Diana, have already conditioned their puppies to the sensation of the leash, so you can actually begin the leash-training process with this very first exercise you share together.

Once you reach your vehicle, open the door or tailgate and lift up the puppy by her scruff, but put only her front two paws down on the car seat or cargo area. This will trigger her brain to automatically want to put all four feet down where the first two landed. You have helped her accomplish this monumental new feat, but you haven't done all the work for her. Instead you've been a *partner* in the learning experience.

Next, the puppy will want to explore the new space, first with her body and then with her nose, so you can use food to lure her into her transport kennel. She'll also be attracted by the item containing the scents of her littermates and mom. Make sure she is relaxed and comfortable inside the kennel before you close the door. Never, ever close a door on an excited or anxious puppy. This can contribute to kennel phobias and even separation anxiety. Finally, position her near enough to smell and see you during the drive home.

Remember, scent and sight are far more important to your puppy than sound! In fact, sound can sometimes reinforce any fear or anxiety the puppy may be experiencing about this first-time adventure. If your puppy is whining throughout the trip and you are constantly repeating, "It's okay, it's okay," what you are actually communicating to your puppy—not with the words but with the energy behind that sound—is that her *discomfort and whining* are okay. Also, try to refrain from using the squeaky, high-pitched cooing and baby talk people seem to slip into when they are around cute baby animals. If you are feeling sorry for the puppy, her first impression of you will be one of a creature with weak energy. As always, silent, calm-assertive energy is better for your puppy than talk or even touch at this point.

To calm a very anxious puppy, I always recommend using scent to distract first, then, once the puppy begins to relax, reinforcing that with a treat if necessary. But petting a fretful puppy can actually create exactly the outcome you don't want—a puppy that always gets upset whenever she is inside a car or her kennel.

INTRODUCING YOUR PUPPY TO YOUR HOME

For those of you who have read my other books about rehabilitating adult dogs, you will be familiar with my instructions for walking a new dog around her new neighborhood for thirty minutes to an hour before inviting her into your home. This begins the forging of a bond and simulates the experience of migration, so that moving into your house feels like migrating from one area to another, and thus makes sense to her on a primal level.

For puppies, I recommend a kind of "abridged" version of this process. Before you bring your puppy inside your house it's important for her to have a sense of the environment she's going to live in, to get a taste of the smells, sounds, and sights of your yard, home, and neighborhood. You must begin to communicate to your puppy that your driveway or hedges or white picket fence marks the beginning of your territory. If your puppy already has had some experience with a leash or is open to wearing one, place a short leash high up on the puppy's neck, so you can have a comfortable amount of control. This is the ideal situation, both to establish a lifetime routine and for your puppy's immediate safety. Next, place the puppy on the ground, then walk toward your home, letting her follow you inside the front door. Do not let her get distracted or sniff the ground. Chris and Johanna Komives describe following this protocol with their new puppy, Eliza: "When I picked her up from the breeder, I put a leash on her—the breeder had already familiarized the puppies with leashes—and walked her briefly before putting her in the car," says Chris. Clearly, Chris remembered the lessons he's learned from six seasons of shooting *Dog Whisperer,* since this is another exercise I always insist upon for clients adopting adult dogs, but it's also a first-rate way to begin the bonding process with a new puppy. "I had her crate in the car and put her in and waited until she was calm before closing the door and driving off," Chris continues. "When we arrived home, I sprayed bleach-water in front of our house and two houses down and walked her this distance before entering the backyard. I let her explore the backyard, and then showed her the area in the back hallway we had prepared for her."

If you live in an apartment, place the puppy a few feet outside the door and wait for her to follow you inside. Patience is key here, because she may be a bit disoriented and a little reticent in the beginning. Hesitancy is normal in puppies, because everything is new to them. As we discussed in the last chapter, your puppy may still be in the "cautious" phase that marks the end of her early socialization period.

Eliza at home

So don't force the puppy inside if she is "putting the brakes on." Remember my formula: nose-eyes-ears. Use a bully stick, treat, scented toy, or the item with her littermates' or mother's scents on it to engage her nose. Eventually she will show natural curiosity and willingness to come in after you. As timid as she might seem at first, it's in her computer program to follow you. It's very important that you remain calm, relaxed, and fully accepting of her natural tentativeness. On the day you plan to bring your puppy home, set aside several hours or even a good part of the day for the process so that you don't become impatient. Remember, the energy you share with your puppy will become her energy. If you are tense and frustrated with her, she will reflect that negativity right back at you. Introducing a puppy to new environments should be a joyful activity for you, not one of frustration and stress.

THE PUPPY-READY HOME

"When someone is buying a puppy, I always give them lots of information about how to prepare their houses," says Diana Foster.

> When people aren't prepared, it's a recipe for disaster. And it's totally unnecessary. It's as if a woman were pregnant for nine months; she goes to the hospital to have the baby; she comes home, but there's nothing ready. There's no crib. There's no playpen. There's no booster seat or diapers. So she just leaves the infant on the floor. That may sound extreme, but there really are people who buy a puppy on a whim and that's the kind of thing they do. Then they wonder why their house is a wreck and they have all these behavior problems. They blame the dog for being out of control. I make sure I never let one of my German shepherd puppies go to someone who's not prepared.

Puppy-proofing a home doesn't have to be a monumental project, especially if you keep your puppy in a confined space for the first few weeks, gradually expanding her territory more and more as she becomes housebroken and starts to feel more at home in your family pack. Finding a secure, limited space in which to keep your puppy—at least during her early months—makes it easier for her to internalize your rules, boundaries, and limitations, gives her a sense of order and structure, and protects your home from accidental destruction. Chris and Johanna Komives prepared an arca in their back hallway (with a dog door to the backyard) where they put Eliza's crate. In our home, all new dogs—including Junior, Blizzard, Angel, and Mr. President— began their residency in their kennels, in our large, well-ventilated garage, with an open door to our side yard and a wall of baby gates as an additional boundary. Of course, our puppies will be staying in that garage with the balanced adult dogs already living there. I don't ever recommend leaving a young puppy crated alone in a garage or a distant, closed-off room, simply because being so completely isolated from the sounds and smells of a living pack will be very upsetting for her.

Diana Foster recommends that families ignore her German shepherd puppies for the majority of their first days home but put their crates in a far corner of a family room or kitchen, where they can feel a part of the pack even while not engaging in the family's activities. This teaches them that excitement in the family doesn't mean *they* have to respond with excitement, a vital skill for powerful-breed puppies that will grow up to be large, brawny dogs. A mudroom or laundry room just off a kitchen makes an ideal place for this kind of setup. Some people bring their puppy's kennel into their bedroom to minimize her loneliness for the first few nights, then decide to leave it there indefinitely. The place you choose should be an area of which you are not

Diana Foster's crate setup for her Thinschmidt German shepherds

obsessively house-proud, so if an accident does occur, you won't lose your temper and blame your puppy for a mistake that is not her "fault."

I am the world's biggest fan of baby gates, be they metal, wire, wood, or plastic. I keep lots of them folded up in my garage and use them for a variety of purposes—as barriers, as "map" boundaries to show where I want the dogs to go, and even as behavioral enrichment tools in obstacle courses for the regular challenges I use to fulfill my dogs' need to work. It's important to remember, however, that a clever puppy can easily push or leap over a lightweight baby gate. It's up to you to set an invisible boundary as well as a physical one wherever you choose to keep your dog.

Spot Check

Although you should always be supervising your puppy in the more open areas of your home, as her confidence grows she will be driven to explore most everything in her immediate environment. Accidents can happen, no matter how diligent you are. That's why it's important to do a puppy-proofing of each room before your bring your littlest pack member home. Pass through each room, checking for loose wires or electrical cords that might appear all too chewable, and move them out of sight or tape them down. Make sure that the food in your kitchen is put away on high shelves or in sealed containers; make sure your garbage can has a firm lid and is out of reach. Put a latch on any low cabinets containing cleaning products, in both the kitchen and bathroom. Examine your bathroom floors and low shelves and clear them of any human grooming products—soaps, shampoos, shaving lotions, loofahs or sponges—that might prove to be temptations. Keep the toilet bowl down at all times. In our garage I have high shelves, locked cabinets, and sealed plastic containers that house any loose odds and ends I don't want the dogs to get near.

Houseplants are a huge enticement—dogs are attracted to anything natural, so the scent of the soil and leaves will be very inviting to them. Terriers like Angel may instinctually want to dig up your prize two-hundred-dollar fern when you're not looking, so be sure to remove plants from the floors of any rooms in which you eventually plan to allow your puppy. There are also a few very common houseplants that can be toxic to dogs, including

Aloe vera	Lilies
Asparagus fern	Mistletoe
Bean plants	Philodendron
Cactus	Poinsettia
Caladium	Potted chrysanthemum
Dumbcane	Umbrella plant
Hydrangea	Various ivies
Indian rubber plant	Weeping fig

Don't forget your backyard in this process. Like houseplants, several common yard plants and trees are poisonous to your puppy, including

Autumn crocus	Lily of the valley
Castor bean	Morning glory
Foxglove	Nightshade
Hibiscus	Oleander
Hyacinth	Precatory beans
Japanese yew	Trumpet vine
Jerusalem cherry	Tulips
Kalanchoe	Wisteria
Larkspur	

The ASPCA's excellent website offers a more comprehensive list of toxic and nontoxic plants, as well as tips on how to spot symptoms of poisoning.[1]

Supplies

In addition to your crate or kennel, you should be prepared with the following items and tools to help both of you adjust to your new life together:

- Healthy puppy or dog food approved by your vet
- Food and water bowls
- Collar and leash
- ID tags (also consult with your vet about microchipping)
- Grooming supplies: nail clippers, brushes, flea comb, dog shampoo, ear-cleaning pads, toothbrush, and dog toothpaste
- Wee-wee pads
- Baby gates
- Natural-material chew bone (I am a big fan of the bully stick, because rawhide can be rough on a puppy's digestion)
- Vet-approved training treats for rewarding
- Plastic bags or scooper for poop
- Dog bed or dog cushion
- A variety of stimulating play toys

A PRESIDENTIAL PUPPY-PROOFING

When Mr. President was three and a half months old, my wife and I took a trip to Australia for business, then went on to Fiji for a short vacation and spiritual retreat. For the two weeks we would be away, Dog Psychology Center director Adriana Barnes took care of the dogs in my home pack, but our hardworking researcher for this book, Crystal Reel, campaigned fiercely for the opportunity to foster our winsome English bulldog puppy. I believe everyone in my human pack should have the joy of spending time with dogs, even if they don't own them permanently, and I encourage everybody who works with me to get hands-on experience practicing the principles of calm-assertive leadership that I teach. But since Mr. President is an accomplished chewer, I instructed Crystal to thoroughly puppy-proof her townhouse before the presidential visit.

Crystal reported later:

My puppy-proofing started with the kitchen, because that is where Mr. President would hang out if I couldn't take him somewhere with me, such as the grocery store or a restaurant—I learned quickly that most people didn't buy the story that he was my Seeing Eye dog! In the kitchen I had to make sure he couldn't get into any of the household cleaning chemicals that I keep under the sink. Baby locks and duct tape work great to keep these securely closed.

Next came the pantry cabinets. Bulldogs might not have the best sense of smell in the world, but Mr. President quickly figured out that his food was in there. I learned the hard way that he could open my pantry cabinet. I set up a webcam in my kitchen so I could watch Mr. President from my computer at work on the rare days I wasn't able to bring him into our very dog-friendly offices. There I was, working away, when I saw Mr. President actually open the pantry cabinet and start pulling out the bags of doggie cookies I had placed on the bottom shelf! I was terrified he would eat the plastic bag the cookies came in, so I immediately jumped up from my desk, hopped into my car, and raced back to the west side, a good forty-five-minute drive. Luckily, Mr. President has good taste—he ate all the treats and left the plastic bag—but still I'm glad I had set up the webcam so I knew what he was doing at all times.

I also puppy-proofed the living room and my bedroom by making sure to hide or pick up off the ground any cables or cords he might be able to chew on, as well as shoes and other things I had on the ground that I didn't want eaten. I then vacuumed everywhere because we have leaves and twigs and such that get tracked in around the front door from outside and I didn't want him to eat any of those either.

The direction Cesar gave me on puppy-proofing was to keep an eye on his chewing and redirect his energy. He told me bully sticks were best because rawhide can be hard on a puppy's digestive system. So I made sure to have a lot of bully sticks on hand, and they really did come in handy!

PUPPY-PROOFING CHECKLIST

- Keep floors free of loose or small items that could become choking hazards: loose change, pens or pencils, paper clips, jewelry, etc.
- Move electrical cords out of the way, tape them down, or cover them with heavy rugs. Purchase plastic outlet covers for open outlets.
- Make sure breakable items—curios, lamps, etc.—are safely removed from puppy's play area.
- Set up baby gates to block off access to forbidden areas.
- Install childproof locks on low cabinet doors, and remove all cleaning supplies or toxic chemicals to high shelves.
- Fence in or cover swimming pools, hot tubs, and other open bodies of water.

(continues)

- Remove potentially poisonous houseplants and outdoor land-scaping.
- Keep toilet seats down.
- Make sure trash can lids are locked and sealed.

BOUNDARIES BEHIND WALLS

Since a recurring theme of this book is "how not to raise Marley," here's another telling incident from John Grogan's poignant and hilarious memoir, describing the very first time he brought their two-month-old Labrador into their small home. "When we got home, I led him inside and unhooked his leash. He began sniffing and didn't stop until he had sniffed every square inch of the place."

A cautious new puppy checking out his new crib—sounds like a perfectly reasonable reaction, doesn't it? What first-time dog owner John didn't realize was that almost all puppies at eight weeks of age will act polite and tentative while checking out an unfamiliar environment. But a casual introduction like this one sets the precedent for a puppy eventually to believe that he should "own" that entire space. Once a dog starts feeling secure and confident within the confines of his new real estate—especially a fast-growing, powerful, and very-high-energy dog like Marley—problems can multiply with lightning speed. True to form, within a few short weeks, Marley was acting like a drunken rock star hell-bent on trashing a hotel suite: "Every last object in our house that was at knee level or below was knocked asunder by Marley's wildly wagging weapon. He cleared coffee tables, scattered magazines, knocked framed photographs off shelves, sent beer bottles and wineglasses flying. He even cracked a pane in the French door."

The Grogans' decision to let Marley explore his new environment on his own is one of the most common errors I see new puppy owners make. And I'm not alone in observing this. "The very, very worst thing you can do to a puppy when you bring it home is introduce it to your whole house," Brooke Walker says emphatically. Diana Foster agrees. "He doesn't need the whole house, and he doesn't need the whole yard. Those are the owners who will call me a couple of weeks later, complaining, 'I thought the dog was supposed to be well-behaved. This dog is out of control.'" Unfortunately, some of the most popular puppy-training books on the market advocate letting a new puppy run free, claiming that you "owe" your new puppy her "freedom." Freedom, in my experience, means something quite different to a puppy than it does to us, or even to an older dog.

Your eight- to ten-week-old puppy has just come from living with her mother, who provided her with specific rules, boundaries, and limitations from day one. Your puppy could romp and play and explore, but there were always limits. She could wrestle, bite, and pounce, but there were always limits. If she had a conscientious breeder, she also learned to feel self-assured within the world of human boundaries. To your puppy, that world of very clear structure has come to represent comfort, safety, and security. Structure gave her harmony, serenity, and a growing sense of self-confidence. If freedom equals peace of mind, then, as it turns out, *structure* actually makes up the foundation of a dog's freedom.

In contrast to the Grogans' first day with Marley, consider Chris and Johanna Komives's first day with Eliza:

When we brought her home, we took her right to the back hall, which we had already set up for her. We had her crate there, her food, and a dog door (but we left it closed until she was crate trained). She stayed in her crate or the backyard for the first week. Then I brought her into the living room on her leash and introduced her to her "place": a dog bed. She was not allowed to leave her place when she was in the living room. We began teaching her commands right away. She learned sit, stay, down, and go to your place. A week or so later, we showed her the kitchen.

The Komiveses may never write a bestseller about Eliza's crazy antics, but they still have an intact home and a dog they can confidently take with them anywhere without worrying about destruction or a lawsuit!

Once you cross the threshold of your domain, it's up to you to supervise and control how your puppy first experiences her new environment. The Komiveses chose a foolproof way of communicating to a puppy the idea that the humans are the ones who control all the space within their walls. To eight- to ten-week-old puppies, the vastness of a strange new environment may seem overwhelming and frightening. Having a well-defined space that they know is theirs is actually a comfort to them. If you have followed my instructions so far, you have blocked off a small area—a "safe" area—in which you've put your puppy's crate or bed. Baby gates are great to use as barriers, because the puppy can have you in her scent and sight but still be in a limited area. The Komiveses' approach involved bringing Eliza through the front door, then walking her immediately to her area.

THE FIRST NIGHT HOME

Bedtime, for your new puppy, will be the moment it really sinks in for her that she will no longer have her mother and siblings around for warmth, company, and comfort. In their natural world, puppies always sleep with their mother and siblings. This transition from her pack to yours is a monumental challenge in the process of becoming your perfect pet. It's where the rubber meets the road.

For a puppy, the next-best thing to having her original pack around is to sleep near or with another dog. If you already have a dog at home, however, you'll have had to introduce that dog to the new puppy, and determine whether or not the dog is receptive and nurturing. Warning: A dog that growls, ignores, or acts wary around a puppy will need a lot more introductory work from you before she can be left alone with the puppy. It's also important that any older dog sleeping with a puppy is compatible in size with that puppy, since a very small puppy can easily be suffocated by a well-meaning but heavy larger dog. If you have any doubts at all about this, check with your breeder or your vet.

Junior slept with Daddy from the first night he came home with me. Daddy and Junior were already used to caring for a variety of dogs in various states of mind and stability, and I trusted them absolutely with the welfare of the new puppies. They became grandfather and big brother respectively to the two-month-old yellow Lab puppy, Blizzard, who slept in his own crate but next to the other dogs' crates in the garage. And since Mr. President and Angel came home with me around the same time, the two of them automatically accepted each other as "stepbrothers" and have been inseparable ever since, always sharing a crate as if they were actually littermates. Thanks to the dogs of my pack, not one of the puppies in this book has ever had trouble adjusting to his new lifestyle. Most likely, however, you don't have another balanced dog that is ready and willing to take on the role of "nanny" to your puppy. It is up to you to reduce any trauma the pup might have on her first night away from her birth family.

When it comes time for sleep, set up the puppy's crate, kennel, or bedding in the area where you want her to stay, making sure to line any hard surfaces with newspaper or a towel. A raised bed in the back and papers on the ground will prevent the puppy from having to sleep in her own excrement, should a nocturnal accident happen. If it does, change all the bedding and completely clean and sanitize the crate the next day, so the puppy never smells her own excrement and becomes accustomed to relieving herself in there. Also outfit the crate or bed with an item with the mother's and siblings' scent on it; a good, smelly chew toy like a bully stick; and perhaps even a soft dog toy with a simulated "heartbeat" inside it, which can be quite comforting for a puppy.

For the first few days or weeks, make sure the location of the sleeping place is not so far away from you that your puppy can't smell or sense your presence—staying in a closed garage all by herself might be fine in two or three months' time, but on night one, it could cause a panic reaction. If you have created a space for your dog in the laundry room or hallway, you can choose to begin the sleeping arrangement or crate training right then and there, but be prepared for a long, restless night. Most puppies will whine, and some will scream, when separated from their packs. To minimize this reaction, make sure your puppy is as tired as possible before her first bedtime. Once she shows signs of slowing down, let her follow you to where her resting place is going to be. Don't just pick her up and drop her in the crate or on the bed; let her find it herself. Use scent, nose-eyes-ears, or just your presence to attract her to settle down in that place. Provide an inviting toy or treat. By going there on her own steam—especially if led by a treat—she will associate her new "den" area with pleasant relaxation. Remember, you may have created the most luxurious, inviting paradise in the world for her to sleep in, but if you introduce it in a negative way, your puppy will never want to stay there.

If the area is a crate with a door that closes, make sure the puppy is lying down and relaxed before closing it. This may involve quite a bit of patience at first. Use a sound or your energy to disagree with any whining, then wait quietly by the crate next to the puppy until she has thoroughly calmed down. She may begin to nod off on her own (remember, puppies need a lot of sleep—nearly eighteen hours a day during their peak growth period). Then quietly close the crate door and leave the room.

At a certain point, your puppy may wake up in the night and begin whining. This may sound horrific, but it is perfectly normal. With the exception of getting up to take the dog out to urinate (some dogs, like

Angel, will already be conditioned to staying in a crate all night; others, like Eliza, will need to be let out every few hours until housebreaking really kicks in), you should not be rushing in to respond to the puppy's mournful cries. Never comfort a whining puppy. I know, I know. It sounds heartbreaking. And, yes, your puppy is going through some distress at this moment, but it's important to let her work through it. The only way possible for her to get past that anxiety permanently is to learn to solve the problem for herself. You must allow her the space and dignity of coming out on the other side of her discomforts, even if it makes you feel bad to listen to her. If you run to soothe her every time she cries, she will learn very quickly (a) that she controls you and can summon you by vocalizing, and (b) that you are *agreeing* with her whining because you are positively reinforcing it with comfort, attention, or a treat. You may also be setting the stage to create a nervous, fearful, dependent puppy. Ignoring at this early stage is also vital to prevent the issue of separation anxiety. For now, buy some foam earplugs at the drugstore, have a glass of warm milk before bed, do a little meditation, and repeat to yourself, "This, too, shall pass." Trust me, it will, before you know it!

To minimize this common first-night trauma, I recommend that people set up their puppy's crate or bed near or in their bedrooms, for the first few nights after arrival. The first night of whining may still keep you awake—and, no, you *still* can't respond to it with cooing or comfort—but if the crate is near your bed, you can tap it once and make the sound you want your puppy to associate with a behavior you don't agree with. This will stop the escalation of the behavior, sometimes long enough for relaxation to set in. If your puppy quiets down for a significant period of time after that, you can reward with praise or even a treat. A bully stick is great for this because it engages the nose and distracts the mind. Only reward a calm state of mind. Then put in your earplugs and ignore.

By the next night, your puppy should have reduced this behavior, or have stopped it entirely. She will begin to find comfort by just being around you or being in the familiar surroundings of her crate. This method also offers the advantage of your puppy's picking up on your human sleeping patterns and learning·to imitate them. If you don't plan to have your puppy remain in your bedroom indefinitely, three days should be long enough to acclimate her to her new style of living. She may again whine through the night when you move her sleeping place, but if you tire her out and make sure she is relaxed before you put her down for the night, it won't take long for her to adjust to the new location.

Don't forget that your own energy and attitude toward your puppy's sleeping arrangements will have a powerful impact on how she herself views them. If you feel terrible about putting your puppy's crate in the laundry room and are wracked with guilt that she'll feel abandoned out there, then your puppy will probably pick up on your negative emotions about the place. Decide on a sleeping arrangement that makes *you* feel that you are providing the best for your puppy, then make sure she is always tired out, relaxed, and submissive before you say good night. This will be your best guarantee for a lifetime of healthy, happy sleeping habits.

CRATE TRAINING

"Crate training is a must," says Brooke Walker. "No dog ever leaves my house without learning to love a crate."

Brooke didn't always feel this way. Before she became a professional breeder, she had bought into the old-school myth that crate training was cruel, that dogs don't like small spaces, that they always needed the run of the house or yard. It was breeding and living with generations of content, calm miniature schnauzers that changed her mind, because she saw such an enormous difference in the behavior and general level of happiness between her dogs and dogs whose lives did not have such predictable routine. In fact, crate training your puppy is one of the best things you can do for her as well as for yourself. Done correctly, crate training provides your puppy with a ready-made "den"—a place that she can associate with safety, tranquillity, and quiet. Instead of calming herself in a destructive manner when she is alone or when you need her to be at rest, the puppy will learn how to soothe herself by going into her private den and relaxing there.

Crate training also provides a familiar surrounding for traveling in cars or for spending nights at friends' homes or pet-friendly motels and hotels. Dogs love adventures, and the easier it is for you to bring your dog wherever you travel, the more stimulating new experiences you will provide for her. Crate training helps maintain a calm-submissive mind and helps prevent all the unwanted behaviors that too much so-called freedom—I call it chaos—can inspire.

"We started crate training the first day," says Chris Komives, now a confirmed fan. "I bought a crate appropriate for an adult wheaten terrier and made a partition to give her an area appropriate to her size. For the first two weeks she was in either the crate or the backyard. I made sure the crate was associated with calmness and safety. At first she was anxious, and I would wait for her to be calm and then go sit with her. She learned that when she's calm in her crate, I reappear. Soon she was quiet when left in her crate."

Teaching your puppy to use a crate requires patience and repetition, but it is not difficult, as the puppy instinctually feels comfortable in a den. If you've adopted your puppy from a breeder like Brooke or Diana, you will already be well ahead of the game. Place the crate in the area that you have chosen for your puppy's resting place. Make sure it is not an isolated area but one in which the puppy can still feel a part of the rest of the pack, even if she's behind a baby gate in her crate. Diana likes her new owners to set up their crates in a corner of the family room, where the German shepherd puppies can share in family togetherness from a distance, but where they won't be constantly distracted by too much activity or foot traffic.

Wherever you choose to place the crate (later you can move it from room to room if you like), take Brooke's advice and use it as the number one destination for rewards or treats. Find a favorite toy or a snack or bully stick—whatever most motivates your puppy—and make the crate the place she is guaranteed to get it.

Begin this crating routine as soon as you bring your puppy home. Let your puppy play—supervised at all times, of course—then when she begins to tire, invite her into the crate and close her in for a half hour. Next time, make it an hour, then an hour and fifteen minutes, and so on. Never close the puppy in if she is excited or anxious, but if she becomes whiny later, ignore her; don't inadvertently reward the behavior by trying to soothe her with your voice. Give her a firm "Tssst," or the sound you choose to use as your "I disagree with that behavior" sound, wait until she calms down, then walk away and ignore. Always reward true calm submission in the crate with praise, petting, or treats. Do this at regular intervals throughout the day. Your goal is to build up to several hours of a peaceful, resting puppy. Having your puppy sleep in her crate facilitates this. After she is house-trained, she will be able to stay in her crate overnight for a full seven to nine hours.

CRATE-TRAINING SUCCESS STORY

Angel's Night Out

My coauthor, Melissa Jo Peltier, can't have a dog in her life right now, because she and her husband live in New York but travel back and forth to Los Angeles frequently for work. While we were working on this book, I offered her the chance to take Angel overnight to stay with them in their small short-term apartment near Universal Studios.

Angel was just four months old and had never been away from his pack overnight before. As part of his learning program, I was curious to see how he would fare.

On a Friday afternoon, we put Angel in a midsize crate and seat-belted it tightly into the passenger seat of Melissa's small convertible. I showed Melissa how to let Angel go into the crate on his own, following a bully stick with his nose. I also provided him a towel with the scent of "home," and she put in a couple of her socks as well, so he could get used to her scent (he already knew her as a regular visitor to the pack). "The moment the car pulled out of Cesar's driveway, Angel looked at me for reassurance, then lay down in his crate and promptly went to sleep," Melissa reported. "He snoozed all the way—despite the stop-and-go rush-hour traffic and the deafening freeway noise, all the more distracting in a convertible with the top down. He only started to rouse himself after I had already exited the freeway and was about half a block from our destination. I believe he was that sensitive to my energy, even though he'd never been where we were going before."

Melissa and her husband spent a delightful evening playing with Angel, taking him to an outdoor café (his first!) while they ate dinner, giving him one long and two short walks on Ventura Boulevard and in a nearby park, and making sure he eliminated right on schedule. "He spent the latter half of the evening getting some decadent belly rubs on the couch while we watched a DVD," Melissa told me. Still, I was a little unsure about how he'd handle his first real sleepaway experience. He was only four months old and had thus far never experienced any traumatic nights, thanks to Brooke's early crate training and, of course, to the comforting presence of the other dogs in my pack. But he was used to sleeping in the same crate as his adopted brother, Mr. President, every single night. How would he fare, all alone in an alien environment, with two complete strangers?

It turns out that Angel was an Angel, even away from home. Melissa reported:

I took him for one last walk outside so he could relieve himself, and did a very short but fast-paced sprint with him to help tire him out. It had been a big day anyway, so when it came time to go to bed, I placed the crate in a corner of the bedroom where I could watch it, and invited Angel in with his bully stick. He was really ready to crash by that time. The crate obviously represented relaxation to him, and he lay right down and started chewing quietly. When I was sure he was relaxed, I closed the door, and we got ready for bed ourselves. Cesar had told me he was worried that Angel might whine if he woke up during the night, but he uttered not a peep. When I opened my eyes in the morning, he was standing up in his crate trying to make eye contact with me, obviously ready to go out, but not at all anxious about it . . . just patiently waiting for me to come get him. It was so sweet! He didn't have a single accident, was enthusiastic during our morning walk, and when it was time to bring him back to Cesar's, he climbed right back in the crate and let me lift it into the car. Once again, he napped through the whole commute.

Angel's "night out" illustrates how incredibly beneficial crate training can be for a dog's well-being, helping him become adaptable to all sorts of new circumstances and opening up the possibilities of a life full of exciting adventures. I was very proud of Angel—and of Melissa, for reinforcing all his good lessons up to that point.

YARD RULES

If you are planning to let your puppy out in your yard, make sure it's been puppy-proofed, and always begin by supervising. If you are going to use a dog door and make the yard a part of the space in which she's allowed free rein, make sure—especially if it's a large yard—that you start her off by containing her in a small part of it. Set up a gate between your yard and side yard, establish a yard pen, or hook up a dog run. The backyard is not supposed to be Chuck E. Cheese, where anything and everything goes. If a puppy has no structure in her backyard wanderings, letting her ramble around your property just because it makes you feel better will actually add stress to her life. She will be like a ship without a rudder, and instead of signifying freedom, the yard will begin to feel like a prison. Never leave your very young pup out in the yard unattended. The outdoor pen and indoor crate or confined, safe area should become the babysitters for your pup.

"There are just so many advantages to confining your young puppy to a side yard, dog run, or penned-off area, " says Diana Foster. "It prevents destructive behavior to the rest of the yard; it reduces territorial aggression; it cuts down on the stress caused by overstimulation, which in turn leads to arousal and barking; it reduces the excitement of jumping on people and annoying visitors; and it keeps your yard cleaner. How can anyone argue with that?"

DRAMA-FREE HOUSEBREAKING

"I think people still have a huge misconception about how to house-train a puppy," says Dr. Paula Terifaj of Founders Veterinary Clinic in Brea, California. "They still use punishment or yelling. Puppies do not understand you, no matter how much you yell or swat at them. Consistency is the best way to house-break a puppy. Get a potty schedule going and the puppy will eventually get with the program."

"I don't understand what the fuss about housebreaking is all about," Brooke Walker muses. "By the time my puppies are ten weeks old, they are all totally housebroken. My clients call me and say, 'My dog has never had an accident inside the house.' I can house-break any dog in three days."

   Like Brooke and Dr. Terifaj, I also have never been able to comprehend all the high drama that people tend to associate with housebreaking a puppy. The truth is, this is a situation in which you have Mother Nature working with you right from the start. When the puppies are first born, they eat and they relieve themselves inside the den, but the mother always cleans them. The mother stimulates their bodily functions, and her environment always remains unsoiled. There is never the scent of urine or feces where the puppies eat, sleep, and live. When they get old enough to follow the mother outside, they imitate her example and quickly learn to relieve themselves in the flora and fauna on the outskirts of their general living area. In this way, all dogs become conditioned never to eliminate in their dens or near the places where they eat and sleep. From two to four months of age, most pups pick up on the concept of housebreaking quite easily, since it is a part of their natural programming.

   Of course, this doesn't always apply to puppies that were raised in puppy mills. Dogs in puppy mills often wallow in their own waste twenty-four hours a day, and even though it is naturally abhorrent to them, it becomes the only thing they know. By the time you bring a puppy mill puppy home, the trauma of its neonatal period may have effectively canceled out many of its natural instincts. This is true of Georgia Peaches, the rescued puppy mill Yorkie in my pack. Her formative months were so miserable, so unnatural, that her common sense in many areas seems to have vanished. I have rehabilitated her to the point where she's about 80 percent consistent, but she's the only one in the pack who has regular accidents. The new puppies all got the hang of our bathroom schedule within a week or two of arriving at my house.

   Another built-in plus when it comes to housebreaking is your puppy's digestive tract, which is extremely quick and efficient. You can set your watch to it. Five to thirty minutes after a puppy eats, she'll want to defecate. From the time you get your puppy until she's about eight months old, you should be feeding her three times a day. I recommend that you keep to a very consistent feeding schedule and that you take your puppy outside immediately after eating and also right after naps, long confinements or trips, or extended play sessions so that it becomes her pattern.

When bringing your puppy outside after a meal, take her to an outdoor area where there's dirt, grass, sand, rocks—some sort of natural surface that will stimulate the instinctual side of a puppy's brain to look for a place to relieve herself. "By the time they leave my house," Brooke states, "my puppies have learned how to defecate on grass, on dirt, on concrete, on brick, and on stone. That way, they are more adaptable when their owners take them places. Some people make the mistake of only potty-training their pups on one type of surface, so if they find themselves in another situation, the puppies don't know what to do."

In the early days of housebreaking, you also want to make sure that the puppy has a place to relieve herself where she feels safe, a place that seems and smells familiar. For a puppy's digestion to be regular, she should feel totally relaxed when she relieves herself. If a dog is panicked, nervous, unsure, or insecure, she will shut down and not be able to eliminate.

As always, remember that your own energy is a big factor in your housebreaking efforts. If you are feeling nervous or impatient or are trying to rush a puppy to relieve herself, that can also stress her out and stop her down. When new owners call for advice on housebreaking their German shepherd puppies, Diana Foster always asks them to check their own energy and behavior, to make sure they are not the ones putting the drama into the housebreaking experience. "You take him out there. You're all excited. You're talking in a high squeaky voice, 'Go potty for Mommy. Go potty—Mommy loves you!' The dog is running around, all excited, and looking at the person, wondering, 'What is she trying to say to me?' You're distracting the dog so much, he can't relax. Then you think he doesn't have to go because he's not going, so you bring him in, and then he pees on the carpet. And the drama starts all over again." If this is your pattern, Diana recommends that you go back inside the house and, if you have a closed yard, leave the dog for fifteen or twenty minutes or wander ten or fifteen feet away, to give him a chance to relax.

While in the early stages of housebreaking, also make sure you're not just rushing outside, letting your puppy go, then rushing back inside. For most dogs, just spending time outside is a reward in itself. If your dog associates holding in her bodily functions with the reward of a game or a walk outside, it will be more motivation for her to practice that self-control.

And then there's praise. "Praising your puppy when he does his business is very important," Brooke Walker says, and I agree. Praise doesn't have to be a big, loud celebration—it can simply be your quiet approval. Your dog picks up on the positive energy in your pleased and satisfied silence, which can be a much more powerful way of communicating with her than screaming "Good girl!"

Treats can also be a way of rewarding good bathroom behavior, though I recommend that you wean your puppy off them once regular patterns have been established. That's what I advised Crystal Reel to do when she took Mr. President home with her. "Cesar told me that Mr. President was very food driven so I should use that when reinforcing good housebreaking behavior. So while Mr. President was with me I made sure to have a few of Cesar's Discipline Organic Dog Treats with Organic Beef on hand at all times. In the beginning, whenever Mr. P. would go poo or pee outside, I would praise him with a treat and my positive vibes. After a while I reduced the treats so he was just feeling my happy energy whenever he went potty outside."

Crystal shares with us the schedule that worked for her with Mr. President, who never had an accident in her house during the week they were rooming together:

- 7:00 a.m.: Let Mr. President out of his kennel. We immediately went to the front door and outside to his designated pee spot. He would pee and I would then put on his leash and we'd walk to his favorite poo spots. He had three general areas that he liked to go poo in.
- If Mr. President didn't go at this time, he'd go at 8:15 a.m. and vice versa.
- 8:15 to 8:30 a.m.: After Mr. President's morning feeding I would take him out to go potty again before we got into the car for the morning commute.
- 9:00 a.m.: I'd take Mr. P. on a short walk before we entered the office. Typically he'd go pee again.
- 11:00 a.m.: Mr. P.'s first potty break of the workday (sometimes he'd go poo at this time; if not now, then at 1p.m.).
- 1:00 p.m.: Mr. P.'s second potty break (also my lunch break, so we'd get out of the office and grab a bite to eat with my coworkers and their office dogs).
- 3:30 to 4:00 p.m.: Mr. P.'s third potty break (generally he'd just want to pee about now).
- 6:00 p.m.–7:00 p.m.: I'd take Mr. P. out for a short walk before we got in the car to go home for the night. He'd generally go pee again.
- 7:30–8:30 p.m.: Mr. P. would go out again after his dinner. This is when we'd take our evening walk.
- 9:30 p.m.: He's in his kennel for the night.

I was very impressed with Mr. President and Crystal for their consistent work during my absence. Remember, this is a three-and-a-half-month-old puppy that adapted right away to a brand-new situation.

By your sharing only calm-assertive energy and a positive outlook, your puppy—like Mr. President—will be able to tune into his natural instincts and learn the lessons of housebreaking smoothly.

Keeping your puppy in the confined space or crate in which she's assigned to stay during the times when you are unable to supervise her is also a huge boon to pain-free housebreaking. "What I try to get through to people," says breeder and trainer Diana Foster, "is that it's all about prevention. If you don't give 'em a chance to pee on the carpet, they'll never even know what peeing on the carpet is. And if you keep that up the first few months, little by little you can start to give them more freedom. When our puppies leave our kennel, none of them ever had an accident in the house. We didn't do anything to them. We didn't scold them or correct them. We just never gave them a chance to make a mistake."

BABY GATES

Angel was only eight weeks old when I adopted him and had only just begun his housebreaking experience when I brought him home from Brooke's. During the miniature schnauzer's first days at my home, he was a little more hyper and therefore more difficult to house-break than the laid-back Mr. President. Although he was always responsive and attentive to the behavioral cues I sent him, the new environment and all the new friends to play with were perhaps a little too much stimulation all at once for the little guy. He was especially attracted to Jack, the four-year-old Jack Russell terrier in my pack. Having just left his own extended family of miniature schnauzers at Brooke's, Angel immediately recognized and was interested in a fellow terrier, but unfortunately, Jack is a bit too hyperactive to be an ideal role model for calm-submissive behavior. All these distractions made the normally medium-level-energy Angel a little more excitable in the early days and therefore a little less consistent with his bodily functions at first, even though he had the other dogs' bathroom behaviors to emulate.

In addition to feeding and exercising the puppies on a regular schedule, setting up a line of baby gates in the garage pointing a clear path to the backyard was a great help in teaching Angel to go outside to pee and poop. This tool has been invaluable for me in keeping so many dogs in my house, garage, and yard. When using baby gates, it's important to understand that puppies don't necessarily see them as boundaries (they can be pushed over, or jumped over) unless you teach them that they are boundaries.

COMMUNICATING LIMITS

With Angel, I set up the gates, then stood on the other side of them and waited for him to try to follow me. I used my body language—stepping forward strongly, putting out my hand, and most important, projecting a blocking energy—to communicate to the puppy that he should not cross the threshold of the gates. When he tried to nudge the gate in order to push it over, I moved toward him even more assertively, establishing an invisible frontier between him and the gates on both sides. With this motion and this energy, I am very clearly communicating to him that he is not allowed to get too close to the gate, even on his side.

I repeated this exercise several times, even though Angel is an amazingly quick study, and I continued to reinforce it again over the next several days. Within three days, Angel totally respected my concept of a borderline that he could not cross. Dogs naturally respect "invisible boundaries"—much more so than man-made ones. They set invisible limitations for one another all the time by using energy and body language. But you must take the time and patience to reinforce the rules until your puppy internalizes them.

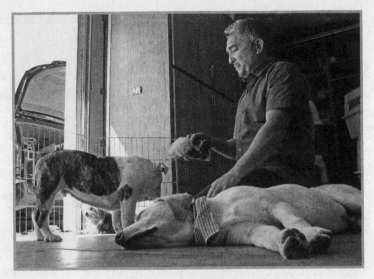

Cesar using baby gates to set boundaries

ROLE MODELS

One of the best ways to teach a puppy about proper bathroom etiquette is to let an older dog lead by example. When Junior first arrived at our home, he immediately learned the good habits of the smaller dogs living at our home back then—Coco the Chihuahua, Molly the dachshund, Sid the French bulldog, and Minnie the Chihuahua-terrier mix. That's also how he learned to use wee-wee pads right away—a big help to me for when I wanted to bring my handsome new pit bull on the road with me and the *Dog Whisperer* crew. When Blizzard came along, Junior was able to impart his good manners to the new little yellow Lab puppy in the family, who in turn was able to influence Angel and Mr. President, both of whom were perfectly housebroken within a couple of weeks. That's a beautiful thing—generation after generation of dogs, all teaching one another to be balanced.

WEE-WEE PADS

Many puppy owners, particularly puppy owners who live in cities, don't want to go through the chore of taking a puppy outdoors five or six times a day, so they choose to use wee-wee pads as a shortcut to housebreaking their dog. Though wee-wee pads are a wonderful invention and my dogs use them all the time when we travel, it's very important that puppies learn to eliminate outdoors as well as behind walls. Your home becomes a big "den" to your dog, and it's not natural for them to eliminate inside the confines of their own personal nesting space. Conditioning a dog to eliminate *only* inside the house goes against your puppy's inborn nature. That's why puppy mill puppies like Georgia Peaches continue to have accidents throughout their life span. Often when people start by conditioning puppies to depend on wee-wee pads alone, they are shocked when the dog won't eliminate outdoors. The truth is, you the owner have created the situation by stifling the puppy's own natural instinct not to eliminate where he lives.

The best way to incorporate wee-wee pads into your housebreaking routine is to set them out only at times when you won't be able to supervise. Set out four pads at first, in order to zero in on exactly the part of the pad where the puppy will relieve himself. As the puppy begins to use them correctly and to refine and mature his behavior, you can remove the pads until there is only one left, at exactly the spot where he will go every time.

In order to attract the puppy to the pad, find a piece of grass or dirt with the scent of urine or feces from another dog on it and place it on the pad. This may sound distasteful to you, but the presence of another dog's excrement will stimulate your puppy's brain to pee right over it. Eventually you won't need to do this, once the puppy is conditioned to the pads.

In the area of my house or hotel room where I keep the wee-wee pads, I always use an air filter to make sure the scent doesn't travel, and I make sure to give the dogs a place to sleep that is far away from the pads, since dogs, like humans, like their bedroom and their bathroom to be in distinct locations. As soon as I get up, I roll up the used pads and immediately mop up the floor beneath the pads so there is no more scent. This is a *must* for using pads, newspapers, or anything you put on the floor for the puppy to relieve himself on: *always* replace the used pad immediately and clean up the floor underneath, because a dog doesn't want to pee on a place where he himself has already peed. In addition to helping train your puppy to use that spot again, you will be keeping your own environment clean and sanitary.

DON'T TAKE IT PERSONALLY

Housebreaking is not rocket science, but if an accident does happen, it's important not to get upset or frustrated. A dog isn't wetting on the floor to hurt your feelings, to get even with you, or because he's angry at you, nor is he telling you that all your previous housebreaking efforts are failing and that you have to go all the way back to step one. Early on, accidents are a part of the process, and the only correct response from you is *patience*. Repeatedly making a big deal out of a housebreaking mishap is one of the worst things you can do, because you will be teaching your puppy that if he pees, he can produce a certain response in you. No matter how young or how old your dog is, he is always reading your emotional state and energy and constantly updating himself about exactly what makes you tick. When your puppy does something that triggers a negative emotion in you, it makes you weak in his eyes, so the puppy learns, "Hey, this is an easy way to control this human!" Later, if the puppy is bored or lonely or has nothing else to do, he can just pee, and you'll provide him with a little gratuitous entertainment. Just like kids, dogs will sometimes choose negative attention over no attention at all.

And never, ever correct or punish! Don't buy into the old-school notion that you should push a puppy's nose into his excrement or hit him if he happens to go in the house. This makes absolutely no sense to him. Instead, remain calm and assertive, and immediately bring the puppy outside to where he is supposed to relieve himself (or to the puppy pad, if that is the only option at the time). If you catch a puppy in the act, use a light touch or a sound simply to distract or snap him out of it, then remove him to his spot outside and wait until he relaxes and finishes his business. You are using the opportunity of your puppy's making a mistake as a chance to reinforce the behavior that you *do* want from him. That way you are telling the puppy, "It doesn't matter what you do. In every situation, I will always have the right answer and I will always share a calm energy." That kind of neutral but reliable response is the nature of true leadership.

Done correctly, housebreaking should not be a turbulent production but just a matter of putting a little extra work into getting your puppy on a schedule during the first few weeks after he arrives at your home. Don't let unnecessary stress over this very natural, uncomplicated process taint any of the joy surrounding your new dog's puppyhood.

DOS AND DON'TS OF HOUSEBREAKING

1. DO bring the puppy outside first thing in the morning, immediately after eating each meal, after he awakens from a nap, and after long play sessions.
2. DO bring the puppy to the same general area outdoors each time.

(continues)

3. DO supervise your puppy closely! You are investing a lot of time in these first months to establish a lifetime of good behaviors. Keep your puppy with you as much as possible. If you can't be with him, put him in a safe, enclosed area or in his crate. If you think you might forget about your puppy's "call of nature," set a timer to remind yourself.

4. DO remain consistent! Daily consistency is the key to good habits. Feed and walk your puppy at around the same time every day. Remember, dogs don't understand the concept of weekends or holidays. If you want to sleep late on a Sunday, take your puppy out first, then go back to bed.

5. DON'T punish a puppy for an accident or do anything to create a negative association with his bodily functions! Stay calm and assertive and quietly remove the puppy to the place where you want him to go.

6. DON'T potty-train a puppy on wee-wee pads alone. It's not natural for a dog to relieve himself inside his "den." Make sure you alternate between outdoor and indoor bathroom habits.

SETTING RULES, BOUNDARIES, AND LIMITATIONS

Many owners will be all too tempted to shower their puppy or new dog with toys, petting, and nonstop attention; to give her table scraps or treats whenever she begs; and to give her the run of the house right away. To our human minds, this is what we do to show a dog that we "love" her. The problem is, your new puppy is coming directly from her first family—her mother and littermates—where "love" equaled order and organization. If she was also raised by a conscientious breeder, she has probably already begun to learn and internalize her very first set of human regulations. "The dog already knows it needs to live with rules and boundaries, as this is all it has known since birth," Diana Foster explains. "This dog is very content, secure, and conditioned to living with certain rules and restrictions."

Now this same dog that equated leadership with her mother's and breeder's calm-assertive energy suddenly finds herself surrounded by unstable, excited energy and humans who either don't set any limits or are mostly inconsistent with the ones they do set. The dog, formerly just one member of a cohesive, well-behaved pack, suddenly sees that all the focus, all the attention, is on her—except when she's expected to be alone. In the brochure that she gives out when a new owner purchases one of her Thinschmidt German shepherds, Diana Foster describes the likely outcome of this situation:

> The dog enters a new home, and this family hugs him, pets him, and talks to him without him having to do anything to earn it. He is given lots of attention, and is barely alone for even a few minutes. . . . Later it is time for bed and the family finally puts the puppy in his crate for the night. So now he has gone from almost non-stop attention to absolute isolation. This is too much of an extreme for any dog, and causes total stress and anxiety. Now you have a puppy who is barking and whining in his crate. Why? He has already made the association that being in your house means freedom to walk around freely and having people with him. Where are all the people? Where is all the attention? The pup wants more of what he had earlier. You have just set yourself up, and you need to ask if it was worth it?[2]

By introducing your puppy to your home on your terms, by crate-training early, and by restricting her territory to a safe, limited area for her first weeks or months at home, you are creating the rules, boundaries, and limitations that will provide the framework for her secure, happy future.

EXPRESSING DISAGREEMENT

Puppies are hungry for direction and are receptive to any limits you might want to set. But how do you express those limits kindly, fairly, and in a language the puppy will understand? A mother dog does not bribe with treats or petting to get good behavior (although she does sometimes reward submissive behavior after the fact with licking and grooming). She does not whine or cajole with her voice. She corrects the behavior of her offspring using calm-assertive energy: body language, eye contact, and touch. The pups always understand exactly what she wants, and she rarely has to correct the same blunder more than once. On the other hand, most humans correct a puppy using frustrated, anxious, or angry energy; jerky movements (such as pulling a hand or an object away, or moving their bodies away); and loud sounds—"No!" "Stop it!" "Bad dog!" You'll hear such humans repeating their admonishments over and over and over again; then they throw up their hands in amazement that their puppy doesn't obey them.

I believe we can help our dogs understand us better by trying to speak with them in their own language. That means I will address an unwanted behavior in a more canine style, using one or a combination of techniques I refer to as "corrections":

1. By using my energy and intention to communicate that I don't agree with a behavior, while never taking the dog's actions personally and always remaining calm and unruffled (what I call *calm-assertive energy*)

2. By using eye contact to communicate my energy and intention

3. By using my body and body language to own my space and to block an unwanted behavior (for instance, stepping forward purposefully into a puppy's space to "own" it, or firmly nudging away a puppy that is trying to climb on my leg)

4. By using touch to communicate displeasure or snap a dog out of an escalating behavior:

- "Touch" never, ever means "hit"! Puppies and most dogs are very responsive to touch at the level of the kind of light tap you might use to get a friend's attention in a darkened movie theater.
- Touch a puppy on the side of its neck or on the side of its hindquarters.
- Use a claw-shaped hand, which mimics a mother's bite on the side of the neck, on the muscle, not the throat. This hand doesn't "pinch"; it is firm, but it doesn't have to use much pressure. The pressure should be proportionate to the level of the behavior (for instance, an adult dog that has escalated into a red zone will need more pressure than a puppy that has just begun chewing a shoe, which will need only a light touch). All dogs recognize this sensation from their early puppyhood and respond in a primal way.
- The timing of a touch correction is crucial; it has to take place at the exact moment of the transgression and end the moment the puppy relaxes and changes her behavior. Waiting until after the behavior is over doesn't make sense to a dog, because dogs live in the moment. Cause and effect have to match in their minds.
- One firm touch is effective; half a dozen small pushes, pinches, or tweaks can make the situation worse.

A mother dog or other adult dog will also sometimes emit a low growl from time to time, using sound to convey disagreement with a pup's behavior. All it takes is the hint of a growl from Daddy to send Junior, Blizzard, Angel, and Mr. President into "Daddy-pleasing" mode—he commands that much respect from all his adopted "grand-kids." As an adolescent, Junior has learned to mimic this growl and that's how he keeps the younger puppies respectful of his role as a "big brother." Taking a page from this section of the canine dictionary, I advise clients to create a simple sound that their dog will associate with the thought "I don't agree with that behavior." Choose another sound that means "Yes," "Come," or "I like that behavior."

- I use the "tssst" sound to represent displeasure.
- I use a "kissing" sound to represent a positive action or a call to follow or pay attention to me.
- The specific sound you choose doesn't matter at all! (There is no magic to the sound "tssst.") It's the calm-assertive energy and the intention behind the sound that carry the communication. Just make sure you use the same, simple sound every time.

Hand correction on Mr. President

• Timing of the sound is essential. It's best to use it early in the escalation of an unwanted behavior. With a positive sound, don't repeat the sound unless your dog is already giving you the positive behavior that you desire. This way, the sound reinforces the action.

• Don't use a dog's name to correct her. Like the positive sound, use her name only when she is giving you a positive response.

There is one more way dogs correct one another, and that is by ignoring. If an unwanted behavior remains at a fairly low level of escalation—especially if the behavior is designed to gain attention—ignoring can be just as effective as a touch or sound correction. A puppy's littermate may turn and ignore her if she starts to play too roughly. If the first puppy still wants to play, she's got to figure out a more appropriate way of getting the other puppy to give her what she wants. In much the same way, blocking and then turning away and ignoring a puppy that jumps up on you when you come through the door can be effective, if the intensity of the jumping isn't too high yet.

The action you take to correct a behavior should always be proportionate in intensity to the level of the behavior that prompted it. The great thing about puppies is that if you supervise them closely in the beginning, you need never let any unwanted behavior escalate to the point where much correction is needed.

REDIRECTING AND REWARDING

It's simple enough to block or correct a dog or a puppy when she is making a basic mistake, but that only stops the behavior; it doesn't change it. In most situations, we also have to offer an alternative behavior. For instance, if a dog is play-biting, a claw hand to the neck can correct the behavior, but a chew toy redirects it. If a dog is trying to jump onto something, we can physically step in between and block the behavior, but if we insist that the dog sit after she has submitted, we have redirected the energy and provided an alternative solution. Once a puppy has agreed to do it our way, then we can reward and reinforce with petting or a treat or a toy, the way a mother dog sometimes rewards with licking and grooming. Reinforcing with something pleasant is a good strategy, but the reward or affection won't be effective unless it's offered *after* the behavior has changed and the dog is in the ideal calm-submissive state of mind. Affection should always come after exercise and discipline. I'll talk more in Chapter 7 about how to use rewards to communicate with a dog and help condition her behavior.[3]

ENFORCING THE RULES

These are the basic skills everyone in the family needs to master in order to manage a puppy's behavior:

1. Have a picture in your mind of the behavior you desire.
2. Clearly and consistently communicate that desired behavior. In this communication, energy, intention, and body language are more important (and more easily comprehended by your puppy) than verbal commands.
3. Ignore very mild misbehaviors using the no-touch, no-talk, no-eye-contact rule (they usually correct themselves when they aren't reinforced).
4. Immediately and consistently give corrections to more obvious misbehaviors.
5. Always apply corrections with calm-assertive energy—never take your puppy's misbehavior personally!
6. Always give your puppy an alternative acceptable behavior every time you correct an unwanted one.
7. Reward good behaviors—with affection, treats, praise—or

simply your silent joy and approval, which your puppy immediately senses and understands.

Whatever rules, boundaries, and limitations you decide on setting for your dog, they have to be enforced from the moment the puppy enters your home for the first time, and they have to be reinforced consistently by all pack leaders in the family. Your dog needs to know where she stands from the very start, how the routine is going to flow, and what is and isn't acceptable with her new pack. By being clear about those rules from day one, you set her up to succeed as a member of her new pack, which is what you want for her—and what she really wants for herself.

PREVENTING SEPARATION ANXIETY

The skills you've mastered in communicating limits to your puppy or new dog will never come in more handy than when you are tackling this very important issue that occurs in every dog's life—separation anxiety. The leash, the rollover, the sit, getting your slippers—whatever behaviors you wish your dog to learn in the future—are all a piece of cake for her compared to being left on her own. This is a very common problem and is to be expected. Dogs are not programmed to live by themselves. In nature, the constant presence of the pack is what shapes their identities. The only time they have to learn to be alone is when they live among humans. We shouldn't be surprised that they are distressed by it. But even though we are asking them to do something unnatural, we can't feel bad about it or stress out about it, because this is the reality of how we live today.

Our modern lives make it next to impossible that our dogs are with us 24/7. But there's a reason dogs as a species have survived millions of years of evolution in just about every environment imaginable, in every corner of the globe. They are among the most adaptable mammals nature ever created. A dog, and especially a puppy, can adjust to this new style of life with very little difficulty, if we help her to do it in stages, and if we stay calm and unemotional about it. That's what we want to communicate to her—to relax.

The puppies I raised for this book lived at my house and were with my pack almost constantly. But they will all eventually find loving adoptive families, and at some point in all their lives they may have to spend time alone. Even Junior, who will always be my dog, will travel with me and, like Daddy before him, may end up spending hours alone in a hotel room while I go to a business meeting or a restaurant. I owe it to all these puppies to begin taking certain steps from day one, in order for them to always feel comfortable being alone and behind walls when I am gone.

Of all the puppies in this book, Angel had the hardest time with separation anxiety. I first noticed that if he was outside in the backyard and the rest of the dogs had wandered back into the house without his noticing, he would look into the window, whine, and bark. Sometimes he'd jump up and scratch at the sliding glass door or the screen. When Melissa took Angel for his little adventure away from home, the only time he whined at all was when she took his crate down to her car, right before he was to come home to me. She left him in the apartment with her husband, John, for a few minutes, and right after she left with the crate, he started to cry and run from window to window, trying to find her. John made the typical human mistake—he went to Angel and starting cooing, "It's okay, it's okay." When a human does this, he is essentially saying to the dog, "Your separation anxiety is okay. I agree with how you are reacting." You are reinforcing the behavior you want to change, and you are not offering leadership, which is the very thing that anxious dog is seeking at that moment.

Angel's behavior illustrates something important for us to understand about separation anxiety—it's in a dog's nature to try to come to get us when we leave. Dogs are programmed to want to be with the pack, to follow the pack, and to try to reunite the pack when separated. If they can't follow the pack, they'll try to call them back with their voice. Much of the time, they succeed in bringing people back this way. What's more, they bring them back upset or feeling sorry for the dog and guilty about leaving. Often the people they bring back also bring them treats. So the message they get is, "They're not here to stop my anxiety, they're here to reward my anxiety." We can't take our dogs' separation anxiety personally or feel that we are doing something awful to them, to "make" them feel this way.

If they don't succeed in bringing us back, it's a logical next step for them to try to dig themselves out from behind walls if they can't find us any other way. In *Marley and Me*, John Grogan wrote that Marley's separation anxiety and fear during thunderstorms became so extreme that he actually made holes in the drywall, digging until his paws bled, trying to get out and find his pack again. The problem was, the Grogans let Marley's anxiety escalate to the point of no return. You don't want to wait until your neighbors are calling the apartment manager or homeowners' association, saying, "That dog's got to go." Instead, prepare your dog for such situations by setting up the separation in stages, so it never turns into full-blown anxiety.

To condition Angel out of his separation anxiety, I would practice putting the other dogs in the garage or in the house, leaving him outside alone. Then I'd hide just out of his sight. It would take him a few minutes, but eventually he would start crying. If I waited too much longer, the crying would become screaming, and I didn't want it to go that far. Instead, I would come back from my hiding place and immediately address his behavior. I stood as far away from him as possible, since eventually I want to be able to be miles away from him, and had a conversation using my "tssst" sound, my body language, and my energy to communicate to him "I don't agree with your behavior. I want you to relax." One finger up means "Sit," and when Angel complied, I would check his energy. At first, even though he was sitting, I saw that he was still in an alert state, yawning. Many people make the mistake of thinking yawning means a dog is relaxed, but puppies often yawn when they are anxious or frustrated by a situation they can't figure out. I could tell by Angel's anxious eye contact and his stiff body that he hadn't relaxed yet, so I stayed where I was until he went into the relaxed state I was seeking. About thirty seconds later, he moved away. I would then go and hide again.

The second time I left Angel alone, after a minute or two he started pacing. Then he started darting to the side of the house. This is typical—he was trying to find a way out. That's the part of his survival programming that says, "I need to find a way to be part of my family again." This is why we have to be very patient, and this is why we have to prepare for separation in stages. In this case, I came back out, addressed Angel again, waited, then hid. Each time, I tried to stand a little farther away when I addressed him. Each time I did the exercise, Angel would stay calm a little longer before he became anxious.

I knew I was making progress with Angel after the third time I corrected him. After waiting several minutes and not hearing any whining, I sneaked back into the room and crept toward the window. There was my little schnauzer, stretched out on the patio, resting in the sun with his eyes closed. This was exactly what I wanted. There was no need to get all excited and no need to reward him, because his behavior—being over his anxiety—was a reward in itself. What I do instead when I see such progress in my dogs is to silently thank God for helping me to teach them that I mean no harm when I leave, that it's not a bad thing, it's just how we live. For me, prayer increases my own relaxation, so my energy creates a more relaxing environment for my dogs and for my family.

5

YOUR HEALTHY PUPPY
Health Care Basics

Cesar stays relaxed while cleaning Mr. President's jowls

This is a book about puppy behavior, not puppy biology, but when you bring any new dog home with you, you are automatically taking responsibility for every aspect of his health and welfare for the rest of his life. That is why preparation and prevention are so important. All it takes is one disease, accident, or injury to bring home the harsh reality of how very expensive caring for a sick animal can be. I've faced it myself many times over a lifetime of living with dogs—emergency veterinary bills can easily run into the tens of thousands of dollars. Of course, once we fall in love with an animal, no amount of money is too much for us to spend to save his life or take away his pain. But we can lower the odds of having to go into debt or empty out our savings for the dog we love if we take certain precautions early on.

SELECTING FOR HEALTH

Prevention starts with the choice of how and from whom you get your puppy. Top-notch breeders like the ones who have contributed to this book keep up with the latest research about genetically transmitted defects or illnesses, and they are meticulous about selecting dogs whose parents and grandparents also have clean bills of health. German shepherds, for instance, have a history of genetically transmitted hip problems. To prevent passing this tendency on to the puppies in their lines, Diana and Doug Foster study a comprehensive pedigree database before selecting sires and dams to mate for their Thinschmidt kennels. Diana says,

> It's time-consuming, but it's really important. It shows you the line breeding, what's coming up, how many generations, the father, the grandfather, all the way back. We have to be careful not to breed too close. Then we have to study, what did both the lines—the mother and the fathers—produce in the past? If there are any issues like the hips, for example, that's a red flag. Don't put that combination together. We breed on the much stricter German standard, where there is a numerical rating system for hip dysplasia, so that's something else we take into account. It's actually a science—we don't just put two dogs together because they both have pretty colors. And a lot of people don't know that. So when they come to us, and they ask, "Why are your puppies so expensive? I just looked at one that's half the price, and it looks just as good," we try to explain to them what goes into cre-

ating a dog that's not only got a great temperament but will have a long, healthy life. They don't always listen, and will go for the cheaper one. Sometimes it's a disaster.

If you do buy your puppy from a reputable breeder, that breeder will want to stay in touch with you throughout the puppy's lifetime and be updated on any health problems that develop. Brooke Walker will even pay for a necropsy on any dogs from her lines if they pass away prematurely, to make sure there weren't any hidden health problems that may affect future generations of her prize miniature schnauzers.

If you are adopting your puppy from a shelter or rescue organization, try to get as much information as possible about the puppy's parents or, at the very least, the area from which he was rescued and the general health of the animals there. Make sure the puppy has had a thorough veterinary checkup, and get all the records that exist on any procedures or vaccines he has undergone since he came to the rescue. You can't ask the puppy, "Did your mom have a tendency toward chronic eye infections?" but the more information you can gather about his past, the better armed you will be if you come up against genetically or environmentally transmitted problems in the future. If you are adopting an older dog from a shelter or rescue, a previous owner or rescuer may have put together important medical information about the dog. Make sure you don't bring your dog home without asking.

PLANNING FOR VETERINARY COSTS

Keeping complete and thorough records is the first step toward safeguarding your new pet's health; the next is taking stock of your personal financial situation and planning for the long-term costs associated with owning and caring for a dog. According to the American Veterinary Medical Association, the average American spends about $350 in medical expenses per dog each year. The American Pet Products Association gives a lower amount, $211, for routine care, but adds $574 a year for surgical costs.[1] Either way, it's a considerable sum.

Most of us don't want our kids to go without health insurance, because we understand the ramifications an unexpected sickness or accident can have on our family bank accounts. The same situation can occur with a pet. We are all struggling in today's difficult economy, but I strongly suggest that new dog or puppy owners create a separate savings fund for their pet that is not to be touched except in the case of animal-related medical expenses or emergencies. Of course, your dog doesn't know or care if you have a bank account in his name, but to my mind, every responsible action we take to protect a dog's quality of life only raises the level of our calm-assertive energy. When we are relaxed and confident about our ability to care for our dogs, no matter what happens, it only contributes to strengthening our roles as their unshakable pack leaders.

A second option is pet health insurance. I am often asked, "Is pet health insurance a scam?" The answer is no, if you do your research, buy from a reputable company, and have realistic expectations. In fact, many progressive employers, including Google Inc., Hilton Hotels Corporation, Ford Motor Company, and McDonald's Corporation, have become so impressed with the practicality of pet health insurance, they have begun to offer group policies for their workers who are pet owners.[2] Pet health insurance is not intended for basic, routine exams or vaccinations—plan to work those into your regular household budget. The American Animal Hospital Association did a study that showed the majority of pet owners felt comfortably prepared for emergency expenses from $500 to $1,000 but had serious concerns about being able to handle anything higher than that.[3] As a result, the AAHA has spent several years working directly with the pet insurance industry to develop smaller-premium, larger-deductible policies. Now that the AAHA and other organizations such as the ASPCA and Humane Society have begun to officially rate and review those corporations offering pet health insurance policies, owners no longer need worry about falling for a potential scam. For a good website comparing what different companies have to offer, check out http://www.petinsurancereview.com.

VACCINATIONS

The first journey you will take with your puppy in terms of safeguarding his long-term health will be the experience of getting him through the vaccination process, to make sure he has adequate protection against a host of common canine maladies. Puppies enter this world without any antibodies at all, meaning they have absolutely no pre-existing immunity to the many viruses and diseases that lurk in our modern world. Nature, however, has provided a natural buffer for their first few months of life. The rich, thick milk called colostrum that a mother dog secretes right after giving birth contains all her own antibodies and provides a temporary shield to protect her offspring. The amount of natural immunity a puppy retains is usually based on a pup's birth order and his inborn energy level, since the most assertive nursers get the lion's share of this limited-offer premium beverage. But the colostrum offers only a temporary protection—every nine days, the pups' antibody levels drop by half until, at around four months of age, the level is too low to protect them anymore, making them easy targets for parasites and viruses. This is why veterinarians prescribe a series of vaccinations, usually starting at around six to eight weeks of age and continuing until sixteen weeks (four months).

Vaccines are spaced out over three- to four-week intervals for the antibodies to take effect, as well as to protect the puppy's delicate system from possible side effects. They are also staggered so that the vaccine won't cancel out the natural antibodies from the colostrum, or vice versa. Never allow a repeat or new vaccine if your puppy was vaccinated less than fourteen days earlier.[4] If you have bought your puppy from a breeder, it's likely that he will already have had at least one set of shots by the time he comes home with you—probably at least one deworming in addition to a DHPP (distemper, infectious hepatitis, parainfluenza, parvovirus) vaccination. Most veterinarians recommend the following protocol.

Recommendations for Puppy Vaccinations

3 weeks	Worming
6 weeks	Worming for the common parasites passed through the mother's placenta and milk, fecal exam for coccidia, and combination DHPP (distemper, infectious hepatitis, parainfluenza, and parvovirus)
9 weeks	Worming, DHPP
12 weeks	Possible worming, DHPP, possible rabies. Leptospirosis and Lyme if in endemic area. (The last two will need to be boosted in three weeks if given.) Possible bord (bordetella) if puppy is going to be boarded or groomed frequently
16 weeks	Possible DHPP, final fecal exam, and rabies if not done previously[5]

Dr. Paula Terifaj, owner of Founders Veterinary Clinic in Brea, California, is a veterinarian educated at University of California—Davis, who describes her approach to puppy care as "integrative-holistic" (combining modern Western medicine with nontraditional therapies), with an emphasis on preventive medicine. Having written a book entitled *How to Protect Your Dog from a Vaccine Junkie,* Dr. Terifaj takes a different approach to the puppyhood shot routine. "I'm very conservative when it comes to vaccines," she states. "I think the earliest a puppy should start a vaccine series is between eight and nine weeks. If we're starting at eight to nine weeks, they should get revaccinated three to four weeks after that. The last vaccine should be given between twelve and fourteen weeks old. We're talking about DHP here—rabies is different. Rabies is at four months and then one year. So ideally puppies should receive no more than three series of vaccines. But I tell people to do their own research. So check with your vet or with a few vets."

When it comes to the vaccination versus overvaccination controversy, I tend to come down on the side of Mother Nature; that is, I want to do all I can to make sure my puppies have full immunity against dangerous diseases, but at the same time, I believe a tendency to overvaccinate has greatly hurt rather than helped many generations of dogs. In my last book, *A Member of the Family,* I chronicle my story of meeting the many learned experts, including premier holistic veterinary pioneer Dr. Marty Goldstein, and reading the convincing studies and research, all of which led me to form this conclusion.

In 2006, the American Animal Hospital Association (AAHA) came down on this side as well. AAHA released a new strategy for vaccinating your dogs, based on years of research supporting the conclusion that overvaccinating dogs contributes to chronic illness, disease, and even death. The new guidelines divided vaccinations into three categories:

- Core: Vaccines that should be given to every dog
- Non-Core: Optional vaccines that should be considered only if an individual dog's lifestyle or risk factors strongly warrant it
- Not Recommended: Vaccines not recommended by the AAHA under any circumstances

Core Vaccines	Distemper* Hepatitis (adenovirus-2)* Parvovirus* Rabies
Non-Core Vaccines	Leptospirosis† Lyme† Bordetella (kennel cough) Parainfluenza
Not Recommended	Adenovirus-1 Coronavirus Giardia *Crotalus atrox* toxoid (rattlesnake) Porphyromonas (periodontal disease)

*DHP—3 in 1 vaccine
†May be considered on a regional basis where these diseases are known to be a true risk

Since a thorough series of vaccines given in puppyhood has now been determined to provide most of a dog's immunity for life, the AAHA recommends revaccination no more than once every three years. Many of my holistic veterinarian friends think that even three years is far too often to risk exposing your dog to the health risks of overvaccination, since multiple studies have shown that dogs properly immunized in puppyhood maintain lifetime immunity to hepatitis, distemper, and parvovirus.[6] A great option for conscientious dog owners is to ask their veterinarian to provide antibody titer testing for distemper, parvo, or rabies, which shows approximately how much disease-fighting immunity is present in your dog's system at the time the test is given. If your dog has plenty of antibodies, then the titer level will be high—proof that the vaccines have done their job and your dog is protected. With a high titer level, you can assume your dog doesn't need a vaccine booster, though even a low blood titer doesn't necessarily mean another vaccine is indicated. For more information about titer testing, contact www.hemopet.org.

There is a short period of about a week during which the puppy no longer has much immunity from its mother left but the new vaccines have not fully kicked in and started working. This window can allow even the best-cared-for puppies to get sick, but the potential danger can be exaggerated, to the point where dog owners will grow paranoid and keep their puppies inside and isolated for months, ultimately creating frustrated and antisocial dogs. "I tell my clients that ten days after the first vaccine, they should begin to get as much socialization for their puppy as they possibly can," advises Dr. Charlie Rinehimer of Northampton Community College. "I counsel them to stay away from places like dog parks—where you have no idea of the vaccination or health status of the dogs—during that time, but going to visit friends with dogs, taking walks on a leash, or going for car rides are all great. After sixteen weeks, anything goes as far as I am concerned."

PARVO

I recently had a frightening experience with the parvovirus that really shook me up. Around the time I began thinking of raising puppies to write about in this book, a friend came to me having rescued two abandoned two-month-old Yorkie puppies from the streets. My wife and I were about to leave for a seminar on the East Coast the following day, but as usual, I could not say no to any abandoned dogs, let alone two tiny puppies. I left instructions for our housekeeper to care for the puppies while we were gone and made an appointment with Dr. Rick Garcia to come by to check them out when I came back in a few days.

We hadn't even been gone a full day when our housekeeper called us in a panic. "The puppies are very, very sick," she told me. "They have really bad diarrhea and they're shaking." I called and asked a friend, *Dog Whisperer* field producer Todd Henderson, to go to our house to get the puppies and rush them to the vet. Todd later described to me the horrible experience of driving beyond the speed limit to get to the animal hospital, while the puppies struggled to stay alive in his car. They both made it to medical care, but one of them passed away shortly after arrival. The diagnosis was the parvovirus, which meant that all the dogs staying at my home had been exposed. Fortunately, they all had full immunization, but we had to disinfect our entire home and garage with the only solution known to kill the hardy virus—one part chlorine bleach to ten parts water. Before we could sleep easily again, I also had Dr. Rick give the rest of the pack a clean bill of health.

This horrendous event demonstrated to me the quick and deadly power of the parvovirus, to which puppies are susceptible during their most sensitive period of development. Parvo is an extremely contagious organism that targets the sensitive intestinal lining of puppies. It can be fatal. Even if caught early, the treatment involves quarantine and is extremely expensive. "I remember when parvo first struck when I was in vet school," recalls Dr. Paula Terifaj. "Puppies would die when we thought they'd live and live when we were sure they'd die. It's a tough thing." Parvo is spread through the feces of infected dogs, and some adult dogs can carry the virus without showing symptoms.

Dr. Paula explains, describing exactly what happened in our home with the Yorkies:

With the parvovirus, puppies are most likely to be exposed *before* they are adopted into their new homes. Kennels, questionable breeders, animal shelters, and pet stores are all breeding grounds for viruses. The exposed puppy will not show signs of illness for five to seven days, which is the incubation period. Often, a healthy-looking puppy is brought into the home and then becomes ill days later. Then people think that they were the ones who exposed the pup, but most times that's not what happened. Most of the sick puppies I see came from a pet shop or the Internet and they are almost always from puppy mills. They are shipped or come from a contaminated facility and stressful conditions. Infectious diseases run rampant in puppy mills but not among puppies coming from respectable breeders, or good shelters and rescues.

Despite my recent experience with the virus, I still believe that many owners become so fearful of their puppies' contracting it that they overprotect them, isolating them indoors for weeks or even months, and depriving them of much-needed exercise and socialization with their own kind. In coming chapters, I'll offer more suggestions on how to safely socialize and exercise your puppy under sixteen weeks of age.

In the case of the Yorkie puppies, I'm happy to say that the little guy that survived received medication and went through a period of quarantine. He is now a much-loved, healthy adolescent, living in the comfortable home of a supporter of the Cesar and Ilusion Millan Foundation.

GENERAL PUPPY HEALTH FAQS

"We generally say, 'Don't treat your puppy like a baby,' but in terms of health, puppies are a little like babies—they do need a certain level of protection. They are vulnerable to the heat and cold and can dehydrate quickly. They definitely need more care and attention than adult dogs," according to Dr. Paula Terifaj. However, because of the excellence of modern veterinary medicine, most of the vets I work with rarely see many sick puppies in their practices these days. "We do see a few health issues, such as diarrhea from worms and upper respiratory infections such as kennel cough," says Dr. Charlie. "There have been a few recent parvo outbreaks in unvaccinated puppies, especially pit bulls, a breed that seems to be more susceptible and often dies. We hardly ever see lepto, hepatitis, or, thank goodness, rabies in puppies." Dr. Charlie's rural Pennsylvania practice has seen a recent rise in Lyme disease cases (also epidemic among humans in that region) but a definite drop in preventable illnesses. "Actually we don't see too many major mistakes made by owners anymore, either. People seem to be more educated on the need for a series of vaccines and heartworm prevention. Most of the mistakes we see are on the behavioral side," he says.

Good nutrition, a thorough vaccination program, regular vet checkups, and a good owner-based health check and maintenance program at home serve as prevention for many of the problems that plagued both grown dogs and puppies in the recent past. Drs. Terifaj and Rinehimer contributed their answers to a few of the most frequently asked questions about puppy health:

Q. *Are there any symptoms in my puppy's behavior that are red flags for health emergencies?*

A. What people have to know is that when a puppy is vomiting or not eating—then you got a sick puppy! Puppies have two settings: play and sleep. If your dog is running around, playing, and just has a little bit of diarrhea, it'll probably be fine. But if your puppy isn't playful, and is vomiting and not eating, then you should see a vet right away.

Q. *My puppy isn't doing so well with housebreaking. How can I tell if it's got a urinary tract infection?*

A. Just because your puppy hasn't picked up on housebreaking doesn't mean he's got a urinary tract infection. Puppies with UTIs will strain to urinate and go frequently. If the bladder is infected, the lining will become inflamed. When salty urine comes down from the kidney, it burns and the dog immediately tries to get rid of it. If there is blood in the urine or if it's unusually smelly, you should check with your vet.

Q. How does a dog contract heartworms and what can be done about them?

A. Heartworms are spread from dog to dog by mosquitoes. The larvae actually have to go through a molt in the mosquito to become infectious. Preventive care is a monthly pill like Heartgard that kills any larvae that are introduced. Heartworm disease can be detected only by a blood test. It can be treated, but the treatment, although better than the arsenic compounds used in the past, is still somewhat risky and expensive. So prevention is definitely the way to go.

Q. How do you protect puppies from flea infestations?

A. Good diet and regular grooming should prevent most flea infestations. Puppies should be brushed with a fine-toothed flea comb. Sometimes you will catch the flea, but often you will find black particles that look like pepper. Fleas suck blood and what comes out the rear end is a black grain. To determine if a speck is flea dirt or just regular dirt, rub a piece in a paper towel with a little bit of rubbing alcohol. If it is flea dirt it will leave a red, blood-colored stain on the paper towel. A spot-type flea protectant like Frontline or Revolution should take care of the problem.

TEETHING

Between four and six months, most puppies will pass through a teething phase. This process is uncomfortable, and the increased chewing binges you'll see in the puppy's behavior at this stage are his attempts to relieve this discomfort—usually on your most expensive pair of shoes, since they are often made of natural materials like leather or suede, and since they carry the comfort of your scent. Don't take any of it personally—pet stores offer thousands of teething toys to help you redirect this behavior. During this stage, all the puppy is focused on is "How can I relieve this irritation that I have in my mouth?" A big no-no at this time is to wear gloves and let the dog chew on them, or to play games where you allow the dog to bite you anywhere on your body. It may seem harmless now, but you will be conditioning your dog to see your hands or your body as a source for relieving his frustration. Teething discomfort can also be minimized through exercise. I've used swimming in the past, and not necessarily in a large pool. A bathtub or wading pool for a puppy or a medium-size dog will get his legs moving in the water, give him something healthy to focus on, and distract him from what's going on inside his mouth. After the exercise, give the dog an object of your choice to chew on, and be relieved that the teething stage for puppies passes quickly—a month or two at the most.

When your puppy approaches adolescence—from six to ten months of age—he will go through a second chewing phase. His permanent teeth are coming in now, and the urge to chew is powerful. Remember to make the appropriate toys available to your "teenager" at this stage, and provide as much healthy exercise as possible. Often, dogs that don't teethe at this stage may have dental problems later in life, so make sure you are seeing your vet regularly and reporting on your pup's teething behavior.

SUPPERTIME

One of the most important lessons I have learned from the many fine veterinarians I've consulted with over the past few years is that a dog is what he eats. As a naive guy newly arrived from Mexico, I used to blindly accept as true all the extravagant claims and promises made by commercial pet foods in their ads and fancy packaging. Back then, I shopped for whatever seemed the best bargain on the shelves. Today, I feed some of my dogs an organic raw-food diet and I'm intimately involved in creating the recipe for my own Dog Whisperer brand organic dog food. What you feed your dog can affect a dog's energy level, his digestion, his immunity, even his susceptibility to allergies, ticks, and fleas. In *A Member of the Family,* I discuss nutrition in more depth, and in *Be the Pack Leader,* I give a thorough description of my own personal mealtime rituals with the pack. In general, however, I recommend that new puppy owners avoid the supermarket and consult with their veterinarians about the many other choices that are available to them in order to safeguard their puppy's long-term health. Instead of the big-box commercial puppy foods, look into the select number of excellent natural, organic, prepackaged pet foods created by smaller companies that you won't see on the shelves of your local supermarket or discount store. Seek out the specialty dog foods at pet supply stores or at natural food stores, and learn how to read the ingredients on pet food labels before you buy.

The first three ingredients listed on the label are critical, as they account for most of what your dog will be ingesting. Look for animal proteins listed as meat. Limit or avoid those with processed cheap grain products. Immediately reject any products with artificial preservatives, food dyes, and any meat or grain by-products.

And resist the urge to overfeed a puppy with a bottomless appetite or indulge in too many between-meal treats, as these are habits that may be hard to break once your pup stops growing like a weed and burning those extra calories. Obesity is becoming as serious a problem among America's dogs as it is among our human population.

Feeding Chart

Age	Stage	Feeding Schedule
0 to 8 months	Puppy	3 times a day
8 months to 3 years	Adolescence	2 times a day
3 to approx. 8 years	Adult	Once a day
Approx. 8 years and up	Senior	2 times a day

MAKING VET VISITS FUN

If you are raising your new dog from puppyhood, you have the perfect opportunity to ensure that you never have a hard time at the vet's office or with groomers. Veterinarians are trained medical professionals, but many of them aren't dog behaviorists. Even if their foundation in dog psychology is sound, they don't always have the time or energy to make sure your dog is feeling his best while they are focusing on his treatment. It falls to you to prepare your puppy for vet visits and to make the ritual of going to the vet or the groomer an exciting journey filled with fun, positive sensations.

The approach I used for all the puppies raised for this book—as well as for all the grown dogs under my care—began with getting them used to traveling in cars, from the first day I bring them home. If a puppy is stressed out by a car, he will be ten times more upset by the time you arrive at the vet's office, so you as the owner must make getting in and out of the car as automatic a response for him as is going in and out of the front door for your daily walks. Going for a ride in a car shouldn't be a traumatic chore for a dog—it should be a cue that he is about to experience something wonderful. I drive everywhere with my dogs, and they have come to associate a trip in the car with fun, adventure, and togetherness. They don't know where we're going when they pile into the back, but they know I will always make it a positive experience.

If your puppy feels hesitant or anxious about the car, condition him to go in and out of the car when you aren't going anywhere. Leave the doors open, offer a treat, and play in the car while it's in the driveway. Once you've repeated that exercise enough to make the transition in and out of the car go smoothly, add a ride around the block to get the puppy used to the sensation of movement. Gradually increase the length of these drives. Finally, once you've successfully passed these tests, add a destination experience to these practice excursions, but vary it, to expose your puppy to as many new environments as possible. Drive to your friend's house, your mother-in-law's, your local library, or your favorite sidewalk café, making sure you are aware and observant of your puppy's level of immunity and therefore his exposure to other dogs. Let the puppy get out of the car, reward him, then bring him back. An important added benefit of these exercises is that they greatly increase your leadership position in your puppy's eyes. The more places you go in which you display calm-assertive energy to your puppy, the more your dog recognizes you as the one who can guide him through any experience, no matter where you go.

However, some owners who succeed in conditioning their puppies to the car create another problem—overexcitement. The puppy gets so hyped up by the idea of a car ride that he can't calm down, creating chaos that can be anything from a nuisance to a roadway hazard. Overexcitement can show itself as barking, whining, hyperactive movements, or even drooling. Crate training is the most obvious way to temper this problem. Once you have conditioned your puppy to remain calm inside his crate, when you move the crate into the car, they both can come to represent quietness. Follow the same procedure as above, but add the crate, and do not pay attention to your puppy until he is calm and submissive in the crate at all times. Correct him with a "Tssst" or a tap on the top of the crate if his excitement even begins to escalate. Then practice the exercise without the crate, using a safety gate or a doggie seat belt.

Chris Komives practiced this exercise with four-month-old Eliza when he noticed her developing a drooling problem in the car. "I put her in the car when we weren't going anywhere, waited until she was calm, and then got out and did it again. We played in the back of the car. It wasn't long before the drooling stopped." I am constantly challenging my dogs to stay calm-submissive inside the car, even in the face of stimulating activity happening all around us. The other day, just for fun, I took a carload of puppies with me to share a drive-through car wash experience, to expose them to all the different sights, sounds, and smells. Everybody—Junior, Blizzard, Angel, Mr. President, and a visiting French bulldog named Hardy—stayed quiet and calm through the entire ordeal.

Once you are certain your puppy is comfortable about accompanying you anytime, anywhere, practice getting him used to your specific vet's and groomer's offices. *Since sick dogs can be present at either location, don't practice this part of the exercise until after your puppy is four months old and his immunization schedule is complete.* I always recommend getting a dog used to the neighborhood of the vet's office, parking a block away, and walking—or even Rollerblading—to the office itself. That mimics the experience of migration to a dog, so it makes sense to him when you arrive at your destination. When your puppy is young and still unsure of new places, don't push him too far. Instead, start with a short walk across the parking lot. Don't let the puppy pull and sniff the ground, but let him take his time at first. Take a few trips to the vet's office, just for fun, and ask the office staff or vet techs to provide your puppy with a treat or a fun toy when he arrives. Remember when you were a kid and your doctor had the best lollipops?

It's also important that your puppy gets to know the vet, and that the vet practices no touch, no talk, and no eye contact at the very first meeting. Finally, check your own energy when it comes to vet visits. Are you the type of person who always becomes tense before your own doctor or dentist appointments? Do you find yourself worrying about how your dog will cope with an examination? Unless your energy is calm and assertive, you can't ensure that your dog will be able to relax either. Your dog will always mirror the energy you share with him. Puppies in particular are absorbing every cue their pack leader sends them about how they should feel and react when they are in strange new environments.

HOME CARE FOR YOUR DOG

The next thing you must do in order to ensure serenity during your vet or grooming appointments is to introduce your puppy to all the different ways a professional might examine his face and body. Since all veterinarians recommend that you perform regular home checks on your puppy's eyes, ears, and mouth and teeth, this is your perfect opportunity to practice this activity. "A puppy's ears should be checked at least once a week," says Charlie Rinehimer, VMD. "More often if the dog is a flop-eared breed like a cocker or springer spaniel. Owners should also check their dog's paw pads after long walks or play sessions on pavement for abrasions and scratches. After walks in the woods or high grass, run a comb through the puppy's fur to check for fleas and ticks." Bath time is another good opportunity to make routine health checks on your puppy. "Another misconception that I see is people don't bathe their dogs regularly, thinking it dries out their skin. Not true! Wash your dog as often as you see fit," advises Dr. Paula Terifaj. "Clean out the ears. Inspect them for redness, irritations. Look in the mouth—look for redness. Smell—is there any discharge? When you wash the dog, feel for lumps. Lift up your dog's tail! I know you don't want to look back there. But you can find things like tapeworms. Starting this with your puppy young will help them get used to it. Get active in your dog's health care! Don't just say to your vet, 'Here's my dog; take care of it.'" Becoming proactive in your puppy's health routine can also save you on vet bills in the long run.

MR. PRESIDENT'S JOWLS

The lovable bulldog is a feat of human genetic engineering so extreme that it requires special health care and maintenance throughout its entire life. English bulldogs tend to have respiratory problems because of their flat noses, which also cause them to snore and drool. Their unnatural body shape can cause them to develop joint problems or arthritis. Bulldogs also require regular, almost daily, cleaning between the jowls and the loose folds of skin on their faces, which can become dry and crusty—or even smelly and infected—if they aren't tended to. It's vital to start this regular cleaning ritual at an early age, even if the folds are fairly shallow and undeveloped. If you wait until the dog is an adolescent, he can interpret your touching his face as a challenge and may become belligerent and fight back. I've rehabilitated many dogs that have had serious issues around being touched on their bodies and their faces, and we've covered many such cases on *Dog Whisperer*. I made sure to start the process of cleaning Mr. President's folds early in his puppyhood, to lay out the blueprint for stress-free vet and grooming sessions for the rest of his life.

THE HEALTH CARE RITUAL

My supplies for this regular ritual are a towel, a little warm water, some cotton swabs, and a cleaning pad with a little alcohol on it, as well as a few tasty treats for rewards and incentives. I begin by putting an organic lavender lotion on my hands. The scent relaxes me, so I can make sure my energy is calm and centered. Always remain peaceful—never rush any kind of grooming or health-related exercise, including bathing. Your dog needs to associate all these experiences with relaxation and he can't achieve this unless your energy is calm first. I always approach these sessions with my dogs like a prayer or a meditation. Another advantage is that I am teaching Mr. President to associate the scent of lavender with relaxation. The memory of the scent becomes much more influential than my saying, "Calm down" or "Relax." I want to create an imprint so that I can use that scent in the car or anywhere else that I need help creating a mellow bulldog.

I do this exercise on a raised table in my garage. After I lift the dog onto the table, I wait until he relaxes before I begin the session. I start with a treat hidden behind the warm-water-soaked towel. I want the scent to get him interested in the towel, but I don't want the treat so close it creates too much excitement. I want Mr. President to see this as a win-win situation; when he entrusts me with his face, he also gets a treat. Mr. President is one extremely food-motivated dog. However, I don't want to give too many treats; I want to create such a pleasant association with this process that eventually treats won't even be necessary.

Gently, I place my hand under his chin and lift his face up. I'm projecting a serene energy that I want him to mirror. I use this opportunity to put drops in his eyes—bulldogs are also prone to eye irritations and infections, and their eyes must be kept clean and irrigated. He gives me a little protest when he feels the first sensation of the drops—just a little curl of the lip—but I soothe him with a deep-tissue massage of his hindquarters. His reaction serves as a good reminder, however—a curl of the lip from a cute bulldog puppy can turn into a growl or a bite from an adolescent or adult bulldog if we don't build the proper foundation early.

Next, it's time for the cleaning pad and alcohol. Since he is naturally going to be repelled by the medicinal smell, I hide a treat behind the pad. This way, the unnatural smell is accompanied by a smell that definitely interests him. It's a simple trick, to keep him engaged, so he wants to find out more about what I am doing, not shrink away from it. When I give him the treat, however, I always use my clean hand, not the one with alcohol on it, so he doesn't accidentally ingest any alcohol. Using the cotton swabs, I wash between his folds. Every time I move toward his face, I reinforce the action with the association of a treat.

At the end of the exercise I clean my hands to remove the alcohol scent, then put some more lavender lotion on to end the ritual in the same way I began it. I give him one last treat, and the fact that he takes food instantly shows me that his mind is not under stress. Finally, I finish with a massage of his whole body and face, so he learns that when I touch his face it can be for pleasant sensations as well. He ends in a relaxed, receptive state—just the way I want him. I lift him back up by his scruff, using my hand to balance his weight, and place him gently back on the ground. The fact that he gravitates right back to me and doesn't try to run away assures me that he had a positive experience.

My hygiene ritual with Mr. President should serve as an example of how to make a pleasant interlude out of any of your puppy's health care and grooming needs. By applying this method, you will prepare him for future handling by other professionals, you'll be taking a proactive role in his health and hygiene, and you'll also be strengthening the bond between you, building a lifetime of trust.

6

CONNECTING, COMMUNICATING, AND CONDITIONING

How Your Dog Learns

Tug-of-war between Junior and Mr. President

A mother squirrel and her baby spent all day on a walkway of the UCLA campus, repeating over and over the same apparently fruitless task—trying to get the baby squirrel to jump up and over an approximately four-foot-high wall. Such exercises in life learning are everyday occurrences in the animal world, but this particular incident was captured on videotape by some fascinated university student, who uploaded it onto YouTube, and it received an amazing 500,000 hits! When I saw the short piece, I was happy to learn that it was reaching so many people. To me, this simple amateur video illustrates exactly what

I want my readers to take away from this book about how animals learn—and how we can help, not hinder, their natural processes.

In the video, the mother squirrel is showing the baby squirrel what it looks like to jump to the top of the wall, teaching by example. The mother squirrel seems to have an endless supply of patience as she demonstrates her graceful moves over and over again. The baby squirrel finally gets up the gumption to try it a few times himself, but he makes it only partway before falling. At this point, the concerned UCLA students watching this unfolding drama decide to get involved. They move a backpack up against the part of the wall that the squirrel is attempting to scale. At first, the squirrel flees the strange object, but after a few minutes, it returns and figures out that the backpack could make a good ladder. The squirrel climbs up the backpack, but the object isn't quite high enough to leverage the baby animal to the top. Another student comes on the scene with a couple of large sandbags; stacked together, they are taller than the backpack. Again, the tiny rodent flees the scene. This time, his mother comes down and escorts him back to the wall for another try. She leaps up and waits just above the sandbags. Then, encouraging with silence and energy, she watches her baby climb up the sandbag, make a last heroic hurdle, and finally succeed in scaling that daunting concrete wall.

My first thought after watching that video was "What if that had been a mother dog and a puppy?" I have no doubt whatsoever that the same concerned students would have simply picked the puppy up and put her on the grass above the wall. They might even have comforted her, petting and cooing as they did so. Then they would've gone on their way, confident that they had "rescued" a helpless animal, while the puppy actually might have missed a learning experience that could one day save its life. The truth is, in most situations, animals—even juvenile animals—are anything but helpless. Animals are smart, resourceful, and all about survival. What we humans interpret as "rescuing" can actually be blocking a puppy from her natural process of learning and growing and mastering a new environment. In the UCLA squirrel video, the animal in question was saved from this fate because of its wildness. The students approached and dealt with a wild squirrel very differently than they would have a domestic puppy or kitten. And what they did with the squirrel turned out to be exactly the right thing to do! They helped the animal, not by rescuing it, but by working *in partnership with it,* giving it direction but not stepping in and solving its problem. A partnership between human and animal is exactly how we need to approach first connecting and communicating with, and finally, conditioning (or "training") our puppies.

CONNECTING

Relationship Is Everything

It was my original ambition in life to grow up and become the best dog trainer in the world, and I have trained many dogs in my life—to perform tricks, to answer to commands, as well as to work as security dogs. Soon after I arrived in America, however, I observed that traditional "training"—meaning sit, stay, come, heel, or answering to other commands—was not solving the problem of an epidemic of unstable dogs. What those dogs needed was for their owners to stop humanizing them, to reclaim a leadership role in their lives, and to fulfill *all* their primal needs—the needs of animal, dog, and breed, in that order. But as you have already learned, a puppy's mother starts "dog training" from the earliest days of her pups' lives. Her training is not done with a high, squeaky, overexcited voice, commands, or bribery by treats; it is done in silence, using energy—a much more powerful tool of communication.

"When I have a litter, they are learning from the moment they are born. They learn from their mother, their siblings, and from me handling them," says my friend Martin Deeley, executive director of the International Association of Canine Professionals and an acclaimed breeder and trainer of gun dogs.

When an owner picks up a puppy for the first time, the pup is already beginning to learn from the owner. The ride home in the car is a lesson. The meeting of the family is a lesson. Dogs are learning twenty-four hours a day. Even when asked to relax and do nothing, they are learning to do this and be patient. Everything we do with a pup from the moment we get that pup is a learning experience. So we actually start "dog training" the moment we get a pup, and in fact we should start teaching ourselves how to behave and how to establish all the good habits before we even get the pup.

A mother dog's "training" is also done through connecting. She has a real relationship with her pups, expressed through constant calm-assertive leadership. This is why I advise all puppy owners to think "connection," then "communication," before they think "training" or "conditioning." Learn to converse with your dog the way another dog speaks to her—using energy, body language, and eye contact—before you ask her to master the intricacies of any human syntax. Your conversations will have much deeper meaning for your dog that way, and you will be sharing a true connection. Connection is the language of energy; it is the cornerstone of the lifelong bond between you and your dog. Connect and fulfill first, then move on to conditioning.

CESAR'S FULFILLMENT FORMULA

Every dog and puppy needs . . .

1. Exercise—in the form of a minimum of two structured walks with a pack leader, twice a day

2. Discipline—clearly communicated and consistently enforced rules, boundaries, and limitations

3. Affection—in the form of physical affection, praise, treats, and playtime

. . . and in that order! Though you may be adopting a puppy in order to give it love, the reality is that puppies need a lot more than love to keep them balanced. A good pack leader shows love by fulfilling the dog in all three areas—in the right order. This fulfillment formula works throughout the entire life of your dog.

LEASH TRAINING

When it comes to bonding with your puppy, once again you have Mother Nature on your side, since from birth to eight months, your puppy is programmed to always follow her leader. Once the natural mother is out of the picture, you become the puppy's default pack leader, and if you direct her with the same calm-assertive energy that she's been accustomed to since birth, your puppy will automatically follow you whenever you wander away. It's as if there were a built-in invisible leash between you and her.

Still, when your puppy is with you in the public, human world, an invisible leash is not enough. There are far too many distractions and dangers out there. Once she enters adolescence, she is going to want to range far and wide. You need to leash-train her from a very early age, in such a way that the leash is barely noticeable and has only positive connotations for the puppy. Done right, leash training strengthens the connection between you and your puppy. It becomes a physical cord through which your energy travels to her, and vice versa.

Many conscientious breeders will begin the leash training for you. Brooke Walker already had Angel well on his way by the time he came home with me, at eight weeks. Brooke starts the process by putting little paper bands on their necks right about the time they are starting to walk. She initially does this for identification purposes—that's how I first met Angel, when he was simply Mr. Green, next to his brother, Mr. Blue, and sister, Ms. Pink. "Since my puppies rarely leave home before three months, I usually start introducing them to the leash at about eight or nine weeks. Just five minutes, twice a day. I'll do short little stints with a treat held close to their nose to encourage them to move forward. I like to compare it to when you introduce a child to swimming and you keep moving backward from them so that they have to take one more stroke to reach you."

Brooke's method of leash training is right in line with my own philosophy of being a partner instead of a dictator when it comes to your dog's learning. I recommend letting a puppy drag around a very short leash for quick intervals while she's playing—supervised at all times, of course—just so she can get accustomed to the unnatural feeling of having something around her neck, while still experiencing the fun and freedom of play. Remember, we as humans are used to getting up every morning and putting foreign objects like clothes, shoes, and jewelry on our bodies, but to a dog, leash, harness, booties, or sweater are just that—completely foreign. Conditioning is the process of making the unnatural feel natural. Trainers who work with wild or exotic animals—for instance, big cats that perform in magic acts—always start conditioning their animals to leashes and collars as young as possible. The younger a puppy is when she gets used to the feeling of a leash, the more normal the sensation will be for her.

As for the tools themselves, I am a big proponent of less is more when it comes to a puppy's leash. In fact, with all the puppies I've been raising for this book, my simple 35¢ nylon leash slipped over the pup's head and held high up on the neck for control has been my number one tool. I am a fan also of "show leashes"—slim-cut, pure leather leashes with a loop at the end that are used in dog shows. They are short, lightweight, and allow a maximum of control with a minimum of tension. If you want to introduce a Halti or gentle leader to your puppy, the correct time to do it is between four and six months of age.

Never use a prong collar or other advanced training tool on a puppy under six months of age, but if your powerful-breed puppy is still exhibiting signs of overexcitement or lunging as she enters her adolescence, consult a professional to help you decide on the appropriate tool to help manage the problem. By preventing any behavioral issues now, in puppyhood, I hope you will be so in tune with your dog that there will be no need for advanced tools or extra help down the line. But if you need help, make sure to reach out before the problems escalate out of control.

And always remember that it's not the tool itself—it's the energy behind the tool that matters! Your energy passes through the leash directly to your dog, so if you are uncomfortable in any way with the training tool you are using, your dog will sense it—and react accordingly.

Another important detail of leash training is that you must always let the puppy come to the tool, never force the tool on the puppy. The first few times, this may take patience. Make a loop that's about one and a half times wider than your puppy's head. Then hold it in front of you and let her sniff it. You can spray it with an organic scent or palm a treat on the other side of the loop. Let the pup examine the tool and feel comfortable with it. Lightly touch it to her forehead and nose. Once the puppy seems relaxed and curious about the tool, hold the treat on the other side and let her put her head through the loop to reach the treat. Then gently tighten the tool. If your puppy is still relaxed, provide a reward—petting, praise, or a treat. The adventure of the walk that goes along with the leash is the biggest reward, giving the leash a positive association. That's why so many dog owners report that their dogs get excited whenever they see the owners going for the leash—the association of the good times that the leash represents.

After a few times repeating this ritual, you may be able to hold the loop of your leash out in front of your puppy and watch her put her head through on her own. If your puppy is wearing a collar and you are simply attaching a leash to the top of it, never chase the puppy around when it's time for a walk. Once again, let the puppy come to you. Using the tried-and-true formula of nose-eyes-ears, engage your puppy's nose and make sure she's standing or sitting still while you fasten the leash to the collar. Stay relaxed and quiet; keep the image of your pup's calm, confident canine mother in mind. And keep your energy positive. Taking a puppy for a walk should be one of life's most joyful experiences!

Puppies have very short attention spans, so when they are young, keep the time on the leash short and sweet—no more than five to ten minutes at first—and fill that time with fun, pleasant surprises, and rewards. When the shorter sessions become easy, gradually lengthen them. This way you'll leave your puppy wanting more each time. She'll actually come to crave the experience of the leash because it will come to represent adventure, exercise, praise, and, most important of all, bonding with you, her pack leader.

MASTERING THE WALK

1. Always begin the walk with calm-assertive energy.
2. Don't chase after your puppy with the tool you are using, be it a simple 35¢ leash like the ones I use, a harness, or a Halti. To your puppy, the tool you are using is an extension of your own energy, so it should have a pleasant (but not overstimulating!) connotation. Let your puppy come to the tool, not the other way around.

3. For your very first walk with your puppy, wait at the threshold of wherever you are leaving from, be it a shelter, your car, or your home. Make sure your puppy is in calm-submissive waiting mode beside you, and then step out the door first. Ask your puppy to follow. Whoever leaves the dwelling first, in the puppy's mind, is leading the excursion. You want that leader to be you.

4. Hold the leash in an easy, relaxed manner as if you are carrying a purse or a briefcase. Hold your head high, put your shoulders back. If your puppy begins to pull, pull up lightly on the leash, then immediately release the tension once the puppy gets back into line. Keep the tension loose at all other times. Your puppy should be walking beside or behind you, not pulling to the side or dragging you from in front. If your puppy doesn't get that concept right away, use an object, like a walking stick or an umbrella, to create an obstacle until she gets the picture. Gently put the object out in front of the puppy's path in order to create a boundary that will soon become an invisible one.

5. If your puppy starts to wander, gets distracted, or seems to balk at moving forward, use a bully stick, a palmed treat, or a scented toy and engage her nose. Then continue to move forward once you have redirected her attention.

6. If a puppy gets excited when she sees a commotion or another dog across the street, this is not a signal for you to get excited, too! Keep your focus and, most important, your calm-assertive energy, and continue walking. A slight side-pull correction on the leash will communicate, "Don't get distracted, keep on walking!" If necessary, turn your puppy's back to the commotion that is causing the distraction, and make eye contact with her. Wait until she sits, relaxes; then continue on with the walk.

7. When you and your puppy have had a successful ten-, fifteen-, or twenty-minute walk, then allow your puppy the freedom to

wander a bit on the end of the leash, to smell the ground *(only if you are in a safe area and/or your puppy has completed her third round of vaccinations)* or pee and poop. This is a reward. After about three to five minutes, return to your structured walk.

8. When arriving at your destination or returning home, repeat the procedure outlined in step 3. Walk through the threshold first, then invite your puppy in after you. Remember, in your puppy's mind, whoever goes through the door first owns that space! Make sure she is calm and submissive as you remove the leash.

Walking correctly with your dog will be the most important skill you can master if you are seeking a deep, lifelong connection. Stick to the basics—always be the first one out the door and the first one to return back in. Always walk with your puppy beside or behind you, never allowing her to pull you from the front or "zigzag" out to the side. Keep the tension on the leash relaxed, and imagine you are carrying a purse or a briefcase. Focus your eyes ahead, don't stare at your puppy. Most conventional schools of dog training instruct you to keep your dog on your left, but in my experience, you can condition a dog to walk to your right, to your left, or even to do both whenever you want. The key is to have her beside or behind, never out front. If you are having trouble getting your puppy to walk reliably on a leash, choose one side and stick to it until she gets the lesson down cold.

Owners I have helped always marvel at the night-to-day differences they see after they finally master the walk with a formerly troubled dog. For adult dogs, I recommend a minimum of at least a thirty-minute walk twice a day, to drain pent-up energy and for the primal bonding ritual that it signifies. Adding a backpack to an adult dog can help intensify the walk, or make up for time if you can't do a longer session. For puppies with short legs and even shorter attention spans, walks can be brief—even ten minutes a time in the beginning

—but they should still follow the outline above, and you must begin the routine of two or more structured daily walks at your side as soon as your puppy comes home with you. It's the structure and the ritual that are important here. You are imprinting on your puppy's malleable brain that this is your routine; this is how one works for food and water.

IMMUNITY AND WALKING

Because a puppy's immune system will not kick in fully until the third round of shots at around sixteen weeks, many modern owners don't believe they have to walk their puppies until they are four months old or even older. In fact, some of them are so scared of parvo and other illnesses that they want to encase the puppy in a protective bubble for its first months home. I will never disagree with the advice of a veterinarian when it comes to the physical health of a dog. But a puppy's psychological development is also a big part of her overall health. From a purely behavioral standpoint, keeping a puppy inside a house and limiting its ability to exercise is a recipe for disaster. Imagine if you had a human child, and you kept him in the house until he was a teenager. What kind of person do you think he'd become? It's likely he either wouldn't have any clue how to deal with the outside world and would be timid and antisocial, or he might go to the other extreme, come away bursting with repressed, frustrated energy, and become a force for destruction the minute he got a taste of freedom. An overprotected puppy can have a similar reaction if it is virtually quarantined through adolescence.

There are so many different ways to keep a puppy safe from disease while at the same time making sure you fulfill all her physical and psychological needs. Try mastering the walk on a back patio or in your yard, on your driveway, on a limited, sanitized area outside your home (Chris Komives used a ten-to-one bleach-water solution to spray and sanitize the short portion of his neighborhood sidewalk where he first started walking Eliza), or even on a treadmill inside the house as a last resort (you can run on the treadmill next to the puppy to simulate an off-leash migrating ritual). Swimming alongside a puppy in a pool—especially a water dog—can have much the same effect. Use your imagination, along with your sense of caution, to begin this bonding ritual and the exercise habit right away.

Says Diana Foster:

> We always stress walking and exercise. German shepherds are powerful dogs, they've got a lot of energy, and they need their cardio. Walk around a parking lot or go down a busy street where there are a lot of cars and buses and noise—you will very rarely see other dogs. Avoid areas where there are vets' offices or pet stores. Of course, you need to keep them on the sidewalk and don't let them sniff the ground. That's not what the walk is for; it's for structure and for training them to be comfortable on the leash. Just make sure you are walking your puppy in a controlled environment. In our group puppy class, everybody's checked for shots. I don't let anybody on the property that is sick at all. If they have a loose stool or a cough or their eyes are weird, they're not allowed on the property. I tell owners, sure, by all means be careful, but you've got to take the puppy out!

OBSTACLES TO THE WALK

Walking a puppy isn't the same thing as walking an adult dog. A puppy is much more easily distracted. You may need to stop, press the "reset" button on her attention, then start again before she gets into the rhythm of it. Using a scented toy, palmed treat, or bully stick to redirect the nose is a great way to distract a wandering puppy and get her attention back on you. But a puppy also has built-in limits as to how far from home it's okay to wander.

Recently my wife, the boys, and I had the delightful opportunity to care for some newborn Chihuahua pups and their mother in our home. It was fascinating to watch the three one-month-old puppies and their different responses to the outside world. While two of the puppies would not leave the bed we provided for the little family, one pup of the same litter jumped right off it and explored by himself to a distance of four full feet away. Each of those three puppies is "normal." But each of those puppies, at three or four months old, will have a different reaction to a walk with a human. When he grows up to be a big boy of three months of age, the "explorer" Chihuahua might follow me half a block away. The other two might not want to go more than a few yards past the driveway.

You as an owner have to be sensitive to your pup's limits. You definitely need to keep challenging her, but you shouldn't push her past what her instincts tell her is comfortable. Instead, add a few extra feet every day to your walk. Increase the distance gradually. But don't force a young puppy into a new place or circumstance if her body shuts down on you. Slow down and let her take in the experience at her own pace. If you continually ignore and block a puppy's instincts, you will never be able to build the trust necessary to connect truly with your dog. And remember, dogs' superior instincts—their original five and vaunted sixth senses—are a very large part of what we value them for.

ANGEL AND THE DARK PATHWAY

When Melissa brought Angel home with her for his weekend night sleepaway experience, she and her husband took him on several walks. At my house, Angel was always very courageous, exploring the hedges and mailboxes of several houses on our cul-de-sac long before his pal, Mr. President, dared venture beyond our driveway. He also ranged farther than the other puppies when left to roam at the new Dog Psychology Center. True to form, Angel was gung-ho and co-operative when Melissa and her husband first walked with him along busy Ventura Boulevard at twilight, crossing a busy, noisy street and parading down and back a long California block with no problem at all.

Later in the evening, Melissa took Angel out to relieve himself, then began a shorter walk in a lighted park next to their apartment building, hoping to tire him out one last time before putting him to bed for the night. He trotted happily by her side for a few minutes, but when he saw that the path ahead led to an area where the glow from the streetlights dropped off into darkness, he stopped cold and wouldn't move forward. "At first, I treated the situation as if it were an adult dog stopping down; I just kept moving forward," says Melissa. "But Angel wasn't going to go. He became even more determined when I tried to bring him with me, creating tension on the leash. I tried the bully stick—that had worked before—but he wouldn't even engage his nose. I signaled him to sit and asked him to make eye contact with me, but his eyes kept darting toward the path ahead. I was wracking my brain for solutions—'What would Cesar do?'"

Melissa decided to respect Angel's instincts. She chose to turn around and walk back toward the building, which was the correct solution. It's not that Angel was afraid of the dark—he'd been out at the Dog Psychology Center in a pitch black night with the rest of the pack. The problem was, this time he was being led by a human—one who may know how to write about dogs intellectually but is not as experienced from an instinctual point of view. On this occasion, Angel's human companion was not checking out the new situation in the way a balanced dog would check it out. Melissa was barreling ahead without taking the time to smell, or let Angel smell, totally unexplored ter-

ritory. Angel could not use his nose to check out the dark path loom-
ing in front of him, nor could he even use his eyes to see it, so he
stopped. That's using good instincts. Even Daddy might have reacted
that way, although as an adult dog, Daddy has learned that he can usually trust the human who is leading him. If Melissa had wanted to
move forward, she would have had to let Angel take his time, moving
a little bit, smelling, then moving a little bit more, smelling. It might
have taken them a half hour to move a few feet forward. That's because Angel was using his inborn common sense and playing it safe,
which is exactly what we want our dogs to do. If we are truly connecting with our puppies and working in partnership with them as they
become more confident about new things like strange new places and
dark, mysterious paths, we will retain their most valuable instincts,
and we will not lose their very precious trust.

ENERGY AND WALKING

In my previous books and on my television show, I continually stress
the importance of walking, especially the energy of the owner during
the walk. *You must consistently project calm-assertive energy to your puppy if
she is to follow you.* It may seem redundant, but there's a reason for
that—I keep coming up against humans who repeat the same ex-
cuses. They actually blame a dog for being a bad walker, giving justifi-
cations like "She just hates to be on the leash" or "She always wants to
pull ahead" when, truly, I have yet to meet a dog of any age that has
been unable to learn how to walk.

The precious months of puppyhood offer you a window of opportunity to mold your walks into the ultimate, most joyful bonding experience imaginable. If you do your job now, even when the rebellious
period of adolescence kicks in, your dog will be programmed to be an
excellent walker. If during adolescence she seems to want to stray, you

will always have the tools to bring her back to the routine. And every successful walk you take brings you closer and closer, pack leader to follower. I credit much of my intimate, almost psychic relationship with Daddy to the thousands and thousands of perfect walks we have completed together. But you have to put the time in *now*.

BLIZZARD LEARNS TO WALK

In the two years since my family and I moved to our Santa Clarita Valley home, our neighbors Adriana and Terry Barnes and their kids, eleven-year-old Christian and fourteen-year-old Sabrina, have become our close and valued friends. When we first arrived, however, Adriana wasn't too thrilled about having the Dog Whisperer living right down the block. She was terrified of big dogs—especially pit bulls. Her blood would run cold whenever she saw me out walking Daddy. But my charming wife, Ilusion, can win anybody over, and Adriana began working with us as we started planning the new Dog Psychology Center on land we had purchased nearby. Adriana found herself around our house—and our dogs—more and more often. Daddy is a pit bull that can change anybody's mind about pit bulls. "There was just something about Daddy's eyes," Adrianna told me. "Such a connection, in those eyes. It made me know I could trust him." Things changed so much for Adriana, in fact, that now she and Terry help me run the new Santa Clarita Valley Dog Psychology Center. Terry was thrilled, because he was a dog person, and his kids desperately wanted a dog. I let them adopt Molly, a mellow, low-energy dachshund I'd rescued from Ensenada. Life with Molly went so well, the kids—especially Christian—started campaigning for a puppy.

Unfortunately, the family had had a bad experience with a Labrador puppy in the past, when the kids were toddlers. "The puppy was just really wild," Adriana recounts. "She'd go after us all the time. To me it was too out of control. We'd leave her in the backyard, and we actually stopped going into the backyard; she ate the whole backyard up. Looking back now, with what Cesar has taught me, I'm sure that it could have been fixed. We were ignoring her a lot, we didn't walk her, we didn't exercise her. We didn't balance her out at all. And I was thinking that she was aggressive, but really she was bored."

I felt that my neighbors had earned a second chance, so when Blizzard, the yellow Lab we rescued for this book, turned four months old, I presented him to Adriana. Because I see so much of the family, Blizzard gets double benefits—the cozy comfort of being a family dog, as well as having access to living and playing among the pack at my house and at the center. Adriana and her family are fast learners, and they have all grown in their leadership skills by leaps and bounds, thanks to the challenges provided by a dog like Blizzard. But the dynamics of the Barnes family offer a great example of how different energies can affect the same dog.

SAME PUPPY, DIFFERENT WALKERS

Fourteen-year-old Sabrina is a Dog Whisperer in training. She's cool, confident, and exudes a calm-assertive energy—really impressive for a teenager. Her brother, Christian, however, is a more laid-back, quiet guy, and when Blizzard first arrived, he was much less self-assured with his new puppy. Blizzard picked up right away on Christian's hesitation. Whereas Sabrina would walk Blizzard without any problem, with Christian, the energetic Labrador would pull ahead or to the side.

"Cesar says that Christian and Blizzard are both the same energy," says their dad, Terry. "So when they're both the same energy, he's not going to listen to Christian. My boy, he's so quiet and so timid, I think that's one thing. Sabrina will get right on Blizzard if he pulls away, whereas Christian will be yelling, "Stop! Don't!" Yelling at him in full sentences. Too much talk. Like Cesar says, 'They don't speak English; they don't speak human.' "

Blizzard hanging out with Sabrina and Christian

Despite Christian's lower energy level, when Blizzard would get worked up, Christian would become nervous and tense. "He's only a puppy," says Sabrina, knowingly. "He's trying to figure out who to follow. He's like a kid. And with Christian, it's like there are two puppies, they're both hyper, and it doesn't really balance out that well."

"I think it's because I have too much tension on the leash," Christian admits. "Then when he goes on in front of me, he starts pulling. Cesar's taught me to relax and let go, to the point where he's right next to me." I began working with Christian on the walk as soon as I noticed this problem, because it's vital that a puppy see every human in the house as pack leader. When I wasn't around to help, his sister, Sabrina, stepped in. Over the past few months, Sabrina has noticed a big improvement in her brother's technique. "I think he's gotten more used to him walking him now. He's giving him more exercise and he's playing with him a lot more. And I guess they're starting to really bond now. Like I can see the trust grow between them."

Trust and respect are the two most important ingredients of a perfect human-dog relationship. Mastering the walk with your puppy each and every day is the single best way to guarantee a great connection for a lifetime.

CONNECTING THROUGH PLAY

While the walk offers a ritualized, structured way to bond with your puppy, play offers you more varied opportunities to challenge and enrich her life and to build an even deeper connection. Puppies begin to play practically as soon as they can walk, but even their first clumsy attempts at recreation have their own natural rules, boundaries, and limitations. The dominance games they play with their siblings become their very first lessons in social restrictions and canine etiquette. Playing with your puppy should be a big part of your bonding with her as well, but follow the example of nature and remember that play doesn't have to equal anarchy. Many owners think "play" means letting their puppy just go crazy. It's better for your puppy's education and for your own sanity that instead of being a free-for-all, a play session challenges her mind as well as her body. Think about it—we send our kids to soccer practice, which has rules, regulations, and discipline, rather than letting their natural energy build up and cause them to tear through the house, destroying things. Both activities could be considered "play," but one is productive, the other destructive.

There are two ways a dog will play—one from the dog side of her and one from the breed side. Learning to discern one from the other is the key to making play a fun and positive learning experience, as opposed to an out-of-control riot that may fuel certain unwanted breed-related characteristics in your puppy.

PLAYING LIKE A DOG

All dogs love to run, they all love to chase things (though not all breeds innately know how to retrieve, any dog can learn), and all dogs can track using their noses. One simple game I use to bring out the dog in my puppies while keeping their breed-related tendencies under control is to attach a string to the end of a long stick, then tie a soft stuffed animal—a favorite is a plush duck—onto the string. Then I dangle the string in front of the puppy and move it around in a circle. The tendency for most people would be to move the stick rapidly, working the puppy up into a lather of excitement. Instead, I maneuver the stick slowly, stopping it and starting it. This way, I stimulate both the play and the prey drives in the puppy. The faster she plays, the more physical energy she drains. The slower she plays, the more mental energy she drains and the more she is challenged, since prey drive involves more concentration. This is a good game to play while allowing your puppy to drag a short leash. In this way, the leash and the duck, as well as you, the one who controls the game, don't come to symbolize overexcitement and chaos. Instead, the entire exercise represents challenge and focus, bringing out the puppy's animal-dog nature.

In playing games like this that engage the animal-dog in your puppy, you can also begin to observe the breed-related traits that the play or prey drive bring out. When they were three and four months of age, I started playing this game regularly with Angel, the miniature schnauzer, and Mr. President, the English bulldog. There was very little difference in how they played as dogs. Both of them stalked the toy like a dog and chased the toy like a dog.

The breed in them, however, showed itself at the moment they captured the toy. Angel would stalk with his perfect show-dog posture, then muster up the energy to pounce on the duck. After wrestling with it a little, he'd gently let it go and direct his attention elsewhere.

Silent Training: Angel Learns the "Down"

Cesar gets Angel's attention to teach him the "down" command.

A yawn is often a sign that a puppy is mentally working something out, or frustrated.

Cesar rewards Angel for displaying the correct behavior or command.

Cesar gives Angel affection for a job well done.

Playing Like a Dog

All dogs love to run, and they all love to chase things. One of my favorite games to bring out the dog in my puppies is to attach a string to the end of a long stick, then tie a soft stuffed animal to the end of the string.

Angel leaps after the toy.

Angel looks to Cesar for direction.

Mr. President waits to pounce.

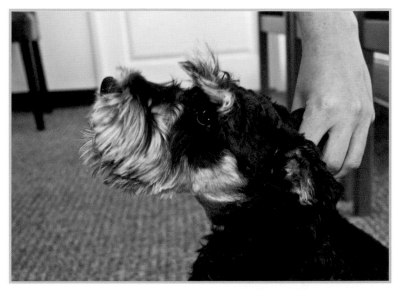

Grabbing Angel by the scruff of the neck.

NURTURING BREED

Once you have fulfilled the animal-dog in your puppy through walks and certain kinds of structured play, next you can introduce her to the world of activities preprogrammed in her by her breed. By fulfilling every side of your puppy's nature—animal, dog, and breed—you will open up a deeper line of communication, a better channel for intimacy.

Blizzard the Retriever

Labrador retrievers are hunting dogs, designed by humans to search out and retrieve prey killed in a hunt. The Labradors have a "soft mouth," which means they carry their prizes lightly so as not to destroy or mutilate them. This also makes them ideal playmates for children, although the soft mouth of a Lab must be cultivated by the owners from puppyhood. "Blizzard likes to play-bite with Christian," Terry informs me. "Sabrina will touch him on his neck and snap him right out of it, but with Christian, he really pushes the limits." My next job is to help the family retrain Christian to provide stronger leadership with Blizzard whenever he begins to use his mouth a little too much.

When it comes to retrieving, all the ingredients are in a Labrador's genes. But what is inborn doesn't always come naturally, as John Grogan discovered in *Marley and Me*:

He was a master at pursuing his prey. It was the concept of returning it that he did not seem to quite grasp. His general attitude seemed to be, if you want the stick that bad, YOU jump in the water for it. . . . He dropped the stick at my feet . . . but when I reached down to pick up the stick, Marley was ready. He dove in,

grabbed it, and raced across the beach in crazy figure eights. He swerved back nearly colliding with me, taunting me to chase him. "You're supposed to be a Labrador retriever!" I shouted. "Not a Labrador evader!"

John's solution to this problem was to tempt Marley with a second stick, based on the theory that a dog tends to want what another dog (or human) has more than he wants the stick he already has in his mouth. After an exhausting day of trial and error, he and his wayward Labrador did make some progress, but his description of the event makes clear two things—one, Marley did not respect John, and two, John was absolutely not his pack leader. Marley was treating John the way he might treat a sibling or a littermate—teasing and cajoling—but a follower does not play "keep-away" from a leader. Marley may have trusted John and been bonded to him, but John didn't command enough respect from Marley to be able to guide the fast-growing puppy into the Labrador his genes intended him to be.

I have good news for all future Marley owners out there: there is a much easier, more straightforward way to tap into a Labrador's—or any dog's—retrieving abilities than playing the frustrating "mine is better than yours" game. It all comes back to the concept of being the pack leader and controlling the game through your connection with your puppy. As soon as Blizzard came home with me, I brought him into the hills at the Santa Clarita Dog Psychology Center to begin unleashing the retriever in his genes. The key—the secret ingredient John Grogan was missing—is eye contact. I take the ball and hold it, immediately getting Blizzard's attention, because whenever an object moves, it becomes "alive" to a puppy. Then I wait until he is seated, active-submissive, looking into my eyes and waiting for my signal. Only when he is fully engaged in full eye contact with me and is in a waiting mode do I throw the ball. I don't throw it when he's overexcited; I don't throw it when he is fixated on the ball itself. To throw a

ball to a puppy when he is fixated on a ball can plant the seeds of obsession. Blizzard is playing the game with *me,* not the ball. I don't continue the game if he doesn't retrieve the ball, but since he has acknowledged, with eye contact, that this was my game to begin with, he naturally wants to bring the ball back and go for another round. The game—like any game I play with my dogs—also has a clear beginning, decided by me, and a clear end, decided by me. I communicate that the game has ended by making sure Blizzard is seated and relaxed, not excitedly twitching around, waiting for one more round. This exercise is an example of where connection, communication, and conditioning all combine to fulfill all the needs of our dogs' natures. The beautiful part is, this behavior is already in a retriever's DNA. My puppy just needs me to be the one to bring it out in him.

You don't have to own a Labrador or other sporting-breed dog to play this game successfully with your puppy. With leadership, eye contact, and lots of repetition, a dog of any breed can use the exercise of retrieving to access the "dog" in him. I have raised Junior to be a top-notch retriever—it's a joy to behold his muscular body racing after the ball, kicking up grass and dust as he sprints over the brown California hills. Pit bulls are not supposed to be retrievers, but Junior always brings me the ball back. In fact, retrieving has become for him a kind of polite gesture of respect for his "superiors"—unbidden, he always brings toys to Daddy, to me, and to any other human he wants to please. Angel, a terrier, is also a great retriever. Using the eye-contact method, he will reliably chase and return any ball. Even Mr. President has learned how to retrieve, with the help of discipline, repetition, and the examples of his fellow pack members. For a born retriever, the reward is in the successful accomplishment of the task itself. For other breeds, you may have to supplement the reward with more praise, petting, or a treat. Whatever breed you may own, don't underestimate the power of the simple game of fetch to strengthen the connection and bond between you and your puppy.

BEHAVIORAL REWARDS OR INCENTIVES CAN INCLUDE

- Praise, approval, smiles, laughter
- Petting, massage, or other form of physical affection
- A favorite toy or game
- Treats or special meals
- The end of a correction (i.e., releasing tension on a leash)
- The joy of the activity itself
- Your silent but powerful approval

Blizzard the Water Dog

If you have access to a swimming pool or live near water, you have at your disposal a wonderful tool to challenge your puppy, drain his energy, and help him get much-needed exercise. Labs, poodles, Newfoundlands, Chesapeake Bay retrievers, German shorthair pointers, Brittany spaniels, and Portuguese water dogs like the Obamas' Bo are all hunting-retrieving dogs that have water activities in their genes, but pretty much any dog will take to the water if you give him a little encouragement. Swimming is an exercise I recommend also to people who are being cautious about the puppy's immune system during his first few months. There is no chance of the puppy's catching the parvovirus in a chlorinated pool, and it is a fantastic way for you to bond with him as well as to get his body moving. Make sure to supervise at all times, however, and remember to keep your pool fenced in to prevent potentially life-threatening accidents.

How does a dog learn to swim? He dog-paddles, of course! Go into the water ahead of your puppy, and let him watch you enjoying yourself in there. That alone will get his curiosity going . . . he may actually follow you in on his own. If not, urge him in by bringing him gently with the leash, or letting him follow his nose to a food treat you have with you. Once he's fully water bound, he may get a little panicky, but don't panic yourself. Instead, hold his body firmly with your hands and let his legs get into a natural rhythm of paddling. Move him around in the water for a while so he gets used to the feeling. Once you sense he is no longer panicky, you can then take him a very short way—maybe two or three feet—from the pool's edge and let him swim back.

"But Blizzard's afraid of the water!" Christian complained to me shortly after he and his family had taken Blizzard into their home, when the puppy was about four months of age. "He just doesn't want to go in the pool." Christian was justifiably upset at this turn of events—after all, one of the attractions of the Labrador breed is their storied history as swimmers and aquatic retrievers. As much as Christian and his sister, Sabrina, loved Molly, the older rescued dachshund they adopted from me, they had been dying to have an active, playful dog that would splash around in their backyard pool with them. I reassured Christian that a little hesitation around water does not mean they have a "faulty" Labrador. As with Marley's first clumsy attempts at retrieving, the genes for Blizzard's water aptitude are preprogrammed within him. The dogs just need guidance and leadership to bring out those qualities.

I decided to initiate Blizzard into my own backyard pool when he was about five months of age, while shooting the *Dog Whisperer* episode in which I was working in the water with a Lab-mastiff mix named Joe. I've turned all our dogs into water dogs. That particular day, Junior, Angel, Mr. President, Jack the Jack Russell, the French bulldog Hardy, and a visiting English bulldog named Chuckie were all

joining in the fun. A pit bull, two terriers, and three bulldogs were all swimming with me in the pool as if they'd been born in the water, yet there was one dog still lingering on dry land, hanging back from the water's edge with his head down and projecting a nervous energy—the only water dog of the bunch, Blizzard.

I placed a nylon leash over Blizzard's neck, to give me a little more control over him, and set out initially leading him with food. As I drew him toward the water where the rest of his pack were splashing around and having such a great time, he began to shut down. From experience, I knew that offering food to a puppy that has shut down results in rejection, and every rejection weakens the trust between me and him—to him, it means that I am not hearing what he is trying to communicate to me.

Abandoning the food strategy, I took my time, getting into the water myself, coaxing him a little bit closer for several minutes. When

Blizzard exploring the pool

he got to the edge, I lifted him up in my arms. I felt his body freeze completely, so I did not put him in the water right away. I held him for about thirty seconds, until I felt him begin to relax, then I went to the "partnership" strategy—putting Blizzard's two rear feet on the pool stairs in the shallow water. I let him balance his front legs on me while he adjusted to the feeling of the water, then I gently let go. He had to put his front legs somewhere, and found himself sitting upright on the stair in the shallow water. He seemed puzzled to be there, but I could read in his body language that he was figuring out, "Hey, this isn't so bad." Clearly, it wasn't the water itself that was so threatening; it was the transition from dry land to water that seemed to confuse him.

I sat quietly with Blizzard for three more minutes, letting him become accustomed to the sensation; then I waded out a little farther into the pool and tugged lightly on the leash. As his body came forward, I caught it underneath and let him paddle with all fours while he figured out the motion of swimming. I then slowly lessened my hold on his body, until Blizzard left my arms on his own and swam toward the edge of the pool. I brought him back, and after letting him rest a moment, stepped backward and urged him to swim out to me. We repeated this several times, and with each attempt, Blizzard was increasingly comfortable in the water and more confident in his movements.

Next, I practiced walking him from land straight into the water, which he managed without the hesitation he had first shown. He did such a good job, I added a toy to the exercise. Instinctually, Blizzard knew just what to do, swimming back to me with the toy in his mouth. That told me that his genetics were beginning to overpower his original fear of the unknown. Next, I threw the toy far out into the water, and Blizzard excitedly swam right out to retrieve it. I encouraged him with plenty of praise. By the end of the session, he was going in and out of the water and retrieving on his own. We worked on this exercise more than ten times, and in the course of a nearly thirty-

minute session, Blizzard went from being a Lab that was afraid of the water, to the water dog he was born to be.

The Nose of a Schnauzer

As a good pack leader, I want to nurture and cultivate all the special skills of the members of my pack, starting early in their puppyhood. Miniature schnauzers got their name from the word *Schnauze*, German for "snout." They were bred to hunt out rats and other vermin in barns, and suffice it to say, they have a powerful sense of smell. When Angel was only two and three months of age, I started scent-related exercises with him in the garage, using a similar but more advanced technique than I used to nurture Mr. President's nose. I would hide his food inside an object—say, a cardboard box—and let him find the food and figure out a strategy for getting it from where it was hidden. Connection and communication with me is a part of the exercise, however; when Angel would find the hiding place, he'd look to me for help and acknowledgment. I want to encourage this part of his genetics that knows to alert me, the pack leader, when he has located the object he seeks. (Mr. President, on the other hand, would simply barrel straight ahead toward the prize.) I would use silence as my training command in this case, communicating to Angel that I wanted him to solve the problem by himself. When he finally figured out how to get to the food, it would be his reward, but I would also praise him.

At four months of age, I began introducing Angel to a more difficult challenge—sniffing out and identifying something that doesn't have the obvious food reward attached. I came up with the idea for this exercise after watching a television documentary about how dogs are trained to sniff out cancer, and decided to take advantage of Angel's recent habit of sniffing out cigarette butts at the park or other locations where I've been bringing him. I wanted to go with the flow

Angel and the baby food jars

of what he'd already been doing to condition him to single out and alert me to a specific scent.

After cleaning out six baby food jars, I laid them upside down, side by side, about two inches apart, and put a cigarette butt under one of them. Then I brought Angel in and held onto him until I could see that his snout was already in searching mode and he was craning his neck toward the jars. The first time, six jars proved to be too much, as Angel became overwhelmed and distracted, so I reduced the number of the jars to four. I watched as Angel sniffed all the jars but nudged and lingered at the one containing the cigarette butt. We repeated the exercise three times, until Angel looked up at me after finding the butt, as if to ask, "So what do I get for finding this?" I rewarded him with a lot of affection, for a very long time. He got the message, "Hey, it only took me a second to find this thing, yet I get all this affection as a reward!" Right away, after the affection, he went right back to the jars, nudged the one with the cigarette butt, and looked right up at me again.

At four months of age, more than ten minutes of an exercise like this will max out any puppy's attention span. But if I continue to challenge Angel with exercises like these, who knows, someday he may be hired by the City of Los Angeles to clean up all the cigarette butts from the beach at Malibu! By nurturing Angel's nose, I both challenge him as a dog and honor his breed as a terrier.

BATTLING BREED

Sometimes you want to do the opposite of nurturing a breed-specific trait in your puppy. With certain breeds, such as bulldogs, Rottweilers, pit bulls, and other powerful breeds, you don't want to nurture the activity that the dog was originally genetically engineered to perform. For example, you don't want your adorable puppy to bring down bears or bulls or fight another dog to the death, yet you do have to be aware of his breed-related needs and find creative ways to exercise them.

Junior is a pit bull, but his energies have been channeled into other productive activities—"dog" activities such as running, retrieving, swimming (he loves to swim more than any water dog I've ever met!), and, like Daddy, helping me to rehabilitate unstable dogs with his calm-submissive energy. I started challenging my slate gray pit bull this way when he was just a puppy, bringing him on *Dog Whisperer* shoots at three and four months of age, and showing him that we don't respond to aggressive dogs, anxious dogs, or overexcited dogs. The last and most important of Junior's jobs is very unnatural for him—or for any dog—as a dog's inclination when faced with an unstable animal is to physically correct it, and if it doesn't straighten out its attitude right away, to attack it. But the mental energy and concentration it takes for Junior to do his job is incredibly fulfilling for him.

COMMUNICATING

Learning to Leave It

Being able to set and communicate boundaries is one of the most important roles that you play as your puppy's pack leader. Communication, to me, first is intent, then energy, then body language, and last, sound. Martin Deeley agrees. "The most important part of a dog's life is to learn limits and boundaries: what is acceptable and what is not acceptable. Without knowing commands, a dog may not always be able to know exactly what you want, but he will quickly get to read your body language and your actions if they are consistent and he finds himself being rewarded in some way by doing what is acceptable to that owner."

From the time Mr. President first arrived at our house at just over two months of age, he would gaze enviously at Junior and Blizzard as they tugged and cavorted with their plush and rope toys. Much more than for his "brother" Angel, his bulldog breed attracted him to their tough, competitive style of playing. When Mr. President was four months old, I allowed him to start getting involved with the "big boys" and their activities, so that I could observe and guide his reactions. I would choose a toy—a plush squirrel with some vanilla scent—and throw it into the fray so that Mr. President would be the first to get it. Even at four months, Mr. President's belligerent bulldog nature would kick right in. He would puff up his body, hunch over the toy like a football center readying for a hike, and fiercely take possession. Then he'd start wandering around with the toy in his mouth, glancing back at the older dogs as they followed him—actually seeking out a challenge.

To many owners, such a tiny bulldog trying to look tough to a huge pit bull and lanky Labrador might look incredibly cute—a subject for some funny home videos, perhaps. The danger is that if you

allow the intensity of this kind of play to escalate too much or too often, you will be nurturing the very worst side of the bulldog genes—the stubborn side that I'm usually called in to rehabilitate. That's why it's important to start supervision and setting limits early, so that your puppy is "programmed" not to play so intensely that it gets out of control. If you hear a low growl or see the dog dominating the toy with his whole body, or if he's ripping at it as if he wants to kill it, it is time for you to step in.

When Mr. President would start getting into this state, I would approach him calmly and squat down next to him. The first few times, he would put his chin on top of the toy; his eye contact with me was intense. He was challenging me, using his bulldog side. If I had food, I could always use his nose at this low level of intensity to redirect and move him away from the toy, but what I really want is to be able to say to him—simply with my assertive presence, my energy, and my firm, focused eye contact—that it's time for him to give *me* the toy, *now*. This is how another dog of higher status gets an object away from another dog in the pack—she doesn't bribe him with food, and she certainly doesn't yell "Leave it, leave it, leave it!" like a distraught human might. She'll just "demand" the object by using eye contact and energy.

An example of this occurred while I was playing with Mr. President, Blizzard, and Junior in the garage. One of our visiting cases from the show, Memphis, a formerly dog-aggressive pit bull, walked into the middle of the game and did just that—told the younger boys to drop the toy, because she wanted it now. She did it with a look, her body language, and energy, and when she moved toward the toy, they didn't hesitate to give it up to her. I know that some people have a hard time with the word *dominance* to describe this kind of behavior; for some, the words *dominance* and *submission* still seem to have negative connotations. Call it what you will. The point is, this is the strategy used across the board, throughout all social species in nature, so that most conflicts can be solved without fighting or bloodshed. There is

a natural hierarchy and a silent negotiation going on, so that those with the stronger energy are able to set the rules and regulations for those with weaker energy. The stronger dog only follows through—first with a correction, last with a fight—if the other dog doesn't agree with or abide by the rules. Among a pack of balanced dogs, this happens very infrequently.

In teaching Mr. President to give up toys to me, I want him to surrender exactly the way Junior and Blizzard did to Memphis—to just drop the toy and walk away. I could try to grab the toy away from him; I could distract him with food, then do a sneak attack by grabbing it when he wasn't looking, but this would defeat my purpose of using play as a way to connect and communicate with my puppy. I don't want to cheat him or tease him; I want him always to trust me to communicate clearly and directly with him, the way another dog would. Therefore, I wait calmly . . . one or two minutes, the first few times . . . until he sees that I am absolutely not going to give up. Voluntarily, he then gives me the toy and walks away.

Some people may want to add a command to the exercise, such as "Drop it," or "Give," or the noise I use, "Tssst," which simply means "I disagree with what you are doing right now," but it's important to remember not to repeat that command over and over while the puppy is still figuring out what you want—he may come to associate those words and sounds with *holding on to* the toy. *Instead, say the command only at the moment the puppy releases the toy; then reward him with praise, affection, or a treat.* Your dog may test your resolve, but if you practice this exercise on a regular basis, he will come to understand that you are the one who controls all the objects in your household. Toys on the floor don't necessarily mean he can play with the toys.

Setting limits in this way works as a preventive measure against creating a dog that snatches and destroys forbidden objects throughout your home. If Mr. President shows this much determination at such an early age, just imagine how much that will intensify as he

reaches adolescence and really starts pushing those boundaries! With bulldogs or other powerful-breed dogs, you must start young, do this and other "ownership" exercises repeatedly, and have a lot of patience. By having the resolve to wait him out now, in puppyhood, I avoid having a power struggle with him when he's an adult that's capable of doing much more damage. This is exactly how I raised Daddy and Junior to be polite and respectful dogs that just happen to be wearing pit bull outfits.

Communicating "Leave It" Without Words: The Concept of Owning Your Own Space

1. Claiming space means using your body, your mind, and your energy to "own" what you would like to control. You create an invisible circle of space around a person, place, or thing that belongs to you—a space that the puppy cannot enter without your permission.

2. When you want to claim space, commit 100 percent to projecting an invisible line around the space or object you do not want your dog to go near. Say to yourself, "This is my sofa," or "This is my ball." You are having a verbal conversation with yourself and a psychological/energy conversation with your puppy.

3. Never pull your hand or any object away from your puppy, and never pull your puppy away from a place, person, or object. When you pull things away from a puppy, you're either inviting her to compete for it or you're inviting her to play. This only increases the puppy's prey drive and ups her excitement level. Instead, step calmly and assertively toward the puppy, making firm eye contact, until the puppy sits back or relaxes.

4. In order to get your puppy to drop an object, you must first claim it with your mind and your energy. You cannot be hesitant, and you must be totally clear about your intention. Don't negotiate or

plead with your puppy, either mentally or verbally. Do not repeat a command such as "Leave it!" if it is not heeded the first time. Your puppy will not take it personally. She shouldn't have a problem giving you what she now knows belongs to you.

Tug-of-War

Tug-of-war seems to be a game that all puppies like to play, so what's the harm in it, right? Personally, I never play tug-of-war with my dogs. Whether it be a Chihuahua or a mastiff, I don't want any dog to think that she can engage in a contest of strength with me, even if I know I can win every time. If you have a bulldog or a powerful-breed dog, I strongly urge you not to get into this habit, no matter how cute your puppy looks as she tries to tear your favorite sock from your grasp. Dogs love these games, but they can often bring out a predatory drive in them, and this can create obsessive behavior that you may find hard to tone down in the future. Sure, you can easily win a tug-of-war with a small puppy, but by the time that dog is six months old, each time he prevails, he will grow to realize that he is able to control you. This nurtures dominant and obsessive behavior in the puppy, which is exactly the opposite of the calm-submissive dog you want to create.

You also never want a dog that thinks it can "own" something that belongs to you. In your puppy's world, *you* own everything and you give him *permission* to play with certain things. If your dog is holding an object and you want it, he has to know that he must drop it the moment you ask for it. This is the rule of law you should set down at an early age, so it will continue throughout your dog's life.

In their natural pack, however, puppies will frequently engage in this kind of game with their littermates. If you have more than one dog, supervised tug-of-war games between puppies can fulfill your

puppy's desire to engage in this kind of sport without teaching him any bad habits that will come back to haunt you later. Dogs love challenges, and competition is always challenging. Anyone who has spent any time among a group of dogs (or preschool kids, for that matter) knows that no matter how many toys are on the floor, all the dogs (or kids) will be interested in the one toy that another has in his possession.

At five, six, and seven months of age, I allowed Blizzard the Labrador to play supervised games of tug-of-war with Junior, to the benefit of both of them. For Blizzard, the benefits were enjoying the game, the sense of excitement and competition, the challenges to his mind and reflexes, the sensation of the rope toy in his mouth, and the ability to "lose gracefully"—in human terms, knowing when to "cry uncle." For Junior, the benefits were learning how to play gently like a Lab and not at the full intensity of a pit bull—though at one and a half years of age, Junior was already far more "dog" than "pit bull." Junior also gained the wisdom that comes from teaching rules, boundaries, and limitations to a younger member of the pack. I always intercede in any dog-dog tug-of-war games, making sure everyone knows that the minute I arrive, the toy is surrendered to me. That way I always have the ability to stop or start a play session in a split second if I sense it is getting out of hand.

CONDITIONING

Training and Commands

The connection and communication skills we develop with our puppies through structured walks, setting boundaries, and playing games lay a solid foundation for what is called conditioning, or dog training. In this book I am more concerned with your puppy's overall psycho-

logical balance, with preventing her from developing issues, and with her understanding of rules, boundaries, and limits than I am with her ability to answer to the words *come, heel, sit,* or *stay.* I have raised all my dogs by using energy, body language, touch, or very simple sounds, in that order. One advantage to the "less sound is more" approach that I apply is that it automatically limits overexcitement. Many people confuse a dog's "excitement" with her "happiness," but the truth is, if a puppy is in a hyperactive, overstimulated state to begin with, she will have a much harder time retaining anything you are trying to teach her. That's why too much excited "Good boy, that's a good boy!" praise from a trainer can actually be a less effective reward than the quiet reinforcement of happiness and approval. The other advantage of being quiet is that I am communicating with my dogs in a way that is much closer to the way they communicate with one another. I am always able to recognize the subtle signals they are sending me, and I respond by telling them with energy and body language, "I hear what you are saying" and either "I agree" or "I don't agree" with it. When we humanize our dogs, we tend to miss these important signals they are sending us every minute of every day. They are trying to communicate with us all the time, but too often we are not listening. When a dog feels you are not listening to her, she is not going to listen to you. By being aware of and responding to all the tiny, seemingly insignificant cues your puppy is sending you, you are opening up the door to a great possibility—the possibility of having a really intimate relationship with her.

Still, most people want to be sure that their puppy can answer to some commands, or at least to sounds. After all, your dog is not always looking at you. As she grows, she may range far away from you, to the other side of the yard or the dog park. She can't sense your energy or read your body language if you aren't nearby, so you will have to use sound in order to communicate what you want. I like to begin with two simple sounds—one to signify a behavior I like (for me, it's

usually a "kissing" sound), and the other to call attention to a behavior I don't agree with (my trademark "Tssst!"). I add the puppy's name as a "come" command later on. Some people use a clap or a whistle as a "come" command. Others prefer to use human language.

As Florida dog trainer Martin Deeley says,

To dogs, words are noises. The words do not have to be specific words. If you choose to get your dog to sit to the word *Christmas*, then "Christmas" becomes the cue for the dog to sit. Any words we use with dogs must come easily to the tongue and we must be consistent in their use for specific actions required. Also it is better to use one word rather than a sentence or even two words because often the dog will hear only the last word. That is why if we wish to use his name, we say, "Ben," to catch his attention. Then a second later, "Sit." Not "Sit, Ben." If we put the name last with every command, all he hears is his name and really that means nothing.

How early should you begin conditioning your puppy to commands? The Grogans were offered some questionable advice by friends who watched the couple's still small but rapidly growing Labrador puppy, Marley, drag them up and down the pedestrian path of Florida's Intercoastal Waterway. "Our friends who were veteran dog owners told us not to rush the obedience regimen. 'It's too early,' one of them advised. 'Enjoy his puppyhood while you can. It'll be gone soon enough, and then you can get serious about training him.' "

If you have read this far into this book, you will immediately recognize the illogic of that statement. Can you imagine saying of a six- to ten-year-old child, "Let him enjoy his childhood; don't worry about teaching him to read and write until after he's a teenager"? Puppyhood—birth to eight months—is the most intense, compressed period of growth your dog will experience, both physically and men-

tally. Between eight and sixteen weeks, your dog's brain is at its peak rate of growth. The results of many behavior studies and EEG measurements demonstrate that eight-week-old puppies function at nearly an adult level in terms of learning ability. However, as puppies mature—in fact, by about sixteen weeks[1]—the ease with which they learn noticeably begins to decline. That's why, when you start early by conditioning your puppy to respect limits, take on new challenges in the form of games or tasks, as well as to respond to signals or verbal commands, you are actually helping the puppy's brain develop to its fullest potential.

"Training is not repressing," says my colleague and veteran Hollywood animal trainer Clint Rowe. "It's developing and shaping an animal's awareness and access to its brain. I think it develops an animal's *self-awareness* because, to learn willingly, they have to be aware of their thoughts and associations and then focus their awareness. The most important thing when training is to be consistent and have a goal in mind. If you don't have a goal for your training, then the animal won't either."

If you have first developed a connection with your puppy, then she will automatically want to please you. Martin Deeley lists enjoyment of the training session as the number one motivator for a pup.

Having fun and being helped clearly and concisely to do what is expected, rewarded with a smile and a happy face. A puppy does not come into this life wanting to be a leader. She looks for leadership and guidance, she looks for a kind yet firm hand that shows her the right ways to do things and rewards her with a nice touch, a smile, an acceptance into the pack. She even expects reprimand—firm but not harsh—and learns from it. Motivation to do an action or behavior is not always prompted by a potential reward but may also come about by a wish to avoid danger, conflict, and what we may call a nonreward.

Even learning her limitations is actually satisfying to a puppy, because it's in her program to internalize rules within a social structure. A peaceful life in a wild canid pack depends upon every member's learning and respecting the group's restrictions and boundaries. A happy puppy is a puppy who clearly understands what behaviors will best ensure approval by the rest of the pack.

SILENT TRAINING

Angel Learns the "Down"

Angel's blue blood—his lineage as the scion of prize-winning show dogs—has already given him a genetic head start in the obedience process. Miniature schnauzers are often regarded as among the most "trainable" of dog breeds. I easily taught Angel how to sit by using a one-finger hand signal almost as soon as he returned home with me. Sitting down is an automatic response for a puppy when he is undecided about what to do, so it took me only a few days of consistently rewarding (giving a treat at first, then just praising) Angel's correct response to my raised finger before he understood it completely. This is exactly how I have conditioned Daddy, Junior, and all the other dogs I have raised to sit on command. By four months of age, his overnight visit with Melissa proved that he had internalized this behavior, as she was easily able to ask him with her finger to sit, and was instantly able to set spatial boundaries using one hand. This is another advantage of early "silent" command training—it is easily transferable to another human who might be caring for your dog.

The "down" is a little more complicated response for puppies to learn, because lying down can feel unnatural to them if they aren't tired. When Angel was just under four months of age, I brought him to the Dog Psychology Center to begin conditioning him to lie down

on command. The gesture I wanted him to learn was a finger raised in the air, then lowered, meaning he was to do the same movement with his body.

My only tools were some training treats and three long folding tables, set up end to end. Setting up a "runway" of tables is a wonderful way to work with a puppy, because you can maintain eye contact with a small dog without having to bend over and strain your back. It also forces the puppy to stay focused on you, because you are his only way back to the ground and because he can't wander off the tables if he becomes bored or distracted. It's important that you use the "teamwork" approach to getting the puppy up on the table; use either a ramp or steps and lead him forward with scent or a treat (palmed behind your hand so he won't grab at it but must sniff or lick) or, as I did with Angel, lift him by the scruff of his neck, putting only his front legs on the table so that he can figure out how to get his back legs up by himself. This keeps your puppy an active, willing participant in the exercise.

To begin the session, I chose one end of the table and engaged Angel's nose with a treat in my hand. I let him smell the treat but not have it, then I squatted down, holding it in my hand just below the table surface. I made eye contact with him, and slowly moved my finger from a high to a low position. Then I waited for him to figure it out. I could easily have pushed his rear down to create a lying position, then given him the reward, as a way to illustrate what I wanted. This is the "rush" method that some training facilities promising "instant" results for your dog will use, and there's no saying that it doesn't work. But it is my belief that if the dog comes up with the strategy on his own, it imprints on his mind in a deeper way and he remembers it more profoundly. It also raises his self-esteem because I have given him a challenge and he has come up with a solution by himself. This will empower him to try and solve any other problems I give him.

Once again, I made eye contact with Angel and then asked him to

watch my hand as I mimed the motion of lying down. He sat and yawned—as I've mentioned, a yawn is often a sign that a puppy is frustrated, mentally taxed, or working something out. I let him lick my hand but did not give the treat. I was silent and patient. Finally, Angel's lightbulb moment arrived—he lay down and I gave him the treat. To me it felt like forever, but when I looked at my watch, it had taken only just over four minutes for him to get it!

Next, I walked to the far end of the table to repeat the same routine. This time, it took him just a little over forty seconds to lie down and earn the treat! I decided to push the envelope and put him through the exercise a third time, but after about a minute, he began to get distracted and wandered to the other end of the table. This is typical for puppies—ten minutes of focused training is a very long time for them. "In the beginning," says Clint Rowe, "keep training sessions from one minute to five minutes long. Puppies get mentally tired. They need to rest afterward. In my thirty years of training experience—and there's no empirical data I can come up with for this—but during resting, I swear, connections between the brain cells are actually growing and new connections are being built." I could recognize Angel's mental exhaustion in his more frequent yawning. What he was communicating that day was "Right now, I can only give you this behavior twice." This told me I could work with him on it again twice the next day, then add one more time the day after that, and so on and so on, but at that moment, I couldn't end the exercise by letting him fail, because that would be the lesson he would remember. We have to overcome our own impatience and always wait for our puppies to finish with success.

To give Angel his big finish, I made my "kissing" sound, which immediately called him back to my side of the table. When he arrived, I rewarded him with a treat for answering to my call. Then we took one more stab at the down. Angel sat in front of me, yawning and sighing at first—he was one tired, bored puppy at that point. But exactly one

minute and ten seconds later, he completed the behavior. I not only rewarded him with the treat, I gave him an overabundance of affection. The little trouper deserved it!

This training session, as short and sweet as it was, turned out to be very meaningful. We created the blueprint of the motion for the down, plus we reinforced commands he already knew—that moving my finger forward means "Sit down," that moving my finger to the side means "Follow me," that my "kiss" sound means "Come." That's four lessons on one table, in one ten-minute session. If a puppy takes off running after a session is over, you know you've pushed too hard. I knew I had been successful and not overworked him when Angel gravitated right back to me after I took him off the table. The tables now have a positive association for him. "This is the place where I get to spend focused time with my human, where my mind gets challenged, and where I get delicious treats."

METHODS OF TRAINING

While setting limits for a puppy often involves some sort of correction—whether through energy, sound, spatial body language, or a touch—training or conditioning needs consistent reinforcement to keep the dog enjoying the behavior it's performing. Clint Rowe has taught animals from dogs to wolf hybrids to bears to perform all kinds of conditioned behavior for movies, using a wide range of different tools, depending on the animal. When Clint taught Wilshire, an eight-week-old Dalmatian puppy adopted by a Los Angeles firehouse, the behavioral combination of "stop, drop, and roll," he started by rewarding with treats, using a clicker as a signal that Wilshire had successfully completed his task. Eventually, the treats get phased out, and the sound of the clicker becomes the reward. "A clicker is just a cue to them that what they've done is correct and a reward is coming. Saying

'Good' acts as the same thing, or even not saying anything and not cueing them can act as that. Remember, they are artists at watching your body language—they know when you are happy. What eventually happens is, the state of mind is shaped by the reward and doing the behavior eventually becomes part of the reward."

There are many different approaches to training, so do your research, use your best judgment, and, most important of all, know your puppy. Several excellent books on puppy training are listed in the appendix. "What works best is a good trainer using the right tools to gain the right behaviors on the dog he is training at that time," Martin Deeley insists. "No matter what the tool or the approach, the aim is always to have a well-behaved dog that responds to commands willingly and understands limits and boundaries in everyday life. The tools can change depending upon the dog, the trainer, the situation, the owner, the task being taught, and the complexity of the task, so the best way is the one that works."

TWELVE TIPS FOR SUCCESSFUL CONDITIONING

1. Remember that everything you do or say around your puppy is "training."
2. Start shaping your puppy's desired behaviors as soon as you bring her home.
3. Set a clear goal for what you want from your puppy and stick to it.
4. Remain consistent in the commands, signals, or body language you use.
5. Keep sessions short and sweet and learn to recognize when your puppy is overtaxed.
6. Leave your puppy wanting more!

7. Master the art of patience and waiting; your puppy won't learn from a frustrated leader.

8. Be a "partner" in your puppy's learning; let her figure out solutions on her own whenever possible.

9. Don't overstimulate your puppy with excited outcries or too many treats; she may lose the lesson in the confusion.

10. Find the rewards that work for your puppy.

11. Always end a session with a success.

12. Keep training sessions fun and joyful for both of you!

7

THE SOCIAL PUPPY

Getting Along with Both Dogs and Humans

*Mr. President and Cesar socializing with the staff of
Highland Park Animal Hospital*

Just the other day, I popped into a small pet store to pick up some bully sticks for the puppies, when I ran smack into what was billed as a "puppy class," intended for the purpose of socializing young dogs. There were eight or ten people there, and each of them had a puppy. There were a Siberian husky, a Chihuahua, a Lhasa apso, a golden retriever, a Jack Russell, and a few other puppies of breeds that I don't recall. The owners were gathered around in a circle, and the puppies

were just going wild in the middle. There was no guidance whatso-ever. The puppies were all different ages, different levels of energy, and all over the map in terms of social skills. To put it simply, it was chaos. I watched the Chihuahua—isn't it always the Chihuahua?—taking over the class, dominating and then attacking the Siberian husky puppy. It wasn't play anymore, it was escalating into an actual fight. The teacher cried out in a teasing, high-pitched voice, "No, no no! We don't do that in class!" Then, after the owner of the Chihuahua had pulled her puppy away, the teacher said, "Now let's all give our dogs a cookie." I wanted to cry out, "What for? What are you rewarding them for?"

Fortunately, I reminded myself that I was at the store as a customer, not as the Dog Whisperer. I bit my tongue, paid for my bully sticks, and retreated back to the safety of my car, where I took a deep breath and thought long and hard about the meaning of the term *puppy class*. To me, a puppy class should be about reinforcing manners, fostering calm-submissive energy, and teaching proper social behavior. My dream puppy class would mirror the kind of education a puppy would get in a natural pack, where there'd be a wise old senior dog like Daddy, an adult dog—maybe a mother dog with great caretaking skills—and a higher-energy, adolescent dog like Junior. The adult dogs would all be balanced and experienced, show the puppies limits, and offer them good role models to emulate. There would be a few puppies, of course, and at least one experienced human to supervise. That's the kind of puppy class I would like to offer at the new Dog Psy-chology Center, a class in which puppies can practice social behavior with their peers but be overseen by older, wiser dogs—as well as re-sponsible human pack leaders.

Dogs are among the most social of all animals. That's one of the things they have most in common with humans, and it's one of the reasons our two species have become so bonded over the past tens of

thousands of years. You may have trained your puppy to sit, stay, come, heel, get the paper, carry your slippers, or turn out the light before barking "Good night," but if he doesn't get along well socially with humans or other dogs, you haven't got a balanced puppy. And if your puppy isn't balanced, he won't grow up to be a dog that gets to experience all the joys and adventures of life.

INTRODUCING PUPPIES TO PEOPLE

Socializing your puppy to people should begin from the first moment you arrive at your home. All the members of your family, including all children, need to understand how to greet the puppy, and how to share calm-assertive energy. You need to explain to even your smallest children that your new puppy is not a toy but a living being, and that in order to acclimate him to his new home, they will need to refrain from showering him with all the affection and excitement they surely must be feeling, at least at the very beginning. Everyone in your home, from the youngest child to the oldest grandparent, needs to be educated in and committed to the rule of *no touch, no talk, no eye contact.* When the puppy arrives, children should not be crowding around it to pet and play with it. Instead, they should quietly allow the puppy to smell them, then let the primary caretaker put the puppy in its safe place or crate.

"The new pup needs to associate entering your home with calmness, not excitement. He may be stressed and not feeling well due to the change in environment and from the car ride," advises Diana Foster. "He doesn't need to be petted at this point. He needs to be left alone to adjust at his own pace. You will have this dog for many years, and there will be plenty of time to pet him and be with him once he has adjusted to his environment, has bonded to you, and respects you

as leader. All these things take time and there is no need to rush it." But even after thirty years of success in training and breeding prize German shepherds with calm, even temperaments, Diana still finds that new puppy owners take offense at this counsel.

> I have kids crying when I'm saying this. "Oh, she's so mean. We can't play with the puppy." One guy was in my face, saying, "You guys are out of your minds! If you think that I'm going to tell a nine-year-old girl not to touch this dog, you guys are nuts! I thought I was getting a well-bred dog. I didn't think I had to do all this work." People don't think about what is the best thing for the dog. That's why the shelters are packed. People create a dog that's out of control, then they don't want it anymore.

It's not easy for a child to hold back from playing with a new puppy, which is why parents need to be educated in order to supervise. Puppies coming into a new home are often in their reticent stage, as well as naturally unsure about the new situation. Children coming on too strong to a timid or insecure puppy can intimidate him, and such affronts, if repeated, can create a dog that is either too shy or fearful or, worse, fearfully aggressive. This can lead to a bite, and the tendency is to blame the puppy for being aggressive. On the other hand, an outgoing, active puppy may tempt children to play too vigorously, raising the puppy's level of excitement to an intensity that may be hard to temper as he grows bigger and bigger. "The biggest problem we have is kids on the floor, with roughnecking, tug-of-war, play-biting, and scratching, and the dog gets too rough," says Diana. "It's all about prevention. And the kids, it's so hard nowadays because parents tend to spoil these kids. They let them do whatever they want. Then the dog gets big and out of control and starts hurting the kids. Now the family doesn't want him anymore, because he's not cute and fun; he's doing damage."

TIPS FOR CHILDREN AND PUPPIES

- Don't introduce an excited child to a puppy. Teach your kids early about the concept of calm-assertive energy.
- Teach children how to greet a dog properly, by using the no touch, no talk, no eye contact rule until the dog signals that it wants to have more interaction.
- When the puppy first arrives, make sure the children limit their engagement with it for the first few days, and that they always interact in a calm, quiet manner.
- Educate your kids about leadership, and show them how to block a puppy's excitement if he begins to play too rough. It may seem cute in a tiny puppy, but it could become dangerous as the dog grows up.
- Don't ever let a child tease a puppy.
- Discourage rough games such as wrestling, tug-of-war, keep-away, and play biting, and encourage your children to master the walk and to engage in challenging activities such as fetch, swimming, and agility games.
- Teach children that all games with a puppy need to have a be-ginning and an end.

INTRODUCING A PUPPY TO A BABY

The best strategy for preparing a puppy to meet a baby is by getting the puppy used to the baby's scent, using a towel or T-shirt. Then take the puppy for a walk beside or behind you while you push the baby's stroller up front. As always, the walk is the best way to create any kind of bond with a dog. But often, circumstances bring puppies and babies together face-to-face. Learning how to introduce your

puppy to a baby is an important step toward socializing him to be polite and respectful of all children.

To demonstrate how to introduce a puppy to an infant or very young child, I asked *Dog Whisperer* field producer Todd Henderson to lend me his wife, Lindsey, a vet tech and experienced dog owner, and their new son, Hunter, just three months old. The wonderful thing about both a puppy and a baby is that each starts with the advantage of not having any issues. Our job is to help them to grow together with that same mentality.

To begin the exercise, Lindsey sat on the floor of my family room with Hunter in her lap. The baby had just eaten and was in a beautifully calm-submissive state. To this peaceful tableau I added five-month-old Mr. President, who came in with a totally different energy—a classic, pushy, bulldog way of being. At first, Mr. President got excited by the baby and ran right up to him, putting his feet on Lindsey's leg and starting to lick Hunter's face. Some parents might think, "Oh how cute," but Lindsey knew better—that kind of approach is too much, for both puppy and baby. With a firm touch, Lindsey made Mr. President step back, creating an invisible boundary around Hunter's space. Once he stepped back, however, Mr. President became very uncertain about Hunter. He growled, then started to bark excitedly. In translation, Mr. President was expressing his uncertainty, fear, or mistrust of the baby—the baby was a new scent for him, something he didn't understand. His bark was also an expression of alert—since we don't have babies in my house on a regular basis, Mr. President was alerting his pack that "something new is in the house!" We needed to help Mr. President lose that uncertainty, because that could become aggression toward this baby or toward babies and children in general.

I often get letters and e-mails describing real-life situations similar to our little experiment with Lindsey and Hunter. People write, "My puppy started growling at my baby; what do I do?" Often when this

happens, people become afraid and react very emotionally. They start having negative feelings about the dog and creating bad energy. At this point, owners need to stay absolutely neutral and try to understand where the dog is coming from.

What I did in our exercise was to address the barking and growling immediately, with the calm-assertive sound "Tssst," which tells Mr. President that I don't agree with his state of mind. He turned away from Hunter, but he relaxed. This was progress, from fight (aggressively confronting the baby and growling), to flight (running away from the baby), to avoidance (being near the baby but ignoring him). Finally, I got the reaction I was seeking—submission—when Mr. President plopped down and stretched out right in front of the baby. Still, I maintained an invisible boundary between him and Hunter. This is so important to teach puppies. All dogs must understand the "bubble of respect" that surrounds all human babies.

Next I gave Lindsey some chicken to hold in her hand. Mr. President never met a piece of chicken he didn't like. Eating the chicken just outside the baby's "bubble" but next to him created a different state of mind in Mr. President, as well as a pleasant association with the baby.

But Mr. President's state of mind isn't the only thing we need to pay attention to here. Hunter had maintained a mellow, laid-back energy since the beginning of the exercise. He lives among three dogs, so this wasn't a completely new experience for him. And Lindsey, whose energy Hunter is going to mimic, remained totally calm and relaxed. As long as we don't change the baby's state of mind, we can always influence the puppy. If we panic or become anxious, then the baby will pick up on our energy and get scared, too. Never introduce any dog to a baby who is upset or to a mother who is nervous or worried. Always bring the dog to the child only when the dog is calm and submissive, not tired, cranky, or overexcited. Dogs are easier to influence than humans, and once again, remember that a four-month-old puppy is maturing much, much faster than a three-month-old baby.

Angel respectfully sniffs Baby Hunter

As a final addition to the exercise, I took out Mr. President and brought in Angel, who was the same age as his bulldog "brother" and had the same lack of experience around babies. Angel's reaction was ideal. When confronted with the novelty of Hunter, Angel first looked to me, to get his bearings. Then he became curious about the baby and leaned forward toward Lindsey and Hunter to smell them. When he got a little too close, Lindsey gently blocked him, and Angel got the message immediately, opening up more distance with his body, just stretching his neck out a little more. His sniffing was delicate, respectful, polite. After getting his fill of the new scent, Angel stepped back and gave mother and baby their space. I rewarded his alert but relaxed state with copious petting and affection. He picked up right away on Hunter's gentle energy and mirrored it back, in a very nurturing, respectful way.

MEETING NEW PEOPLE

From the time he was three months of age, I was taking Junior out with me, Daddy, and the crew on *Dog Whisperer* cases. Since I wanted Junior to follow in Daddy's footsteps, it was important to me that he become comfortable with as many new types of dogs—as well as people—as possible. During his most formative months, Junior met various dogs with aggressive, fearful, obsessive, and overexcited energies, and learned to stay calm in spite of them. He also met a few people whose issues were as challenging as those of their dogs. But he always had me to supervise both his behavior and the reactions of the various humans that wandered in and out of his life.

If a human got too excited over Junior's cuteness and started invading his space, I'd remind them of the no touch, no talk, no eye contact rule I enforce whenever one of my dogs meets a new person. If the new person had an all too common "Oh my God, is that a pit bull?" reaction, I'd counsel them on how to relax and share a better energy. Then I'd let Junior do the sniffing himself, and signal to me that he was comfortable with the person, before I'd allow their relationship to progress. *Our puppies are counting on us to keep them safe and to listen to them when they tell us that they need a new human to back off a little during a first encounter.* Of course, Junior always had Daddy's behavior to emulate. And Daddy is so confident, he's comfortable with just about anyone.

DANGEROUSLY ADORABLE

"One thing about Angel—his cuteness is definitely a liability," Melissa Peltier said to me, reporting back from her overnight visit with my blue-blooded miniature schnauzer. She and her husband, John Gray, had taken Angel with them to dinner at a busy outdoor café—his first

extended experience in such a hectic public setting. The little guy did fantastically, drinking water from a dish under the table and sitting back—alert but still relaxed—to watch all the interesting goings-on around him. The problem was, Angel is such a good-looking dog, every other passerby seemed insistent upon petting him. Melissa explained,

We couldn't eat our dinner in peace, because people were just going gaga over him. "Oh my God, that is the cutest puppy!" "Can I pet him?" With the adults, they would talk to me first. And he would get a chance to observe them and their energy and smell them while we were conversing. If I said it was okay to approach him, if they did it gently, he was fine, and even a little curious about them. But one guy came by with two kids, about eight and ten years old, and while the dad was talking to me, the kids just charged in and reached toward Angel to pet him. And I could see him getting overwhelmed. There was a complete change in his whole body language—he tensed up and started to shrink into himself. So I said, "He's still a little shy; he's just a puppy. I think that's enough for him." I was beating myself up afterward because I thought I should've known that ahead of time and warned the kids not to approach him like that. Because they invaded his space. And I could just see how, if an owner let that happen to a sensitive puppy like Angel too many times and didn't pay attention to his communication, that dog might grow up to become fearful or even a fear biter. That is definitely a danger when a puppy is as cute as Angel.

READ YOUR PUPPY'S ENERGY

Melissa and her husband learned firsthand another lesson about how adults as well as children need to learn to read a puppy's energy and

body language before they attempt a more personal relationship with him. Melissa's husband, John, is a kind, gentle man, but he's also a fairly well-built guy who exudes the natural leadership energy that comes from being a successful writer-director of movies and television. Angel seemed comfortable with John right away; in fact, he responded to John as a calm-assertive leader much more quickly than he did to Melissa. But once they got back to their apartment for the evening, John wanted to roughhouse with Angel the way he had played with his late, much-beloved terrier mix, Bob. John got down on the floor in the canine play-bow posture, inviting Angel to mix it up with him. Angel stiffened and backed away a little. While John's body language was playful, Angel was reading his very dominant, male energy and didn't know whether or not to interpret the invitation as purely recreational or as a challenge.

I explained to Melissa that John's behavior, though good-natured, made him claim a lot of space. His invitation became like a tsunami instead of just a little wave. Angel has been taught by the adult dogs around him—especially his adolescent "big brother," Junior—that he is always to be respectful of his superiors. He is to keep his head low and go under, not over, until he knows he has been accepted. Not being familiar with John, Angel's first response was the correct one based on what he had learned in his pack—to be polite and respectful with older, more dominant dogs. John seemed a little let down that Angel didn't take him up on his offer right away, and Angel picked up on that disappointment, becoming even more tentative because of it—remember, puppies only want to please pack leaders! Melissa instructed her husband to lie on his back and let Angel come to him. John complied, but when Angel got closer and started to relax, John reached over and grabbed him, eager to begin the game. Once again, Angel backed away.

"John was trying to do too much too soon with Angel," I explained to Melissa, after she related her tale of the visit. "He should have waited

and let Angel come and gently lie on top of him and become familiar with him in that way. If John had waited in that position, instead of going into the playful position—which is almost like pouncing—he would have allowed Angel to explore him, head to foot." What Angel was trying to say to John was, "I mean you no harm," "I respect your space." If Angel had sensed that John got his message and was also respecting Angel's space back, he would have felt free to engage in play with him.

The irony, of course, was that Angel was all too eager to play with Melissa, jumping on her leg and trying to "play-dominate" her; so much so that she had to keep turning around and disagreeing with him by asking him to sit back and relax. I see this dynamic all the time in families where the male is very male and the female is very female. The puppy just gravitates to the female, which the female may interpret as "he likes me more" when, really, he is seeing her more as a peer than a pack leader. Then the puppy grows up to push the limits around the female but always behaves obediently around the male. This occurs with kids, too. In families like the Barneses, the genders are reversed. Blizzard takes advantage of eleven-year-old Christian's softer energy, while he gives space and respect to fourteen-year-old Sabrina's more assertive demeanor. If Melissa and John were to spend more time with Angel, the solution would be for the two of them to try to meet in the middle. John would hold back a little, and Melissa would be a little more assertive. That way, Angel would see them both as pack leaders; he would be a little less threatened by John's unintentionally dominating presence and wouldn't feel he could take advantage of Melissa.

"Angel doesn't care how many books about dogs you've helped me write," I reminded Melissa. "He only cares about the energy you share with him in that very moment."

SOCIALIZING WITH OTHER DOGS

The puppies in this book—Angel, Mr. President, Blizzard, and Junior—have all had great advantages in life. They've not only been cared for by a human who understands dogs, they've been raised by and around other balanced dogs, in an environment that's as close to a dog's natural style of life as possible. Angel was the shyest of his littermates, but in spending time in the pack, he automatically gained confidence every single day. In fact, he grew to be so confident that sometimes he'd act too cocky around more dominant pack members. Then Junior and whatever adult dog happened to be around at the time would discipline him quickly, reminding him not to get too big for his britches. In the case of Mr. President, if he hadn't been raised among dogs, he might have turned out to be an overconfident, blustery bulldog—perhaps a magnet for conflicts or even fights.

Visitors to my house often comment on how intelligent all the puppies seem and how quickly they seem to learn things. I tell them it's because the pack and I have raised them in such a way that their natural method of social learning has been nurtured, not damaged. Too many times, when puppies grow up without the contact of other dogs, they lose their inborn common sense; they become rusty at speaking their natural language. Imagine moving to a foreign country where you never really learn the language—and then returning to your homeland having forgotten most of your native tongue. You would certainly be very uncomfortable in social situations on either shore. When we raise puppies without other dogs around, it's vital that we take extra steps to socialize them early so they will always be able to read the signals and understand the important etiquette of their own species.

SOCIALIZATION AND IMMUNITY

Once again, owners' worries about a puppy's immunity can thwart the dog's social education. Some paranoid owners actually choose to keep their puppy away from other dogs until he is six months old! By isolating a puppy during those crucial eight to sixteen weeks, when his immunity is still developing but his brain is rapidly growing, we run the risk of creating a puppy that will be antisocial with his own kind. This is certainly not the time to bring your puppy to a dog park, but there are several ways you can support the socialization process while still keeping your puppy safe.

- Invite a friend's healthy, vaccinated, *balanced* older dog to interact with your puppy at your house. If you are still concerned about immunity, make sure the dog hasn't just come from the dog park and that it has clean feet and a clean face when it plays with your puppy.
- If the puppy or the adult dog seems reticent at first, pick up your puppy by his scruff and present him to the dog, rear first, the way I introduced Blizzard to the pack at the Dog Psychology Center (see Chapter 1). Let the adult dog sniff the puppy until he becomes relaxed and comfortable around him.
- Set a play date with a healthy puppy of the same age, with the same level of immunity. If this goes well, add another puppy and an adult dog or two to the mix. This way, you create your own "minipack" or dog park, in your home or yard. The adult dogs will serve as "monitors" and role models for the puppy's social behavior, although you must still retain your own calm-assertive energy and supervise the visit.
- Sign your puppy up for a *real* puppy class, such as the one offered by Diana Foster at the Thinschmidt kennels. Such classes are not

free-for-alls, but rather are supervised and taught by experienced professionals, and all animals are prescreened for health problems.

Of course, the owner's energy and response at the time of the socialization encounter will have a huge impact on how the puppy re-
acts to the other dogs. Socialization presented *Dog Whisperer*
cameraman Chris Komives with his first real stumbling block in raising Eliza.

The first dogs she met were two golden retriever puppies that my
neighbor brought home around the same time as Eliza. They
were all at the same place in their inoculations, so we introduced
them to each other. Eliza was hesitant at first, so I encouraged
her to meet them. In my desire to help her overcome her anxiety,
I encouraged her to play too excitedly with these puppies. As
Eliza got older, she started to dominate them and became territorial about their yard—more so than our house! So I had let her
go too far in the other direction. I had to claim the yard and supervise their play. With the help of my neighbor, I'd make them
stop playing and be calm together before resuming play. They
play together successfully to this day.

After Eliza's last set of shots, I invited Chris to bring Eliza with him
to the center on a shoot day, so I could supervise her introduction to
the pack. I handled the introduction. At first Eliza was very anxious
and fled to a corner. Chris wanted to step in, but I ordered him to ignore his puppy; I didn't want him enabling her insecurity. Eventually a
member of the pack sauntered over, sniffed her, and invited her in. By
the end of the day, Eliza was running with the pack and playing with
Junior.

"Encouraged by how well she did with the pack," Chris told me

later, "I took her to the dog park the very next day. Unfortunately, the dogs there were not balanced, and sensing her weakness, they rushed her. She ran away, scared, to the first human she could find. After that, she overcompensated by becoming much more forward in approaching dogs." The next time Eliza came to the center, I could see that she had become much too excited around other dogs. Chris, in his desire to encourage Eliza's sociability and to help her get over her shyness, had let other dogs represent too much excitement to her. I showed Chris how to wait for her to be calm first before I allowed her to enter the yard. By taking the time to balance her energy before she greeted the pack, Eliza was able to be her naturally exuberant self, and she played contentedly with the pack for the rest of the day.

INTRODUCING PUPPY TO THE DOG PARK

Just because your puppy has great social skills within his own pack of humans or dogs doesn't necessarily mean he knows how to interact with strange dogs. It's important that puppies learn how their social skills will translate to dogs outside their home pack. As soon as their vaccination protocol was finished, I brought Angel and Mr. President to Central Park in Santa Clarita, to supervise each of them in their first official dog park experience. I decided to begin with Angel this time. There was still dew on the grass, but the spring sun already blazed down on us as we approached the fenced off-leash area. There were only a handful of dogs and their owners in the park—perfect for a nonthreatening introduction.

I unlatched the gate to the area of the park designated for smaller dogs, happy that Central Park blocks off separate spaces for smaller and larger breeds. If you bring a puppy into an area where there are too many large dogs playing, he may feel intimidated right away. We don't want our puppies to get a negative first impression of anything

during this crucial stage of their lives. I could feel Angel's tiny heart beating faster as I gently set him down inside the outer gate and unfastened his leash. He was feeling safe with me but starting to be a little unsure around the smell of strange dogs. It's important to recognize these physical symptoms in our puppies—they give us our first clues as to what to watch out for in their behavior.

It's also vital that the moment you let your puppy inside the dog park, you check your *own* energy. If you are tense or distracted or, like Chris Komives, overly worried about managing your puppy's experience, the puppy will sense it and react accordingly. Remain calm and neutral, communicating to your puppy that whatever happens, you will come up with the right solution. I sat down on a bench at the side of the park and happily observed my miniature schnauzer experience this new adventure.

Two beagles came running up to greet Angel as he entered the park. I was impressed at how polite and quiet the beagles were; they were the perfect ambassadors. Angel was curious but still hesitant around the two older dogs, sniffing them but not asking them to engage in play. The fact that he was so respectful in this new situation reaffirmed to me how much Angel understands manners and social limits. He was saying, "I'm not 100 percent sure about this, but I am curious about it." Perfect! However, he did wander over to the side of the park, lift his leg, and mark—a very mature gesture for a four-month-old.

A tiny white dog that looked like a toy poodle mix wandered over toward Angel and the two sniffed each other cautiously. "I'm not sure about you," the white dog was saying. Angel's response was "I'm not sure about you, either!" After the first round of introductions, Angel made an invitation to play, but the offer seemed a little too dominant for the white dog, which backed away. Would I have to intervene? It turned out that the little white dog could take care of himself. He ran away, communicating to Angel, "I don't want to play with you because you're a little too harsh for me." But Angel did well in that he didn't try

to force the issue. He took no for an answer. That's great canine etiquette. Instead, he came back to me for reassurance. I gave him a treat
for returning, letting him feel "It's okay, whenever someone doesn't
want to play with me, I can always come back to my owner and get re-
inforcements."

We didn't spend more than fifteen minutes inside the dog park for
this first visit. That's plenty of exposure for a four-month-old puppy.
But we left on a happy note—my little Angel proved he has the perfect
manners for many more successful dog park visits.

Next it was Mr. President's turn. As soon as we got inside the outer
gate, the blustery little guy ran smack up against the fence to meet the
beagle greeters, using his eyes, not his nose, and starting to get a little
overexcited by puffing up his chest in that typical bulldog way. This is
an example of how a bulldog's biology and body language can accidentally send a challenging message to other dogs, even if he doesn't
intend to be threatening. This isn't a good way to enter a new social situation, so I knew I'd have to be a little more vigilant with him than I
was with Angel. I waited until Mr. P. had relaxed a little, then let him
inside the park.

Mr. President took off running, hurrying after the same little white
dog that had just rejected Angel. His ears were back, signaling a submissive energy, but again the approach was very forceful, very bulldog. The little white dog turned around and gave a warning snap—he
really didn't want to play with him. I was proud of Mr. President because, just like Angel, he got the message right away and respected it.
Unfazed, he then trotted off to investigate the beagles. He greeted
them in a very polite manner, and they engaged with him informally.
They seemed to feel more comfortable inviting Mr. President to play,
probably because he was less mature at this point, not lifting his leg
yet, and giving the beagles the feeling that they could control the play
more. I heard them howl for the first time, but it was a playful howl. I
liked the fact that Mr. President was experiencing this, because we

don't have beagles at home. He was being educated in the fact that a hound's howl doesn't mean anything threatening; it is just how they express themselves. This is why it's important to introduce your puppy to all kinds of breeds of dogs. It's like introducing your child to many different nationalities of children—they become more tolerant and understand that just because individuals express themselves differently, it doesn't make them a threat.

Mr. President returned to me after playing with the beagles, and after I engaged his nose again, I gave him a treat. I was reinforcing both his willingness to experience this new adventure and his response in staying connected with me. As we left the park, I reflected that the day couldn't have gone better. As different as Angel and Mr. President are as breeds, they both came to a new social situation sharing the same playful yet active-submissive energy.

TIPS FOR INTRODUCING PUPPY TO THE DOG PARK

- Make sure your puppy is in a calm-submissive state before arriving. I suggest that you tire him out with a structured walk and, if necessary, a vigorous play session first.
- Keep your energy calm-assertive from the time you leave the house. Don't talk to your dog in a high, squeaky voice on the ride over. Before you enter the park, go on another short walk, so that he's not springing out of the car full of energy.
- Check out the park before you go in. If you sense there are too many large dogs or the atmosphere feels too unstable, save the experience for another time.
- If necessary, keep your puppy on a leash and walk him over to the dogs in the park that seem most stable and balanced.

(continues)

- Supervise from a distance, but be ready to step in and block or redirect if you sense your puppy isn't reading other dogs' signals, or that they aren't reading his.
- Don't "rescue" your puppy from challenging situations by grabbing him and carrying him away. Instead, use your body and energy to prevent escalation of a challenging situation.
- Check your own energy at all times. If you are tired, nervous, or impatient, your puppy will mirror those emotions.
- Be a "partner" to your puppy's experience, not a rescuer or an enabler of bad behavior!

My dream is of a world where there are fewer dogs accidentally biting children, fewer dog altercations, and no more fatal dog attacks. By socializing your puppy to dogs and people when she is young and making sure her manners are in order with both species, you are not only shaping a better life for the both of you, you are also contributing to the pro-dog society that I am committed to helping build.

8
PROBLEM-FREE PUPPIES

A sleeping Blizzard

Juliana Weiss-Roessler, the writing and research director for my Internet newsletter and blog, conducted an online reader survey, asking our subscribers to list the most common and frustrating issues they have had with their puppies. Here are the results from the 1,342 top responses, along with my solutions for raising a problem-free puppy.

COMMON PROBLEM 1

Jumping Up on People (51 Percent)

When a puppy comes running up to us and jumps on us, we think, "She loves me, she is so happy to see me!" We feel special and chosen and cherished. And who doesn't thrill to watch puppies jumping and leaping about in play? They are so carefree, so full of the joy of life. These are the reasons we want puppies in our lives, to bring us that enthusiasm, that appreciation of the everyday things we take for granted.

But clearly, 51 percent of our newsletter survey respondents have had more than enough of their puppies' jumping on them. Generally, when jumping up on people is a chronic problem for a puppy, it will continue to be problematic as she grows older and larger. "A German shepherd puppy jumping on you may seem cute," says Thinschmidt German shepherd breeder Diana Foster, "but a 120-pound German shepherd dog can actually knock you down and injure you." Puppyhood is the best time to nip this behavior in the bud.

Since puppies' strongest ability is their sense of smell, and since their primary purpose during the first eight months of life is to investigate and learn about everything in their new world, they will naturally want to check out and smell every human that comes into their environment. As humans, the strongest scents we project come from our genital areas and from our mouths. We've all had the experience of a less-than-well-mannered dog sniffing our crotch areas—though within the dog world, sniffing genitals *is* considered good manners! Puppies need to stand up on their hind legs and put their paws on a person in order to get close to those areas. Since we tend to cover our genital areas with clothes, the next strongest scent for a dog to check out is coming from our mouths. Puppies and small dogs will want to jump up to get closer to our faces and find out what's going on there.

It's a challenge for humans not to see a puppy jumping on them as an "I love you" or a "hug." The truth is, sometimes puppies are just anxious, and they have learned that if they jump on the human, the human will pick them up and bring them toward them and calm them down. A lot of people say, "Well, as soon as I pick him up, he calms down." Unfortunately, this is a Band-Aid solution. The behavior you want to remove is not gone. It's only put on pause. When you stop a puppy and scoop her up in the middle of an anxious moment, you are never allowing her to develop the vital life skill of learning to calm herself down, on the ground.

As always, I advocate that prevention is the best medicine. You can avert a jumping-up problem from day one by practicing the simplicity of the no touch, no talk, no eye contact rule whenever you first greet your puppy. This sends a calming signal and helps a puppy to stay focused on her nose. Her nose will keep her on the ground, and her eyes and ears will react differently. Chris and Johanna Komives took the prevention route with Eliza from day one, and the results have paid off. "We don't give affection if she's jumping on us. We wait until she's seated (or better, goes to her place) before acknowledging her when we return from work."

The second step is to really claim every step you make. Own your space and ignore or actively discourage the jumping behavior by moving through it calmly and assertively. When Angel had his "sleepover" at Melissa and John's apartment, he never even attempted to jump on John, but when in a playful mood, he attempted to leap at Melissa's legs as she walked through the apartment. Right away, he was able to distinguish John's stronger energy from Melissa's softer energy—even with her experiences working with me for nearly six years!

Although Melissa could not change her essence, she did have the education and knowledge to know how to *refocus* her energy and stop the unwanted behavior. All she had to do to discourage Angel's jumping was to turn around, look him in the eye, and put the palm of her

hand out in front of her, a gesture Angel immediately recognized as meaning "stop." She would wait until he backed out of her space, sat down, and relaxed, and only then would she go on about her business. It took doing this several times over the course of his visit, but eventually she was able to stop him right at the moment he looked as if he wanted to jump. "Patience and repetition" were the solutions, she reported. "I had to stay consistent with my discouragement of his jumping, even though it looked so adorably joyful."

Ultimately, that is the key to stopping any unwanted puppy behavior—making sure you don't go into your own emotional fulfillment mode and get caught up in how extremely cute the puppy is. Yes, she may be the cutest thing on four paws. But as a pack leader, you have to go beyond that and really honor what the puppy needs from you at that moment.

COMMON PROBLEM 2

Chewing (38 Percent)

For a puppy, the activity of chewing serves three important purposes. First, they're exploring new things, and since they don't have hands, they use their mouths. By touching with their mouths, they learn "this is okay, this is not okay." Puppyhood is an era where everything new is an adventure, and it is in the puppies' natures to be curious and use their noses, then their mouths, to investigate.

One of the wonderful things about my new Dog Psychology Center is that it is in an area with many varieties of fauna—plants, trees, and grass—for my pack to play in and explore. When Mr. President was about four and a half months old, I observed him following his idol, Daddy, up to the grassy ridge at the top of the property. Daddy would poke his nose through the grass and, using his fifteen years of

wisdom, smell a few different varieties of weeds before deciding on the right one to chew. Mr. President watched him closely, his attention rapt. Daddy would go to one piece of grass, smell it, then move on to another and chew on it. Then Mr. President would do exactly the same thing—smell the first piece of grass, move on, and chew only the grass that Daddy was chewing. In all my years working with dogs, this kind of simple moment never ceases to amaze and inspire me. Daddy was actually teaching Mr. President which grass was okay to chew on and which was not. That's a real-life puppy class right there.

If your puppy doesn't have a role model like Daddy to look up to, it falls to you as her owner to make sure she is not chewing on anything that could be harmful or poisonous. Puppy-proofing your home and yard are the first steps in this direction, but puppies seem to be able to find trouble anywhere, even when you've gone to great lengths to protect them. If your puppy puts her mouth on a potentially hazardous or valuable item, a gentle touch on the rear or neck or an interesting scent or treat will redirect her attention and get her to drop the object.

Mr. President

I prefer a touch to a treat in these circumstances, because that's what another dog would offer, and you don't want your puppy to associate chewing something bad with getting a treat reward. It's also my experience that you should never take an object away from a dog; you should make the dog leave or walk away from the object. Supervision is key, as is having plenty of allowable, safe chewing objects on hand for your puppy to investigate.

Number two, chewing relieves anxiety or boredom. Some breeds are more driven than others to chew as a way to release tension—as you recall, chewing was Mr. President's Achilles' heel. Chewing can become a behavior a dog turns to in order to calm herself, or it can also be a way to control you, the human in her life. Many a puppy has learned that if she grabs an object, it becomes a way to get a human to come to her. It's very similar to the way that puppies learn that if they're excited, jumping up and down, the human will pay attention to them. In these cases, your puppies are training you to respond to them, not the other way around.

Finally, chewing is important to a puppy between the ages of four and six months because it relieves the pain of teething. It is absolutely not natural, especially during this crucial time period, to ask a puppy not to chew at all. Instead, have plenty of different acceptable chew toys on hand that you can use to redirect the behavior. I always prefer something more natural like a bully stick, or even a plush toy with something hidden inside it, instead of a rubber object. The more natural the object or the more layers the puppy has to chew through to get to the scent or taste inside, the more it will engage her mind . . . that's the reason why your puppy always digs through your closet and pulls out your very best leather shoes—because of the challenge of the hunt, and because they have the most natural material in them. I'm a big fan of bully sticks these days because in this economy, it helps that they are so long-lasting. One seven-dollar bully stick can last up to six

months—nearly all of your dog's puppyhood. By your hiding the bully stick inside or behind something, burying it, or otherwise finding a new way to challenge your puppy, the same chew toy can be used over and over in new and stimulating ways.

Before leaving Crystal with Mr. President for the two weeks my wife and I would be away, I made sure she was aware that he was very much a bulldog when it came to expressing himself through chewing. "I'm really grateful Cesar warned me about this ahead of time," she recalls.

> I used a light touch on Mr. President's neck or hindquarters to get his attention. Then I could claim whatever object I wanted Mr. President not to mess with and introduce an appropriate object for him to chew on. The biggest challenge I encountered that week was claiming my space in my car. At first Mr. President really wanted to chew on my gear shift, emergency brake, door handles, and seat belt release. I had to use my energy because I couldn't use eye contact to claim my space while driving. Treats didn't work because they were only a quick distraction and I think they were even reinforcing the bad behavior. But if I gave him a bully stick when we first got into the car, he'd forget all about chewing on the seat belt.

If you do come home to find your dog destroying your best leather purse, try to keep in check any immediate anger you might have. Take a deep breath, stay calm and assertive, and remember there is nothing "personal" in the puppy's actions. Do not carry the puppy away from the object or yank the object away from her. Instead, calmly correct and redirect. With puppies, redirecting with scent is almost always effective. Utilize the momentum of the puppy's nose and let her get engaged with the new, acceptable object. Then immediately claim the

forbidden object as your own. Fortunately, normal puppies have short attention spans, which you can use to your advantage when you want to guide them away from unwanted behaviors.

Remember, dogs naturally understand the concept of ownership, of claiming an object or space. They do this with one another all the time. Chris Komives used the power of "claiming" to nip Eliza's anxious chewing in the bud:

> The only times Eliza ever destroyed anything, I've chalked it up to anxiety. She chewed the power supply to Johanna's laptop when we went to a concert and left her alone all day (approximately twelve hours). We figured the power supply smelled like Johanna, so she relieved her anxiety on it. The next day I brought out a pile of wires and taught her that they belong to me. I thought her chewing wires might mean she needed more metal in her diet, so I started feeding her liver as a treat. She hasn't touched a wire since. She's also chewed a couple of shoelaces (but left the shoes alone). I repeated the wire exercise with the laces and she's left them alone ever since.

COMMON PROBLEM 3

Barking (32 Percent)

If you were to drive by very slowly or walk past my house with your dog, you would probably have no idea that the Dog Whisperer and his many dogs live here. Meanwhile, there's a single dog a few streets over that we can hear from our house, constantly yapping away.

What's the difference? Simply rules, boundaries, and limitations. And the fact that the dogs in my house are always active, fulfilled, and balanced.

We have to remember that a dog's bark is something that early man encouraged in the wolflike ancestors of modern canines thousands of years ago. The fact that a dog could alert them to danger in their camps, settlements, and farms was one of the many qualities of dogs that brought our two species together. In short, the reason dogs bark is as much our doing as it is theirs. Some people, especially people who live alone or in remote areas, want to encourage their dogs to bark every single time something new happens or someone unexpected stops by. Others prefer a loud dog with a tough, territorial bark to scare away possible intruders. Then there are those who live in close quarters— apartment buildings or condos—whose dogs' chronic vocalizations could land them in deep trouble with the landlord or the neighbors.

How many barks are too many? It's simply a matter of preference, but in my opinion, when it goes beyond four barks, it can turn into more than simply the alert to the pack that barking was intended to be. Obsessive barking can turn into a conversation, and the dog is really trying to tell you, "I'm not happy with my life right now. I'm bored. I'm unsure. I'm frustrated. I'm not getting enough exercise. So the only activity I have available is to bark for thirty minutes." When a dog barks for extended periods of time or barks at any little disturbance, it's usually speaking the canine language of anxiety or frustration.

In my house, one bark is enough. That's it—one bark. In my pack, it's usually Coco the Chihuahua who will pick up on a strange presence, scent, or vibration, and then he will alert the pack. Once I tell Coco to be quiet, none of the other dogs will imitate his bark. But all the dogs will then indicate to me where the object or person or animal is coming from and how they feel about it by using body language. Different breeds will sometimes use different body language—holding one leg up or "pointing," sitting down near the spot or lying down, standing in an alert posture, or stalking. With ten different dogs, you will have ten different physical expressions of alertness yet exactly the same energy. But it's my preference that there be no sound after that

first bark. I'm telling the dogs, "Okay, you did your job, now the humans will take care of this." I'm taking the load off their shoulders.

With your new puppy, you make the call—many barks, a few barks, or peace and quiet. But you have to start early. Since you have already taught your puppy to associate a certain sound or word with something you don't agree with, consistently correct using that sound. If your puppy's intensity level has escalated to very high, you may need to use a firm touch to snap her back to your attention. But don't stop there. Your puppy may pause and then go right back to what she was doing. She may be sitting back, but her brain is still on alert. Be patient. Wait until she completely relaxes before you go back to what you were doing. You can also reward with affection or a treat, but only after your puppy is completely quiet.

If your puppy is barking over and over again at the same object, person, or place, then it's time to step up and claim that item as your own. Use your body, your mind, and your calm-assertive energy to create an invisible wall that your puppy is not allowed to cross. This kind of focused energy and body language is exactly what your puppy is looking for you to give her—a direction. But remember, with puppies you have a chance to prevent unwanted barking before it becomes a habit or a chronic way of relieving stress.

COMMON PROBLEM 4

Nipping (24 Percent) and Mouthing (19 Percent)

Nipping, or play biting, is something that puppies do with their littermates, and it is a very instinctual behavior for them. It's a form of social interaction as well as playful practice for survival in the wild. In nature, a dog's siblings, mother, or older dogs in the pack will quickly

teach her how hard is too hard. Junior loves to roughhouse with Mr. President and Blizzard, but if the pressure in their mouths gets a little too aggressive, he'll shut them down in an instant. It's important to keep in mind that a bite that a strapping adolescent pit bull finds to be too much would be extremely painful, perhaps even wounding, to a human. Mouthing, like chewing, is a natural way for puppies to explore the world with their mouths. Neither behavior necessarily indicates an aggressive or dominant temperament. But if you constantly allow your puppy to play-dominate you with her mouth while her harmless baby teeth are tiny and soft, she will learn to use it as a tool to control you when she's big enough to do some real damage. "If allowed to continue, this playful biting from the pup often turns into serious aggression as an adult," warns breeder Diana Foster of her juvenile German shepherds. "He has now learned to use his mouth and teeth to get what he wants."

With Blizzard, Angel, and Mr. President, I allowed them to explore my hands in the way they would naturally, but only using a soft mouth—no pressure allowed. When they would naturally start to increase the pressure and test the limits of my tolerance, I would gently but firmly cup their necks or the tops of their heads with my hand curved into the "claw" shape that mimics another dog's mouth. Then I would hold that position until they relaxed. It's natural for puppies to test limits, but it's just as natural for them to accept them. All I am doing is mimicking what their mother or Junior or Daddy or even another puppy would do in the same situation.

It's important, however, that your timing be precise. Don't overcorrect, don't pinch, and don't hold on too long after your puppy has relaxed, because she might interpret that as a further challenge. In attempting this exercise with your puppy, it may be helpful to wear a glove while playing, to make sure you are relaxed and in control at all times. *If you are worrying about your own discomfort or injury, you will be pro-*

jecting a weak energy to the puppy, which she will naturally try to take advantage of! She will not respect any limits you set with her if you are in a weak or unsure state of mind. Puppies are instinctual—if they sense even a split-second gap in leadership, they will move in to compensate for it. Projecting constant calm-assertive energy and a sense of confident leadership during the months of puppyhood is like buying an insurance policy, so that you will continue to be respected in your dog's eyes for the rest of her life.

Another advantage of using a glove when teaching your puppy bite inhibition is that you will avoid the common mistake of yanking or pulling your hand away when you sense the dog's teeth digging into your skin. This kind of motion triggers your puppy's prey drive and will only increase her excitement. "Too much petting—longer than five seconds at a time—pulling the hands away quickly from the mouth, and raising the hand in a repetitive motion above the dog's head, which is something children tend to do, will actually encourage play biting," says Diana. Once Blizzard moved in with the Barnes family, he quickly learned he could dominate Christian with his play biting for this very reason. Blizzard grew at a tremendous rate and was in danger of really hurting Christian. It was actually fourteen-year-old Sabrina who taught Christian how to stay calm during these incidents, and how to make Blizzard submit to him before they continued their play sessions.

COMMON PROBLEM 5

Housebreaking Issues (24 Percent)

We've already dealt with housebreaking earlier in this book, where I've indicated that housebreaking a puppy is not rocket science, be-

cause you've got nature working on your side. Most issues with house-breaking that I see occur because the owners didn't stick to a schedule, didn't properly sanitize areas where accidents occurred, and, perhaps most important, got caught up in the emotion of a ruined piece of furniture or carpet. Your dog doesn't understand that you paid a thousand dollars for that sofa, but she does understand that you are in a highly unstable, emotional state, that you are projecting strong negative energy, and that you are directing it right at her.

In order to prevent this from happening, don't even give your puppy the chance to create an accident of epic proportions in your home. Until you are sure of her elimination habits, keep her in a safe, contained, easy-to-sanitize area when you can't be directly supervising her. Use wee-wee pads if necessary, and always sanitize the area under and around the pads. Set her up for success, not failure. If you reduce the drama involved in housebreaking, you may be surprised at how easily it all comes together.

With all the complaints I hear about the horrors of housebreaking, it's interesting to me that it's number five on the list of most common puppy problems, not number one or two. I chock that up to the fact that in America, people take the condition of their homes very, very seriously. They may be a little bothered by a puppy's jumping, nipping, or barking, but they absolutely, positively refuse to live in a house that smells like pee or poop. They can live with a couple of bite marks on their hands or a few complaints from the neighbors, but a stain on their prized Oriental rug will make them immediately lay down the law. Is there any better evidence of the fact that a puppy can tell exactly how seriously we take the limits we set with her? With all these common problems, if you are on the fence about whether or not you are willing to set the limits necessary to correct them, your puppy will sense your ambivalence, and the unwanted behavior will continue.

COMMON PROBLEM 6

Not Coming When Called (23 Percent)

First of all, we must remember that in your puppy's world, there is no such thing as a "name." Another dog's identity is its scent and energy, and has nothing to do with a sound. We give dogs names for our own convenience, and fortunately for us, dogs as a species are such natural masters of association that they quickly come to connect the unique cadence and syllables of a certain sound with what we want from them when we make that sound. At the Max Planck Institute for Evolutionary Anthropology, in Germany, a border collie named Rico proved he could recognize the unique names of more than two hundred different objects.[1] Dogs don't reason, but one of the ways they constantly amaze is that they are simply brilliant at making connections. When a person says about a puppy, "He already knows his name," however, it's not in the way a child would know his name—that is, assuming it as part of his identity, or his "me-ness." The dog understands its name relative to how, when, and why it is communicated and, most important, the energy with which it is communicated.

When the Obama family named their puppy Bo, I was asked by many in the media, "Won't that confuse the dog, because it rhymes with *No*?" Perhaps, but it's also likely that as long as the name *Bo* was used in relation to positive things such as playtime, feeding time, walks, and praise or affection, he would have no trouble distinguishing it from a word used in relation to negative things, such as "No." A dog isn't a poet—it's not just the word he's concerned with, it's the energy behind the word that sends the message. This is one reason that I always instruct my clients to refrain from using a dog's name when

correcting him. I use my dogs' names when calling them, when praising them, and when we're playing or doing a positive challenge or exercise.

Let's assume you are doing everything right, using your puppy's
name only in a positive context, yet your puppy still doesn't come
when you call her. It's not that your puppy doesn't want to come to
you or is rebelling or challenging your authority. The number one reason why dogs don't come to people when they call is that their noses
are more powerful sensors than their ears and they are distracted
by fascinating scents. Remember, everything to a puppy is new and
exciting. A new scent can so engage and mesmerize a puppy that to
respond to a sound—far less interesting to him—just doesn't get
through to him in that moment. If you yell out your young puppy's
name over and over while she is being distracted by a scent, you run
the risk of her associating that sound with the action of not paying attention to you. Remember, the energy you are projecting when you
call your dog's name is what the puppy actually hears. If all the pup
gets from your calling her name is, "I'm impatient, I want to get out of
here, I'm frustrated with you," that is not a very attractive energy for
her to follow.

Dogs learn in the order nose-eyes-ears. In raising our friends Junior, Blizzard, Angel, and Mr. President, I followed the example of nature and used sound as little as possible in the beginning. Instead, I
engaged their noses. This is especially effective with puppies. If I am
walking Angel and his powerful terrier nose gets distracted by a scent,
I will place a bully stick in front of him until it gets his attention, then
walk away. I will start saying his name or making a positive "kissing"
sound only when he is *already* coming toward me. That way he begins
to associate the name or sound with the *action* of following—"This is
what I hear when I'm following." The connection becomes clear and
unambiguous.

The next level of this exercise is done on a long lead, using sound and your puppy's automatic instinct to follow. Let your puppy wander away from you. Put your foot on the line to anchor it, then turn your back to the puppy and walk away. As soon as he starts to follow you, turn toward him and call his name, or make the sounds that you want him to associate with "coming." Reward him as soon as he reaches you.

Practice using the positive sound or your puppy's name only during the natural times she is following you. When you get her out of the crate in the morning, while you are praising her during potty training, when you are calling her at mealtime, and when you are engaged in activities that she likes. Make sure the energy behind the name is positive as well as calm and assertive. The more scent-oriented your dog, the longer it may take for her to understand that sound trumps scent when it is time to decide upon an action. But with a patient, dedicated owner, any puppy can learn to make that connection. In the meantime, carry a bully stick, scented item, or treat with you, in order to get your puppy's attention. Try to think like a puppy and see the world as "nose-eyes-ears," and eventually your puppy can learn how to think like you.

COMMON PROBLEM 7

Digging (21 Percent)

All dogs are natural diggers. Some dogs, such as the terrier breeds, have that extra boost in their DNA that makes their drive to dig even stronger. For them, digging can become their primary outlet for relieving stress, boredom, or anxiety. We need to provide for our dogs an outlet for this perfectly normal activity.

The area where the new Dog Psychology Center is located is teem-

ing with local wildlife. From the moment two-month-old Angel arrived at the ranch, he began to fixate on my four-year-old Jack Russell terrier as Jack scoured the ranch for gopher holes. Angel's DNA was crying out in recognition—"Digging! That's what I was born for!" But despite the fact that Angel's ancestors were bred to dig for rats and other earthy rodents, I didn't want him to pick up catching gophers as a hobby. I needed to redirect his digging energy in a safer way, while keeping his mind and his genes engaged.

I have created a special area at the center for this very purpose. A tall, sandy embankment mottled with abandoned rodent holes has become the official "digging place" for the dogs, where we do simple activities to fulfill that need in them. I'll take a tennis ball, focus the dogs' attention on it, then stick it deep into the recesses of one of the small abandoned rodent holes in the bank. It's wonderful to watch the puppies' different breed-related talents and tendencies emerge when I do this simple exercise. Junior, with all his brawny pit bull might, will fly at the bank with all four paws, hurling giant chunks of earth behind him as if he were a bulldozer. He'll widen out the hole in no time flat but in a totally undisciplined manner—all agitation and muscle, with very little focus. With Mr. President, it's easy to see why digging and retrieving buried treasure is not a bulldog's forte. He'll try to join in the excitement, but with his flat snout and large head, he can only clumsily poke inside the hole in the general direction of the hidden object. Angel, however, has been a digging star from day one. While Junior is still knocking himself out trying to make the hole in the embankment bigger, and while Mr. President is looking around, wondering if anyone is going to bring the ball back, Angel will simply slip into the hole like a trained navy diver, disappear for a moment, then come out proudly carrying the ball.

For this I reward him with extra praise and affection. It's important that he understand how proud I am of his ability, that I take joy in his joy, and that I'm nurturing the terrier instincts in him—but directing

them in the right way. He is learning that we dig for balls, not for gophers—and we dig only for what the human wants us to dig for. This is prevention at its best; I know Angel is not going to dig up my Zen landscaping in the future, because I am already fulfilling his genetic need in a much richer, more entertaining way.

If you have a terrier breed or another breed with a powerful digging drive, or you are having problems with your puppy's obsessive digging, I suggest you section off an area in your garden or yard appropriate for your dog's or puppy's size. You can also provide a sandbox, if it is deep enough. This will be the place where your dog can dig to her heart's content. Bury something interesting in the area, like a bully stick or a scented toy. Then bring your dog to the area, and let her sniff. If she doesn't begin digging, start moving the dirt yourself, just a little bit. Eventually she'll start to get excited and want to join in with you. If the area you can provide is very shallow, you can participate in the game and re-cover the area that your dog has already dug up—making it more challenging for her. Or you can just leave her to enjoy the adventure for herself, nurturing her achievement when she's brought you the buried object. After the exercise, replace the dirt, sanitize the object, and put the soil back the way it was before the dog began digging, to keep it interesting, as if every day it is still the first time anyone has ever dug in that space.

The next step is showing your dog that your designated digging spot is the only place where she can practice this activity. After she has succeeded in her digging challenge for the day, bring your dog to your garden or any area that you want to be off-limits. Put something in the ground, but block your dog immediately if she even attempts to come near. Direct her attention to you and don't let her engage her nose, eyes, or ears. Use your body language to claim the area as "yours." Then go back to the digging area and repeat the joyful digging exercise. Repeat this process a few times a week or, if your puppy has already lapsed into bad habits, every day, until it becomes clear to you

that the puppy knows the rules, boundaries, and limitations of digging in her environment.

If you live in an apartment, find an area in the park to practice digging exercises, or perhaps a dog-friendly beach. For digging activities indoors, Angel's breeder, Brooke Walker, provides her newborn miniature schnauzer puppies with a labyrinth of carpeted cat tunnels, to nurture and fulfill their schnauzer's "submariner" needs from birth onward. When we fulfill our puppies' inborn needs from day one, we can actually prevent almost any troublesome issue from developing.

COMMON PROBLEM 8

Won't Walk on a Leash (20 Percent)

Angel has never had a problem with a leash in his short life. And one of the reasons for that is his very proactive breeder, Brooke Walker. She has her miniature schnauzer pups wearing colored bands made of paper at four weeks old and introduces them to the sensation of the leash by eight weeks.

When I am walking my pack on the beach, people often come up to ask me questions because it's very unusual to see a woman walking six perfect miniature schnauzers, all well behaved, all in formation. The other day, a woman came by with a schnauzer that was six months old and didn't know how to walk on a leash. Well, that's disgraceful. It turns out she got the puppy at a pet store, which absolutely explains it. A puppy purchased at a pet store at six months has waited too long and never really experienced the world. But walking on a leash, well, that's one of the first skills your puppy has to have. All my puppies are leash trained by the time they leave my house.

A puppy may be leash trained when it comes to its new owners, but that doesn't mean the owners are leash trained. When I saw the CNN newsfeed of the Obama puppy pulling little Malia all over the White House lawn, I knew that the First Family had not taken the time to master the walk. Mastering the walk, which we touched on in Chapter 4, means having your puppy walking beside you, head up, with no tension on the leash between you and her. She is not pulling you or exhibiting the zigzagging behavior that we saw with presidential puppy Bo. Zigzagging (or what one of my more colorful clients calls "fly-fishing") is a sign of an overexcited dog. The walk should not signify excitement to a dog; it should signify structure, and the foundations of structure are laid in puppyhood. In nature, puppies know they have to follow their mother in a disciplined manner, or else they will get lost or left behind. In thinking you need a long lead in order to give your puppy "freedom" to explore out in front of you, you are actually working against Mother Nature. You can take breaks in the walk to allow for exploration time, as well as scheduling play sessions that involve supervised exploration in your yard or in the park. But there is absolutely no substitute for teaching your puppy to master a structured walk.

As she learns to walk on her leash, however, you should expect certain behaviors from a very young puppy. Remember, everything is new to her. It is absolutely natural that she is going to get distracted by grass, by trees, by other dogs, by humans. At those times she will pull on the leash and that will create tension on it. If you pull back on the leash, you only increase the tension, which makes walking with you a stressful experience. Make sure the leash is high up on your puppy's neck. Carry it loosely, like a briefcase or purse. If your puppy sees something exciting and starts to move toward it, keep the tension loose but continue in the direction you are going, focusing on keeping your puppy's head up. Use a scent, a treat, or a bully stick to engage her nose and keep her moving forward; engaging a puppy's nose is a sure-

fire way of redirecting her attention. If the puppy continues to pull, turn around, stop, face her, and make eye contact with her until she sits. Relax all tension on the leash and wait. When she is focused on you again, totally relaxed, only then should you continue the walk. You may have to repeat this several times until your puppy gets the message that you are in control of the walk.

When Crystal Reel brought Mr. President home with her during my weeklong vacation, she had a different issue on the walk. "Sometimes he'd walk as far as he wanted to go and then he'd just sit down. He's not a fan of long, drawn-out walks—especially when it was warm outside and he'd get overheated." We'd had several unseasonable heat waves in Los Angeles that year, and bulldogs are notoriously sensitive to the heat. Crystal solved her problem by adapting to Mr. President's physical needs. "On hot days, I tried to break up our walks into smaller ten-minute walks throughout the day. I would also use the scent of food to get him up and moving if he sat down."

Another behavior that is totally normal occurs when a puppy gets a little unsure in a brand-new place and doesn't want to keep moving forward. When Melissa took Angel on his overnight adventure, the first thing she did was bring him to an outdoor café at the top of a flight of marble steps, something he'd never experienced before in his life. Angel merrily trotted across the parking lot on his leash, but when he saw those stairs, he balked. This is perfectly natural, and it's a sign of good instincts, good common sense. Here is a four-month-old puppy with a brand-new person, in a new situation that he is unsure of. Instinct is telling him, "Use your nose, check it out, don't do anything rash." You never want to discourage a puppy that's listening to its instincts.

Melissa handled this situation correctly, stopping and letting the tension fall on the leash while Angel took in the stairs. Then, before he could become too overwhelmed, she put the bully stick in front of his nose, then brought him up one step, let him sniff, then another, let him sniff, and so on. After the fourth or fifth step, she upped her pace,

and Angel—still a little tentative but now back in the mode of moving forward—followed along quickly behind her. The same thing happened in her apartment building, but by the third time he faced a flight of stairs, Angel was going up and down like a pro.

COMMON PROBLEM 9

Crying or Whining (18 Percent)

When puppies are separated from their pack in the wild, they will cry out or whine to get their mothers' attention. When your puppy cries, it's usually just to get your attention, because of either loneliness or a need to eliminate. It's normal for a puppy to whine a little on her first few nights away from her mother and siblings—remember, we are asking dogs to do something very unnatural when we separate them from their packs—but they do adjust quickly, and being alone comfortably is a skill they are going to need for living with humans the rest of their lives. You want your puppy to develop this ability as soon as possible, to prevent the issue of separation anxiety later. If your puppy starts to cry a little during her first few nights, ignoring is the best medicine.

One way to prevent the situation of a puppy that whines or barks from her crate is to make sure she is calm and submissive before you close her in. *Never* shut the door on an excited, anxious puppy. Wait next to her in silence until she relaxes, then gently close the door and walk away. Make sure to drain the puppy's energy before bed or quiet times, especially in the early days when she is first getting used to her new environment. If she's happily exhausted, she'll have a lot less energy for whining and be more inclined to simply crash for the night. Also, make sure she pees and poops on a regular schedule so that she's not physically uncomfortable in her crate or sleeping place.

Most of my clients with puppies admit that they have a very hard time not responding to a puppy's pitiful cries during those crucial first nights. Diana Foster of Thinschmidt German Shepherds is adamant that new owners take a "tough love" stance, for the good of the dog, not for themselves.

It is very important to completely ignore all the noise, regardless of how loud it gets. When dogs are stressed and are trying to work out their frustrations, they will try as hard as they can to get their way. Their behavior will escalate and continue to get worse instead of better. Dog trainers call this "extinction burst." Unfortunately, it is just at this point when frustrated owners "give in" to their dogs' demanding behavior, as they just can't deal with it. Had they waited it out for just a short time longer, the behavior would eventually improve. Interrupting the escalation reinforces the exact behavior people are trying to avoid. Soon after it reaches a peak and the dog is absolutely out of control, he will give in and start to settle down.

COMMON PROBLEM 10

Excited (15 Percent) or Submissive (11 Percent) Urination

Like housebreaking issues, unplanned urination, whether it is excited or submissive, is another behavior that owners will take serious steps to correct. Again, it seems to be a universal human motto: "You can drag me all over the dog park—you can even eat my shoes—but don't you dare stink up my living room."

Excited urination is exactly what it sounds like—an overstimulated dog gets caught up in the moment and forgets to control or loses

control of her bodily functions. It's the canine version of "I was so excited, I wet my pants!" Since it's easy to overstimulate young puppies and since they are still new to their elimination routine, accidents can happen. The most obvious solution to this problem is to closely monitor the intensity of your puppy's play, not letting her get too overwhelmed by people, places, or things. If the problem seems chronic, you should see your veterinarian, to make sure your puppy doesn't have urinary tract problems or a neurological inability to control her bladder when excited.

Submissive urination is usually found in fearful, nervous, or very submissive dogs that are sensitive and easily overwhelmed. They urinate under stress in a way to overcompensate, by showing complete submission and respect. If a dog is overly shy or submissive, make sure all new people she encounters practice the no touch, no talk, no eye contact rule until the puppy is ready to meet them. If someone in your household or immediate social circle has an overbearing, high-octane, or very assertive energy, that can also ignite the problem, even if your puppy is familiar with that person. Instruct people who seem to trigger your puppy's issues to ignore the dog until it becomes absolutely clear that the puppy is comfortable with them.

9
SMELLS LIKE TEEN SPIRIT
Adolescent Challenges

Mr. President in a car kennel

When I first noticed that four-month-old Angel was already lifting his leg to pee and showing early signs of marking behavior, it felt to me like the canine equivalent of the time my nine-year-old son, Calvin, told me he thought it was about time he got himself a girlfriend. I felt that twinge so common to parents everywhere: the wistful realization that my children were growing up all too fast.

You won't get a firm consensus from dog behaviorists about the exact moment when canine adolescence begins. The onset of this

stage can begin as early as sixteen weeks—as with Angel's premature marking behaviors—or it can begin to show as late as eight months of age. Generally, smaller dogs mature sooner than larger-breed dogs. Male and female dogs also tend to grow at different rates. I'm not a dog biologist, but from my years of experience, I've come to view a dog between six and eight months old as a "tween," because at six months, the mating urge is just beginning to form. At six months of age, my sweet Angel turned into a little devil that started humping anything that moved, but because of his general puppy way of being, his behavior wasn't threatening to the other dogs around him. If Angel were a human boy, this would be a little like his becoming curious about a *Playboy* magazine but unsure of what to do about it yet. I consider eight months to be the average age when true adolescence kicks in, a period of sometimes daring and unpredictable behavior that can drag on until your dog is two to three years of age. During this phase of his life, your dog's brain is still maturing, but his body is nearly full grown. From six months to eight months, your dog will still look and act like a nice, big, cuddly puppy. But one day, you'll wake up and suddenly you won't see a puppy anymore. Your dog won't play like a puppy. He won't growl like a puppy. He won't bark like a puppy.

"Only in adolescence did Eliza begin barking," Chris Komives told me, when his wheaten terrier was nearly a year old. "It's mostly in the house, so I think she's become a little territorial now that she's older. When she barks, I tell her no, and then ask her to go to her place and relax. Unfortunately, as an adolescent, she made up her own interpretation of that command. She learned to leap into the bay window, bark her head off at the dog passing by, then run to her place and lie down. I realized I'd confused dog training with dog psychology. We now correct her at the window and make her calm down at the spot where she became excited and started barking."

Eliza's "interpretation" of Chris's command in order to suit her whim is a prime example of an adolescent dog who knows the basic

rule book but is still trying to see how much she can get away with. As a puppy, your dog was reliant on your constant input and completely driven by the innate desire to follow you and to fit into your pack. An adolescent dog has a mind of its own. The dog begins to test every single limit that you've worked so hard to impose during those previous, formative eight months. If you waver from the program and your dog begins to believe that the rules apply only sometimes, you'll risk establishing negative patterns of behavior that could haunt you for the rest of your dog's life. If you go back to basics and stick to the guidelines you've already set, however, you will have the chance to establish an even deeper bond with your dog and to build a more mature, more meaningful connection.

I'm saddened by the harsh fact that far too many owners just give up and fold when a previously well-behaved or at least manageable puppy triples in size and starts pushing the envelope at the same time. The owners have been lulled into a sense of false security and suddenly feel they can't handle all these new challenges. "You only have to look at the main age group of dogs surrendered to shelters," says my friend Martin Deeley. "Eight months to two years.[1] This is also the time a dog becomes a backyard dog because he causes too much trouble in the house. It is an indication that something changed in that period. What really happens is that after beginning well, owners relax because the pup is good, is small, and any developing issues are rationalized away as just being 'puppy behavior.' In a very short time the dog becomes larger, stronger, more mature mentally, sexually (if not neutered), and personality-wise more active or even hyper. Now we have the makings of a teenage rebel." This is exactly why I urge my clients to focus on preventing issues or stopping them early on, before they become chronic. They must lay down a solid foundation of rules, boundaries, and limitations in puppyhood and never waver from those basic guidelines, no matter how big or defiant their adolescent dogs become.

PHYSICAL CHANGES

Your adolescent dog isn't being willful just to spite you. There are a number of significant changes going on in his brain and in his body that are driving some of these frustrating new quirks in his behavior.

• His permanent teeth either are all the way in or finish coming in, so he goes through a second, sometimes more destructive, chewing phase.

• He may be growing so fast that he has literal "growing pains," which can range from mild to severe.

• His defense drive begins to develop and mature, so fears he may still harbor from a younger age can show up again, as either shy or aggressive behaviors.

• Rapid growth causes joints and plates to become unstable and susceptible to injury, which means that certain vigorous activities may have to be put on hold until his body matures a little more.

• Older dogs begin to hold the adolescent dog more accountable than they did the puppy, which means new conflicts can develop, seemingly out of nowhere.[2]

SEXUAL MATURITY

One of the hallmarks of this period is the dramatic rise in the role that sexual hormones play in fueling your dog's behavior. An intact adolescent male dog produces testosterone at a rate several times higher than that of his adult counterpart, which means he will act out his urges in ways that may seem extreme or exaggerated unless he is neutered. Unneutered, a male dog will escalate his behaviors of terri-

torial marking and roaming, and some will start displaying an aggression toward other male dogs—or even humans—that they didn't exhibit during puppyhood. While sniffing another dog's urine on a walk, the sexually intact male dog may fixate on it, stare off into the distance (tracking the direction of the dog that left the mark), and either seem unwilling to leave the landmark or act all too willing to tear off in pursuit of the mysterious female whose perfume still lingers. Even the best obedience training during puppyhood will often fail to temper this powerful urge.

The body of an unspayed female starts gearing up for its first heat cycle when she is only about six months old. If you're looking for warning signs of your female preteen's first heat, one of the earliest and most obvious will be the different ways that male dogs react to her—they'll focus in on her right away, usually acting more agitated around her. The female starts sending a scent even before she is fully in heat; it's nature's invitation to male dogs to find and breed with her. Even these premature hormonal cues can aggravate competition and aggression in male dogs, and even neutered male dogs will show some reaction to it. The female in heat may also act a little more playful or "flirty" with males, standing very still with her tail straight up in the air like a flag to let them smell her. Some female dogs will show swelling in the vulva area, and once the heat begins, there is a little blood discharge. Frequent urination and touchiness—sort of a "canine PMS"—are also common red flags of estrus.

THE ETHICS OF SPAYING AND NEUTERING

Next to the food drive, the drive to mate is nature's most powerful passion. A dog's biology dictates that he or she mate every six months. When the mating urge is not fulfilled, incredible tension and frustra-

tion build up in the bodies of dogs—especially male dogs—that are often discharged as serious aggression. This is when the true primal predator self surfaces in previously peaceful dogs, and they can actually kill each other. In rural Mexico where I grew up, dogs don't get neutered or spayed. The whole countryside becomes one giant dog park to them. They tend to live very instinctive lives because they do mate freely on the schedule nature intended. For these dogs, there is no sexual aggravation to turn into aggression. On one hand, this more natural lifestyle has created a terrible problem of dog overpopulation that developing nations desperately need to address; on the other hand, dogs in Third World countries definitely live much shorter lives than dogs in America.

Like their Mexican counterparts, dogs in America have both the ability and the desire to mate, but unlike them, they don't have the opportunity. In the Westernized world, our lifestyle, our leash laws, and the way we've made dogs members of our families—not to mention the enormous tragedy of abandoned and homeless dogs in America—make it completely unrealistic for us to allow our pets to mate at will. That's just reality. And that is why I firmly believe that here in America, spaying and neutering is the *only* ethical choice for those of us who are not professional breeders. We owe it to our dogs to prevent them from having to undergo the extreme physical and psychological suffering caused by not being able to mate when their bodies are screaming at them to do so.

When is the right time to spay or neuter your adolescent or "preteen" puppy? In my opinion, the ideal time is at six months of age. Almost all of your dog's major growth has concluded by this point, but the sex hormones have not yet taken over driving his or her behavior. Some breeders of show dogs who are looking to mold perfect physical specimens believe in waiting a couple of months longer, to ensure that the dog has finished maturing physically. But I believe that by spaying and neutering at six months, we are blocking the brain from receiving

those forceful signals from the hormone world. This way your dog never has to endure the suffering and frustration of needing to mate but lacking the opportunity.

There are so many myths about spaying and neutering—that it changes your dog's personality, that it stunts your dog's development, that it will make your dog fat. If I have earned any influence at all by my work as the Dog Whisperer, I want to use it to help dispel those myths. "There are so many health benefits to early spaying and neutering," Dr. Rick Garcia, one of my favorite vets, agrees. "We're preventing testicular cancers, mammary tumors, and other reproductive-system cancers; we're preventing perianal hernias and blocking the development of many other conditions a dog can develop from having too many sex hormones building up in its system over a number of years. Some say that dogs are at more risk for obesity if they're spayed or neutered, but if they are fed the correct diet and given regular exercise, there should be no issue with this at all."

In my time in America, I have helped hundreds of dogs and owners better understand the operation and prepare psychologically for it. For every one of them, the process has been a positive experience. Nothing physically, psychologically, or spiritually negative has occurred from the operation. "The behavioral advantages are huge," Dr. Garcia adds. "Neutering prevents marking with urine in the house and around the dog's territory, and the accompanying aggression, which can lead to dominance issues and violence toward other dogs and even members of the family. Neutering them makes dogs more manageable, more trainable, and more placid pets at home. The only real downside to neutering is that you can't breed the dog. Overall, the benefits far outweigh that."

Of course, spaying and neutering do not promise you a "magic pill" to relieve all unwanted behaviors. Your role as a calm-assertive pack leader and your consistency in fulfilling all your dog's other

needs through exercise, discipline, and affection remain your only guarantees against bad habits or issues. But spaying and neutering do ensure that you are removing the rush of hormones to the brain that drives dogs to want to mate, as well as the consequences of their acting out of frustration when they can't.

DADDY'S CANCER: A CAUTIONARY TALE

The issue of spaying and neutering became an even more passionate cause for me after my pit bull, Daddy, developed a cancerous transmissible venereal tumor. He survived this life-threatening disease but had to endure surgery, several days of chemotherapy, and an intensive follow-up holistic regimen with Dr. Marty Goldstein to help his body recover from the toxic aftereffects of all the chemo. Daddy was twelve years old at the time and had not been neutered because Daddy's legal owner, a rapper named Redman, was very much against the procedure. Even though he truly did love Daddy, Redman's desire to leave him intact came from an emotional place. With good intentions, he wanted Daddy to have the experience of siring puppies, but Redman forgot to ask himself the question, "When I'm *not* breeding Daddy, how's that going to affect his quality of life? What will become of that frustration and that powerful drive to mate?"

We can't say for sure that Daddy's being intact "caused" his cancer. From a holistic viewpoint, sexual frustration leads a dog to build up excess testosterone as well as negative energy in his body, which can contribute to creating cancer. Soon after Daddy was diagnosed, I adopted him legally and finally had him neutered. It was very painful seeing a dog that I love so deeply suffer so much. Because I loved him, I was going to spend whatever it took to save his life. It ended up costing more than ten thousand dollars. Of course it was worth it—but

that ten thousand dollars could have been put toward my mission in life, which is saving more dogs' lives.

MR. PRESIDENT GETS SNIPPED

When Mr. President reached his six-month birthday, I decided it was time for him to go under the knife so that he could go on to live a long, healthy, frustration-free future. "Oh, how could you do that to such a perfect specimen of dog as Mr. President?" an extremely uneducated stranger asked me. The answer is that even though Mr. President is a very handsome dog, there aren't a lot of appropriate females available for him. You don't just go out and place a personal ad for a genetically perfect female English bulldog. I am not a breeder. Lots of people think it's a great idea to breed their dogs, but as you learned in Chapter 2, avoiding the pitfalls of genetic illnesses and behavioral problems is a complicated, scientific task that should never be left to amateurs. I come from the point of view of wanting to prevent unwanted puppies growing into dogs that we put to death, simply because we can't find homes for them. To me, this is the only real moral outrage, something that creates negative karma for our entire species. By leaving breeding to the pros, we create only healthy dogs for future generations and prevent unwanted dogs from being born into lives of suffering.

A Trauma-Free Procedure

Dr. Rick Garcia of Paws and Claws Mobile Veterinary Hospital has been a great friend and supporter of both the Dog Psychology Center and the *Dog Whisperer* television show for many years now. Dr. Rick has known Mr. President since early in his puppyhood, so I arranged

to bring my growing bulldog to his mobile operating hospital on a sunny April morning.

In order to ensure that a spaying or neutering—or any veterinary procedure for that matter—is an effortless, positive experience for your dog, it's crucial that you, as the owner, have your emotions in check. Simply put, if you are feeling unsure or guilty about the operation, your dog will feel even worse about it. I hope that by educating yourself on the many benefits of spaying and neutering, you will be going into the situation in the same state of mind in which I approached Mr. President's procedure—I was truly happy and excited for him and proud to be able to contribute in this way to his future as a stable, balanced bulldog.

When we arrived at Dr. Rick's, Mr. President was his usual, playful self. All the work that I had done by exposing him to a variety of people, places, and things during his puppyhood was paying off now, with the little guy seeing all new experiences not as scary threats but as exciting, new adventures. He had no idea he was going to get neutered—all he knew was the thrill of coming to yet another new environment. Dr. Rick had instructed me not to feed or give water to Mr. President twelve hours before surgery, but I had brought along one of his favorite toys, a stuffed squirrel, coated with a special organic scented spray I have developed, so that I could keep his nose engaged right up until the moment he went to sleep. I would be there to wake him up in the same way, to ensure his waking up in the same state—calm, content, and submissive.

When we got to Dr. Rick's mobile van, Mr. President jumped right into it—it's a familiar place to him and the rest of the pack, and has always had good, happy associations for him, right from the beginning. He immediately started strutting around, making himself right at home. Dr. Rick and his vet tech, Lizette Barajas, marveled at how much he had grown since the last time they'd seen him. He weighed in at a whopping 39.2 pounds! I engaged Mr. President's mouth with the

toy while Lizette petted him—remember, we had spent many months of his early puppyhood getting him used to being touched in all different parts of his body and associating that with rewards and affection, so when the first injection came, he didn't even notice it. Rick and Lizette were both charmed by Mr. President's bubbly personality; he is a naturally happy-go-lucky guy who simply loves all new humans. "Not all dogs act like this in the vet's office," Dr. Garcia remarked. But then, not all dogs were raised from the point of view of becoming the role model for the perfect dog!

After his first shot, Mr. President seemed just as joyful and curious as when he first came in. He watched Dr. Rick fill his syringe with medication as happily as he would watch me preparing a treat or toy for him to play with. The vet tech held Mr. President's body and I massaged his jowls and redirected his attention toward me as Rick swabbed his front leg to put the IV in. One more shot, and he quickly drifted off into the land of pink elephants.

Once he was asleep and his body totally relaxed, Dr. Rick began the intubation process. "For bulldogs, with their unnatural body designs and short noses, it's extra important for us to keep their airways open and keep their necks extended during the whole procedure," he explained. They also made sure to keep his eyes lubricated. In the operating area, Lizette laid Mr. President on a heating pad to keep his temperature constant (anesthetic drops a dog's temperature about five degrees) and hooked up his intravenous fluids. Dr. Rick made a delicate elliptical incision around Mr. President's entire scrotal area. He cut out the skin sheath first, then detached the small ligament that attached each testicle to the genital zone. Finally, he stitched up the incision. Because I had asked Rick to take off Mr. President's entire scrotal sac to leave him looking "clean and sleek" as well as to prevent some of the skin irritations that can develop when a dog is left with the extra sac hanging, the stitching took a few extra minutes. Even then, the entire procedure was done in just about fifteen minutes.

There was one final shot—twenty-four hours of pain and anti-inflammatory relief plus penicillin. Last, before taking Mr. President to his recovery area, a cozy blanket in a corner of the mobile unit, the vets also drew some blood so they could check his immunity titers.

Less than twenty minutes after his surgery began, Mr. President began waking up, trying to sit up right away. He trembled a little bit at first, partly from cold, partly from his body working to release the anesthesia from his system. I engaged his nose with the toy, which caused him to perk right up—even in his groggy state, his spirits were just as high as they were when he arrived. Then, as the best medicine, I brought in his best buddy, Angel, to help cheer him up. Angel approached his friend very delicately. Of course, Angel had no clue that his "brother" had just been neutered; he just knew that he smelled different and was in a different state.

After a moment or two, we carried Mr. President outside wrapped in his blanket and laid him on the grass in the toasty glow of the sun. Dr. Rick was amazed at how hardy Mr. President was and how fast he was snapping back. "If he can stand up, he's okay to go home," he told me. Almost on cue, Mr. President leapt to his feet and tried to run . . . but he was a little wobbly on his feet and plunked down on his bottom after a few woozy steps. Undaunted, he sprang right back up again, chasing after Angel, who was encouraging him to play. After a few more steps, once more, plop! "That's okay," Rick said. "Running around will bring his circulation back faster." As I took out a treat for Angel, Mr. President instantly reacted to the sound of the wrapper—just the idea of food woke him up even further. Though he would not be allowed food or water (except a little to keep his tongue from drying out) for another three hours, Mr. President—still swaying slightly—trotted after me, Angel, and the tempting treat as we returned to my car. In a procedure that took less than half an hour, I had given my young bulldog the gift of a lifetime of better physical and psychological health.

Dr. Garcia checks up on Mr. President after his surgery

TACKLING TEENAGE REBELLION

Neutering a dog doesn't guarantee psychological balance, nor does it ensure a smooth and stress-free adolescent phase. Even a spayed or neutered dog is undergoing other physical and psychological changes that require extra vigilance and patience from you, the owner, to help guide him through this eventful life stage. This is no time to lose sight of your calm-assertive energy—in fact, now's the time you will need it more than ever. But be assured that, if you have set down a firm foundation of rules, boundaries, and limitations, it's only a matter of reminding, rather than teaching, your dog what to do.

"In the home it may be necessary to go back to the training stages," advises Martin Deeley. "The crate or restricted area may be essential to avoid chewing, running crazy around the house, and even slipping out of housebreaking habits. This is when a dog may decide the sofa or even the bed is a good place to go to the bathroom. Attach a leash to

your rebellious teen, even in the house, so that you know where he is and can be aware of what he is doing and—with luck!—even what he's thinking of doing. In this way you can step in early to correct any attempt at naughtiness." Hollywood trainer Clint Rowe agrees. "Your pup will have to have boundaries refreshed or redefined. Just stay with the training you've done since it was young. Don't put the pup in a situation where you cannot back up what you command. Don't put the animal in a situation where it can ignore you or be noncompliant at these stages. Never threaten. Follow through calmly, consistently."

DISTRACTIONS

An adolescent dog is seeing and reacting to the world around it in a fresh, new way, and may not find you as endlessly fascinating as you seemed to him back in the days when he was working his hardest just to keep up with you. Now he is already wise about his environment and infused with extra energy for exploring it. When you get to the dog park with an adolescent dog, he is all charged up: "Okay, let's run!" But the dog doesn't want to just run at this stage, he wants to *zoom*— and suddenly he notices he can't get the human to practice that activity. The dog is saying, "What's the matter with you? Run with me!" And when he sees the human lagging behind, texting on her Black-Berry, he realizes he is faster than the human. This may make him feel a little cocky about his own physical strength versus the human's. He begins to see other dogs as more attractive companions, because they can match his intensity. At this point, many owners protest, "He used to listen to me but I can't get him to come anymore!" This "distracted" complaint is probably the number one grievance listed by owners of adolescent dogs.

"I have noticed this difference, especially with working dogs I train for hunting," Martin recounts.

Here I lay a very solid foundation of obedience and then develop their skills in the field. I have had females who after their first season—usually around the nine-month mark—suddenly appear to have learned very little. It is as though they have lost their memory, their personality changes, and it is not until after their second season that they begin to "click" with me again. That makes six months of—dare I say it?—"dumbness." They may begin to find that a sniff is more important than the work you are doing and become easily distracted by a favorable odor when it is not the one you want them to be interested in. It may become more important to cock a leg on that tree rather than hunt around it for a retrieve. And this is where we learn whether we have built a solid foundation during the puppy stage and whether we are respected by our dog, as both a partner and a person who should be obeyed.

The solution to a distracted dog is a four-part formula—leadership, consistency, persistence, and patience. When Junior entered his adolescence, the way I managed his drifting attention and the growing intensity of his pit bull energy was to fulfill those cravings for exploration—by taking him with me to as many new situations and environments as possible. Every time I went to a new place with my adolescent dog, it gave me a new opportunity to show him that I was in control, which served the purpose of keeping his mind both challenged and submissive at the same time. While an adolescent dog may be feeling totally like the master of his home domain, a new environment can send him back into a more receptive learning mode.

But the challenges are not just physical ones. When he travels with me, Junior is playing the role that Daddy has played for the first five seasons of *Dog Whisperer*—he is modeling calm-submissive energy for unstable dogs with many different issues. The energy that another pit bull might channel into fighting is channeled into self-control and

healing, and to accomplish that—for any dog—is very, very hard work. And those mental exercises that I put him through constantly reinforce my position as his leader.

Clint Rowe has the same observation of the dogs that he has trained for Hollywood films. "Often, the best way to challenge an adolescent is to work him mentally. Do some structured training while walking; do sit, stay, down, wait; and have him thinking and watching you. Make it fun. If he will fetch, do a few retrieves but again, structured so he has to puzzle it out for himself; he has to sit before being sent for a retrieve, or sit and down and then come back to a sit. Vary it so he has to concentrate. And stop when he is still happy doing it with you. You start the game and you stop the game. That is what leaders do." The more consistent leadership you practice with your dog, the less erratic behavior you will see.

SOCIAL SLIPS

At seven months of age, Mr. President was among a group of powerful-breed dogs I was working with for a recent *Dog Whisperer* episode. Being new to the Dog Whispering game, Mr. President and the other puppies didn't yet understand what Daddy and Junior had learned—that we accept new dogs into our pack and help them adjust. Instead, when I wasn't watching, Mr. President reverted to his natural desire to tell strange dogs to go away, attempting to convey that message to Troy, a large adult German shepherd. Unlike the previous adult dogs in Mr. P.'s life, Troy did not view Mr. President's outburst as the move of a cute, nonthreatening puppy. When Mr. President pushed his buttons, Troy pushed back and nearly got in a bite! I stepped in right away, but it was clear to me that Mr. President was actually revved up for more. He was breathing heavily, his eyes were red—he went from dog to bulldog in a split second. By the end of the exercise, they were walking together like

HOW *to* RAISE *the* PERFECT DOG   269

old friends, but Mr. President's actions were typical of the potentially
calamitous social slips dogs can make during the transition from adolescence to adulthood. Now that he's nearly grown, when Mr. P. shows
too much of that bellicose bulldog style, he's in serious danger of tick-
ing off other dogs. It becomes even more crucial that I supervise his social interactions during this phase, until he begins to understand that
adult dogs expect a different set of manners from him now than they
might have when he was a puppy.

Chris Komives faced a similar social hurdle with the newly spayed
Eliza when he brought her to the dog park. "As Eliza became an adolescent, she lost her timidity and became more forward," he says.

> When she was a puppy, I was concerned she was avoiding inter-
> acting with other dogs and so encouraged her to get out there.
> Now that she's an adolescent, I have to remind her to slow down
> her approach with other dogs, or she can be overwhelming. If
> she's on leash, she'll get excited to meet the other dog, then gets
> frustrated when I restrain her. She begins huffing, growling, and
> spinning, which sounds intimidating to the other dog owner. To
> work on this, I took her to different dog parks and kept her on
> leash. I corrected her when she'd start huffing and growling and
> rewarded her when she entered a calm state by letting her run
> and play. We've made great progress, but I had to learn to ignore
> the woman who yelled that I was a control freak and should just
> let my dog play and the couple I overheard saying they hate peo-
> ple who do dog training in the dog park.

As Chris learned, it can take real commitment to remain a calm-
assertive pack leader in the face of unpredictable adolescence. The re-
bellion is a natural part of the process. As a leader, you always have to
be aware of what is happening with your dog. You have to remain
calm and confident, assertive and positive, to ensure that you are in a

position to minimize problems and that all conflicts end with good behaviors being reinforced. Be ahead of your dog; see potential problems coming and avert or manage them so that you always remain the leader in his eyes. "What we have to realize is that behavior is always changing and dogs are always learning. Training happens twenty-four hours a day and training never stops—maybe adolescence never stops—we all become older teenagers," Martin Deeley observes. "If we accept this as a normal phase in our dogs' development, then we can be prepared to work with them to ensure that good habits are not lost and even better ones are created for life."

TIPS FOR TEENAGERS

- **Be consistent.** If you set a rule, boundary, or limitation, don't waver from it. Intermittent reinforcement creates an unpredictable dog.
- **Follow through.** Don't give a command you're not prepared to back up with a consequence. Make sure all interactions end on a positive note, with the right behavior being modeled.
- **Be persistent.** No matter how rebellious your teen, prove to him that nothing in his behavior can rattle your calm-assertive authority.
- **Be patient.** Your dog won't be an adolescent forever. The results of your hard work will be more apparent with every success you share. By the end of two or three years, you will have established the good habits to make your dog your ideal life companion.

All the members of the Barnes family are delighted to report that the payoff for seeing a dog through a sometimes rocky adolescence

can be enormous. At ten months of age, following his neutering at six months, Blizzard the yellow Lab has actually grown into an even more laid-back, happy-go-lucky version of his puppy self. Christian and Sabrina noted that he seems to have formed a more complete understanding of his boundaries in the house, he has become a more accomplished retriever, and he now responds in a more mature way to the other dogs at the dog park. "He's still at such a young age," their dad, Terry, marvels, "but his breed, his Labrador breed, is coming out where his fetching and his walking next to you is just automatic. It's really amazing to see the whole process unfold."

PASSAGE INTO ADULTHOOD

The Perfect Dog Revealed

As the adolescent phase nears its end, your dog will challenge you once again. This time, you've got more to fall back on than just those eight crucial months of puppyhood and the blueprint you created; you also have two to three years of successfully met adolescent challenges behind you. When your dog asks you with his behavior, "Okay, can I do this now?" you have a whole lifetime of a balanced upbringing to support you in your response. I silently ask my dogs, "What are you going to listen to? What you want in this moment? Or what you've learned in the past three years?" I know the answer, because I believe that every test gives me a new opportunity to strengthen my leadership position.

The compensation for your hard work and caring these many months is a mature dog that demonstrates a steadiness and calm confidence that the younger one did not have. He is able to maintain focus and an open, submissive state of mind in a range of both familiar and new situations and environments. "When they're young, a butterfly can take over their mind state. That's all that exists in their mind, their

world," Clint Rowe explains. "When they mature, they're able to watch a butterfly and also be aware of other things in the environment. One particular stimulus usually does not dominate them. They have awareness of their own states more readily. Awareness and wisdom just keep expanding." This is the end result of spending the first eight intensive months of puppyhood, then another two or so years in adolescence, fulfilling your dog's needs through exercise, discipline, then affection—and setting and maintaining basic rules, boundaries, and limitations that establish your permanent leadership. It's that relentless consistency that creates a Daddy or a Junior or whatever role model you want to shape your dream dog to emulate.

This is your reward when you set out and follow through on creating the perfect dog. Congratulations. It's now much more than a possibility—you've actually accomplished it.

10
EPILOGUE
The Puppies Grow Up

Cesar with Junior and Daddy

Over the course of this book, I've had the joy of watching all the puppies featured here mature from clumsy childhood to gawky then almost graceful adolescence. All the dogs I have had the honor of raising educated me further about the nature of both their breeds and their species, adding new insight and depth to the work I do every day. Blizzard, Angel, and Mr. President each left me with such special gems of wisdom. And now, nearly a year after my "puppy project" began, these puppies continue to impart their wonderful gifts to the new humans in their lives.

BLIZZARD THE YELLOW LAB

Adolescent Blizzard

The first member to join the puppy pack has found pack life to be so good that he's going to stay. As the newest member of the Barnes family, Blizzard now spends his days hanging out with Adriana Barnes, the director of my new forty-three-acre Dog Psychology Center, which means he's got the great outdoors to romp in and a bunch of boisterous fellow canines for playmates. That suits Blizzard fine, because he has matured into the ideal yellow Lab: happy-go-lucky, friendly, slightly goofy, and amenable to new adventures. He's always popular among the pack—the regular fixtures and new visitors alike—although if his energy level gets a little too high, there's always someone like Junior or Angel to remind him to tone it down.

Blizzard is as warm and welcoming to humans as he is to members of his own species. At night, he cuddles up with the rest of the Barnes family, including Molly the dachshund, to enjoy one of their favorite family activities—watching movies together. He's overcome his fear of the water and loves to splash around in the pool with Christian, whose pack leader skills are gradually improving. Blizzard has truly become what I had hoped he would grow up to be: the model yellow Labrador and living proof that there is indeed a better way to raise Marley!

ELIZA THE WHEATEN TERRIER

Teen Eliza

A full-fledged teenager now, Eliza has grown into the physical "springiness" that her breed is known for. She now flies through the air on jumps at her weekly agility classes and gracefully sails over the blockades in the house that used to keep her in her place. Chris and

Johanna Komives learned to set stronger boundaries—and also bought taller gates ("We had to buy one designed for Great Danes," Chris marvels). Chris says Eliza is the perfect dog 80 percent of the time, but he is still working to balance her ebullient energy when she's around other dogs. "My goal is for both of us to be calm enough that she can hang out with Cesar's new pack while we're shooting this season's *Dog Whisperer*. Her excited energy could get her into trouble with some of the red-zone cases. When she's more like Junior and Daddy, I'll feel more confident in having her with us."

Other than Eliza's tendency to be a little too exuberant around other dogs, Eliza's life is a terrier's dream. "We get up every morning for a walk before feeding. On weekends, if I'm not up by seven, she comes to the bedroom door and waits. She's allowed to sleep in the living room. During the day, she stays in the backyard and the back hallway. From what I see on the webcam we set up to watch her, she sleeps most of the day, gets up around three p.m. and goes outside. On weekends or days I'm not working, I take her on a couple hours' hike to Runyon Canyon or up in the San Gabriel Mountain or to the dog beach. Basically now on my days off, I think of things I can do with Eliza. I definitely get more exercise than before she came along. In the evening I take her for a walk or run, then feed her and groom her. On Wednesdays, we go to agility class. Life's a lot more entertaining with her around. She's a joy to have in our house."

Ultimately, Chris has learned as much about himself as he has about raising a puppy from his experiences with Eliza. "Even though I told myself I was being calm-assertive, the fact that my dog is excited means I am feeding that energy. Now, when she's excited, I ask myself consciously, 'Am I really calm?' Then I relax, and she relaxes. I probably dote on her too much. Johanna feels if our house were on fire, I'd run in to save Eliza first and then her. I probably should work on this."

MR. PRESIDENT THE ENGLISH BULLDOG

Teen Mr. President

As a purebred bulldog puppy, Mr. President started life genetically imprinted with a few bulldog traits that don't always make for the best well-mannered pets: he'd throw his weight around at mealtimes, he'd hog toys, and he'd approach new dogs chest out and eyes first. I'm delighted to have coached this little guy into becoming a true canine good citizen worthy of his illustrious name. He's learned to wait for his food and play nicely with others, and he's beginning to meet and greet new dogs like a pro. I'm particularly proud of how Mr. President has learned to use his nose almost as well as the other members of his pack—a skill that will go a long way toward keeping him balanced for the rest of his life. He's also developed into the best and most enthusiastic swimmer of any bulldog I've ever seen!

Researcher Crystal Reel had been enamored with our little English bulldog since the moment she first laid eyes on him, and after fostering him while Ilusion and I were away on our trip, she began mounting a fervent campaign to become his official adoptive owner. While I wasn't certain at first, Crystal persisted and proved to me without a doubt that she has what it would take to be pack leader to a strong-willed bulldog. Now that he's officially her dog, he's still very much in the *Dog Whisperer* extended family. When he's not on location with me and the rest of the pack, Mr. President is hanging out in the office with Crystal and the many other office dogs at MPH/CMI, including Angel, where his days are filled with naps and belly rubs.

But Crystal also learned that despite his excellent breeding and background, Mr. President couldn't escape the curse of allergies that bulldogs are prone to. "He's fully recovered now," says Crystal, "but Dr. Garcia tells me that bulldogs have special needs when it comes to skin allergies, and it's just something we'll have to monitor through his life. Thanks to his upbringing with Cesar, however, I have to say that going to the vet doesn't faze Mr. President one bit."

Thanks to his adoring new owner, the adolescent Mr. President is now enjoying the classic LA lifestyle. "He hangs out in a production office all day," Crystal says, " then he has his assistant (me) drive him to the set, where he tapes a hit TV show. I don't think life could get any better for this bulldog."

ANGEL THE MINIATURE SCHNAUZER

Now a full-fledged teenager, Angel has hit a few monumental milestones. First and foremost, he has found a forever home with my close friend and the producer/director of *Dog Whisperer with Cesar Millan*, SueAnn Fincke. After months of spending time with Angel on shoots, SueAnn knew she couldn't part with him. Brooke Walker, Angel's breeder, couldn't be more satisfied with the match: "I'm so happy Angel will get to stay in the *Dog Whisperer* family." Angel will continue

The Proper Way to Lift a Dog by the Scruff of the Neck

Reaching toward Angel.

Mr. President examines the toy.

Mr. President and the toy.

Picking up Angel with one hand while the other supports the hindquarters.

Mr. President was calmer than Angel during the stalking phase, but once he got hold of the duck, he would continue to maul it unless I stepped in immediately to make him let go. This is where I have to make sure he plays like a dog, not a bulldog. If he gets into a bulldog state, his play will have no limits. He will actually try to "kill" the toy. It's much more difficult to remove the toy when a powerful breed's behavior escalates to that level. If Mr. President—even as a four-month-old puppy—were to get fully into his bulldog state, even food wouldn't distract him from tearing apart the toy. As long as the puppy's play stays in the "animal-dog" zone, you can always use the nose to distract him.

A NOSE FOR PLAY

All dogs are born exploring the world first with their noses, then with their eyes, then with their ears. Challenging your puppy's nose is a wonderful way to engage the "animal-dog" in him—even if he's a flat-faced dog like a bulldog or a pug. Because of the shape of their noses, these breeds aren't as sensitive as normal dogs to the scents around them, and they can become addicted to using their eyes as their primary senses in interacting with the world. This in turn can cause them problems. Socially, they can be perceived as more "challenging" to other dogs. It can also lead to behavioral issues if they are frustrated—for example, when bulldogs get obsessed with fast-moving objects such as skateboards and bicycles.

In raising Mr. President to become more dog than bulldog, it was my goal to get him always to use his nose first. One way I went about doing this was through making a game out of hiding his food. I built obstacle courses in the garage, using barriers, boxes, and containers. Then I rubbed the scent of food in several spots throughout the "course" but made a point of hiding the main meal in the toughest place to find. Since Mr. President's food drive is mighty powerful, this is a wonderful way to get him to engage his nose more than his eyes. This is an exercise I do with all the puppies—with Angel, it is also a way of getting him in touch with the terrier breed in him—but for Mr. President, it will go a long way toward freeing him from the sometimes destructive pull of his bulldog genetics.

OBSTACLE COURSE

An obstacle course is another great way to challenge the animal-dog in your puppy. This is another instance where you don't need to spend hundreds of dollars on expensive tools and toys—you can use your imagination. An emptied-out box, an old tire, a two-stair stepping stool—anything and everything can be a way to mentally stimulate your dog and challenge her agility. Begin by using food or scent as a lure, then progress to the point where you save the food reward until the end.

Knowing he'd adopted a high-energy terrier with a mind that would need constant challenges, Chris Komives set up his own agility course for his wheaten terrier, Eliza. "Eliza has a strong play drive. I built jumps, tunnels, and other obstacles in our backyard so she could be challenged. She has balls, Frisbees, rope toys, and other toys that are her reward for running through the course. In the evening after returning from our walk but before her dinner, we'll do some practice for ten to fifteen minutes. On weekends or days I'm not working, we'll do agility work in the afternoon—again only ten to fifteen minutes at a time." Chris points out another thing owners must remember when doing mentally stimulating games or conditioning sessions with their puppies: "Being obsessive by nature, I think she was done before I was. If anything, I had to be aware of when I was overtaxing her." With puppies, short and sweet is always best; think of the old showbiz motto, Keep the audience wanting more.

Adolescent Angel

to enjoy hanging out with me on location, along with the familiar company of all the dogs in my pack—including his best friend, Mr. President, from whom he is still inseparable. He remains well behaved, respectful, curious, and always eager to learn something new.

Now that Angel has been adopted by SueAnn, she made the important decision to have him neutered. "I knew he was going to be a family pet and not a competitive show dog, so I thought it best to have him fixed," she says. He's also got a new name: Sir Albert Angel, or Albert for short. His favorite past-times are walking, fetching, playing with his chew toys—and going to the dog park. "In his spare time, he likes to relax on the couch, which he knows he shouldn't do . . . since it only occurs if we've been out of sight for a while. We have given him the nickname Pigpen because although he is a fancy purebred he misses no opportunity to roll in as much dirt and mud as possible. He gives you these looks that make you wish you could read what's going on in that funny, adorable mind of his."

JUNIOR THE PITBULL

Junior in action

Junior, well into his adolescence and careening toward adulthood, gets along with any new dog or human that comes into our lives, while always remaining attuned to his instincts and alerting me to any negative energy that might be coming from either species. He can play equally happily with a terrier like Angel, a Lab like Blizzard, or another pit bull, such as Memphis, or another visitor to our pack. Much more "dog" than "pit bull," Junior is actually a more enthusiastic water dog than Blizzard the Lab! To watch the gusto with which he dives into our backyard pool and retrieves balls and toys is to witness the purest kind of bliss imaginable.

But beyond being a happy, well-adjusted dog, Junior has been shaped into something much more rare through Daddy's and my hard work and guidance. Junior is becoming more than just an enabler of balance; he's becoming an actual source of balance itself. He seems deeply aware of his purpose: to use his abilities and power to help others. He has gone beyond the programming of his breed and even of his species to become a real ambassador to the world at large—a canine Gandhi or Martin Luther King. I feel we're seeing only the beginning of what Junior will accomplish in his life.

As Daddy settles into semi-retirement, Junior is coming into his own as the next leader of the pack. In any new situation, I can sense Daddy's wisdom mirrored in Junior's feedback and intuition. Breeders try to pass on the genes of a dog from generation to generation, but with Junior, I've aimed to pass on Daddy's psychological and spiritual essence instead. As sad as I am that Daddy is facing the sunset of his days on earth, I am comforted by the knowledge that his legacy will live on—not just in my heart but in the impact he has had on Junior, and in the influence Junior will have on the world. Junior will take Daddy's gifts to the next level, having the added benefit of an owner who is older and wiser—as I certainly hope I am!—plus a full pack of committed humans, including my kids, to support and nurture his purpose. That's what we all dream of, isn't it? The next generation getting better and better? Through Junior and the future generations of puppies that Junior will inspire, Daddy and what he stands for will live on forever.

I am so proud to have had the opportunity to share all these dogs' carefree, joyful puppyhoods with my readers and with the world.

APPENDIX: RESOURCE GUIDE

CHAPTER 1: MEET THE PUPPIES

Grogan, John. *Marley & Me*. New York: HarperCollins, 2005.

Southern California Labrador Retriever Rescue
www.scllr.org

Brookehaven Miniature Schnauzers
brookehavenminis@yahoo.com

CHAPTER 2: PERFECT MATCH

Thinschmidt German Shepherds
www.assertivek-9training.com

The Monks of New Skete. *The Art of Raising a Puppy*. New York: Little, Brown and Company, 1991.

Last Chance for Animals
www.lcanimal.org

Humane Society of the United States
www.hsus.org

The American Kennel Club
www.akc.org

Petfinder.com
www.petfinder.com

Pets911.com
www.pets911.com

CHAPTER 3: MOTHER KNOWS BEST

The American Society for the Prevention of Cruelty to Animals
www.aspca.org

CHAPTER 5: YOUR HEALTHY PUPPY

The American Veterinary Medical Association
www.avma.org

The American Pet Products Association
www.americanpetproducts.org

The American Animal Hospital Association
www.aahanet.org

Pet Insurance Information
www.petinsurancereview.com

Terifaj, Paula. *How to Protect Your Dog from a Vaccine Junkie.* Palm Springs: Bull-
    dog Press, 2007.

Animal Blood Bank
www.hemopet.org

CHAPTER 6: CONNECTING, COMMUNICATING, AND CONDITIONING

International Association of Canine Professionals
www.dogpro.org

The Monks of New Skete. *The Art of Raising a Puppy.* New York: Little, Brown
    and Company, 1991.

————. *How to Be Your Dog's Best Friend: The Classic Training Manual for Dog
    Owners.* Boston: Little, Brown and Company, 2002.

Rutherford, Clarice, and David H. Neil. *How to Raise a Puppy You Can Live With*. Loveland, Colorado: Alpine Blue Ribbon Books, 2005.

Kilcommons, Brian, and Sarah Wilson. *My Smart Puppy: Fun, Effective, and Easy Puppy Training*. New York: Warner Books, 2006.

Cesar Millan's Sit and Stay the Cesar Way: Vol. 4 Mastering Leadership Series. http://www.cesarmillaninc.com/products/dvds.php

Deeley, Martin, and Cesar Millan. *Working Gundogs: An Introduction to Training and Handling*. Marlborough, England: Crowood Press, 2009.

CHAPTER 8: PROBLEM-FREE PUPPIES

Dog and Puppy Tips
www.cesarmillaninc.com/tips/

CHAPTER 9: SMELLS LIKE TEEN SPIRIT

Paws and Claws Mobile Vet
www.pawsandclawsmobilevet.com

NOTES

INTRODUCTION

1. Dogs' life spans vary according to their size: smaller breeds have longer life spans (twelve years or more) than larger breeds (approximately ten years). The Humane Society of the United States, *Dog Profile*, http://www .hsus.org/animals_in_research/species_used_in_research/dog.html.

CHAPTER 1: MEET THE PUPPIES

1. Sharon L. Peters, "Bulldogs Sitting Pretty on Top Dog List," *USA Today*, January 17, 2008, http://www.usatoday.com/news/nation/2008-01-16-favorite-dogs_N.htm.

CHAPTER 2: PERFECT MATCH

1. Susan Kauffmann, "Interspecies Friendships: When Cats Join the Pack," ModernDogMagazine.com, http://www.moderndogmagazine.com/ articles/interspecies-friendships-when-cats-join-the-pack/270.
2. John Grogan, *Marley and Me* (New York: HarperCollins, 2005).
3. Monks of New Skete, *The Art of Raising a Puppy* (New York: Little, Brown and Company, 1991), p. 76.
4. American Kennel Club, *AKC Meet the Breeds: Soft Coated Wheaten Terrier*, http://www.akc.org/breeds/soft_coated_wheaten_terrier/.
5. "Questions All Reputable Breeders Should Be Able to Answer" list courtesy of Jeri Muntis, http://www.mojaveschnauzers.com/.

6. The Humane Society of the United States, *Policies and Guidelines*, http://www.animalsheltering.org/resource_library/policies_and_guide lines/guidelines_for_animal_shelter_policies.html.

7. Clarice Rutherford and David H. Neil, *How to Raise a Puppy You Can Live With*, 4th ed. (Loveland, Colorado: Alpine Publishing, 2005), pp. 136–146.

CHAPTER 3: MOTHER KNOWS BEST

1. Bruce Fogle, *The Dog's Mind: Understanding Your Dog's Behavior* (New York: Macmillan, 1992), p. 74.

2. Miniature schnauzers were exhibited as a distinct breed as early as 1899. American Kennel Club, Miniature Schnauzer History, http:// www.akc.org/breeds/miniature_schnauzer/history.cfm.

3. According to Bruce Fogle, socialization to dogs is four to six weeks and to humans is four to twelve. It's safe to say that puppies interact primarily with their littermates and mother between two and six weeks. Bruce Fogle, *The Dog's Mind: Understanding Your Dog's Behavior* (New York: Macmillan, 1992), p. 69.

CHAPTER 4: PUPPY COMES HOME

1. American Society for the Prevention of Cruelty to Animals, *Toxic and Non-Toxic Plants*, http://www.aspca.org/pet-care/poison-control/plants/index .jsp?plant_toxiciy=non-toxic-to-dogs&page=14.

2. Diana Foster, *Arriving Home with Your New Pup*, Thinschmidt German Shepherds, 2009.

3. For more in-depth information on the different theories of discipline and rewards that apply to how I rehabilitate dogs, see my book *Be the Pack Leader*, chapter 2.

CHAPTER 5: YOUR HEALTHY PUPPY

1. www.americanpetproducts.org.

2. James McWhinney, "The Economics of Pet Ownership," Investopedia .com, http://www.investopedia.com/articles/pf/06/peteconomics.asp.

3. The American Animal Hospital Association, "AAHA Seal of Acceptance," http://www.healthypet.com/sealofaccept.aspx.

4. Paula Terifaj, *How to Protect Your Dog from a Vaccine Junkie* (Palm Springs: Bulldog Press, 2007), p. 42.

5. In 2006, the American Animal Hospital Association revised its guidelines on the use of vaccines in dogs. *2006 AAHA Canine Vaccine Guidelines Revises,* retrieved May 5, 2008, from http://www/secure.aahanet.org/web/startpage.aspx?site=resources.

6. Paula Terifaj, *How to Protect Your Dog from a Vaccine Junkie* (Palm Springs: Bulldog Press, 2007), p. 17.

CHAPTER 6: CONNECTING, COMMUNICATING, AND CONDITIONING

1. Clint Rowe, *Critical Periods in Canine Development,* http://www.wrimclubamerica.org/yourwein/development1.html.

CHAPTER 8: PROBLEM-FREE PUPPIES

1. Max Planck Institute for Evolutionary Anthropology, http://www.eva.mpg.de/English/research.htm.

CHAPTER 9: SMELLS LIKE TEEN SPIRIT

1. For more in-depth information on pet overpopulation: Elizabeth A. Clancy and Andrew N. Rowan, *Companion Animal Demographics in the United States: A Historical Perspective,* HSUS.org, http://www.hsus.org/web-files/PDF/hsp/soa_ii_chap02.pdf.

2. Kathy Diamond Davis, *The Canine Behavior Series,* http://www.veterinarypartner.com/content.plx?P=A&A=1701&S=1&SourceID=47.

ILLUSTRATION CREDITS

INDEX

ABOUT THE AUTHOR

Founder of the Dog Psychology Center in Los Angeles, CESAR MILLAN is the star of *Dog Whisperer with Cesar Millan* on the National Geographic Channel. In addition to his educational seminars and work with unstable dogs, he and his wife have founded the Cesar and Ilusion Millan Foundation, a nonprofit organization dedicated to providing financial support and rehabilitation expertise to shelters. A native of Culican, Mexico, Cesar now lives in Los Angeles.

MELISSA JO PELTIER, an executive producer and writer of *Dog Whisperer with Cesar Millan,* has been honored for her film and television writing and directing with an Emmy, a Peabody, and more than fifty other awards. She lives in Nyack, New York, with her husband, writer-director John Gray, and stepdaughter, Caitlin.

www.cesarmillaninc.com

Also by Cesar Millan with Melissa Jo Peltier

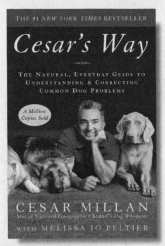

CESAR'S WAY
The Natural, Everyday Guide to Understand-ing and Correcting Common Dog Problems
$13.95 paperback (Canada: $16.95)
978-0-307-33797-9

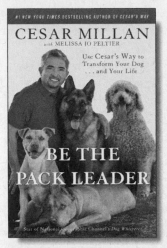

BE THE PACK LEADER
Use Cesar's Way to Transform Your Dog . . . and Your Life
$14.00 paperback (Canada: $17.00)
978-0-307-38167-5

A MEMBER OF THE FAMILY
The Ultimate Guide to Living with a Happy, Healthy Dog
$15.00 paperback (Canada: $18.95)
978-0-307-40903-4

CESAR'S RULES
Your Way to Train a Well-Behaved Dog
$15.00 paperback (Canada: $17.00)
978-0-307-71687-3

MILLAN FOUNDATION